Violence and Miracle in the Fourteenth Century

MICHAEL E. GOODICH

Violence and Miracle
in the
Fourteenth Century

PRIVATE GRIEF AND PUBLIC SALVATION

THE UNIVERSITY OF CHICAGO PRESS

CHICAGO AND LONDON

MICHAEL E. GOODICH teaches in the departments of History and
General Studies at the University of Haifa, Israel.

THE UNIVERSITY OF CHICAGO PRESS, Chicago 60637
THE UNIVERSITY OF CHICAGO PRESS, Ltd., London

© 1995 by The University of Chicago
All rights reserved. Published 1995
Printed in the United States of America

04 03 02 01 00 99 98 97 96 95   1 2 3 4 5
ISBN: 0-226-30294-6 (cloth)
0-226-30295-4 (paper)

Library of Congress Cataloging-in-Publication Data

Goodich, Michael, 1944–
    Violence and miracle in the fourteenth century : private grief and public
salvation / Michael E. Goodich.
        p.   cm.
    Includes bibliographical references (p.) and index.
    1. Saints—Europe—Legends.   2. Hagiography.   3. Social history—Medieval,
500–1500.   4. Popular culture—Religious aspects—Christianity—History.
5. Violence in literature.   I. Title.
    BX4662.G65   1995
    282'.4'09023—dc20   94-39199
                                                         CIP

Portions of chapter 4 were previously published in slightly different form as "Family,
Sexuality, and the Supernatural in the Fourteenth Century," *Journal of the History of
Sexuality* 4 (1994), 493–516. © 1994 by the University of Chicago. All rights
reserved.

For Claudia and Marian

Contents

Preface

The past several years have witnessed a marked revival of interest in medieval hagiography. The long-held view that the saints' lives and miracle stories are hopelessly naive and partisan defenses of some of Christianity's more fantastic claims has been replaced by a wide appreciation of the wealth of unmined material which may be found through a critical reading of such sources. The first stage of this reevaluation has led to the growing use of saints' lives in order to investigate such themes as the composition of the medieval family, the efflorescence of female piety, and the social structure of the medieval church. Miracle collections had long been treated suspiciously owing to what appears to be an almost slavish repetition of stereotypical themes by their medieval reporters. The typical miracle story is often almost devoid of specific reliable data, including the elementary "who, what, when, and where" of any historical document, and historians have thus often despaired of exploiting such a source for social history. Nevertheless, more daring scholars have attempted to use miracles and visions as evidence of an underlying *mentalité* which unifies the medieval centuries. It has been suggested that while the *vitae* increasingly represented the ideological views of the learned and the higher ecclesiastical ranks of the church, the *miracula* voice the beliefs of the unschooled, and suggest the continuing hold of a pre-Christian culture.

This book focuses on the intersecting point of two primal human emotions, belief in the transcendent and fear of death. The fourteenth century has long been characterized by historians as one of the most uncertain, fear-ridden periods in European history, when many of the traditional foundations of the medieval consensus had broken down, and the lives of many were endangered by war, pestilence, famine, and other ills. It has often been viewed as a transitional phase between the waning middle ages and the nascent Renaissance. Nevertheless, despite the despair and hopelessness with which many were gripped, faith in the restorative power of God remained. The "rescue miracle," in which an innocent victim is saved from a violent death, found an increasing place in miracle stories; and, owing to the greater accuracy and specificity of such reports, it may be regarded as a reflection of the fears and conflicts which characterized a turbulent age.

The theme of this book has been long in the making, and although I had been fitfully collecting material for several years, it is only recently that I have had the opportunity to put together the raw material in some cogent form. Over the years, I have had the privilege of encountering, either by means of the printed page or through direct discourse, many distinguished scholars whose work has, often imperceptibly, made an impact on my research. The list would be too long to do justice to each one. Nevertheless, I wish to acknowledge with gratitude the following persons who have read parts of the manuscript, or who have offered fruitful suggestions: Ronald Finucane, George Ferzoco, Karlfried Froehlich, Jocelyn Hillgarth, Bernard McGinn, Robert Muchembled, Caroleigh Neel, Sherry Reames, Andries van Aarde, and Michael Vertin. Portions of this work have appeared in slightly different form in the *Journal of the History of Sexuality* or have been delivered as a conference paper at Kalamazoo in 1993.

In addition, I would like to thank the staffs of the following libraries for their kind assistance in allowing me to pursue my research: Haifa University Library, Columbia University Library, the Library of the University of California at Los Angeles, the Huntington Library, the Morgan Library, the British Library, the Bibliothèque Nationale, the Index of Christian Art, the Bibliothèque Ste. Geneviève, Speer Library of Princeton Theological Seminary, Firestone Library of Princeton University, the Alcuin Library of St. John's University (Collegeville, Minn.), the Hill Monastic Manuscript Library, the Bodleian, Exeter College Library (Oxford), and the Stella Maris Carmelite monastery (Haifa).

A special thanks should be accorded to the Institute for Ecumenical and Cultural Research at St. John's University in Collegeville, Minnesota, for providing my wife and me with hospitality and a stimulating spiritual and intellectual environment during the academic year 1992–3; and to the members of the institute, whose varying backgrounds and perspectives often provided valuable and fresh approaches to universal issues of scholarship and religious faith. Thanks are also due to the Princeton Theological Seminary for extending its hospitality during the summer of 1993, and to the University of Haifa Research Authority for their research funds.

Carol Saller and the staff of the University of Chicago Press deserve credit for assisting in the preparation of the text for publication.

Finally, the encouragement and perseverance of my wife, Marian, has remained a steady support of my work, without which what seemed like an insurmountable task would never have been accomplished.

ONE

Cult and Miracle in the Fourteenth Century

I n the late thirteenth century, under the influence of Aristotelian philosophy, such scholastic theologians as Thomas Aquinas, Albertus Magnus, and Engelbert of Admont had attempted to reduce the number of phenomena properly termed miraculous.[1] Nevertheless, the view that the immanence of divine justice guaranteed that wrong would not go unpunished remained largely undiminished, particularly among the popular classes, and served as continuing solace against the disorder and violence of the world.[2] Such faith in the superiority of divine over human institutions was voiced, for example, by a poor woman of Polizzi (ca. 1320) who had been forcibly expelled from her home and could not afford a lawyer to defend her rights.[3] Gandolph of Binasco appeared posthumously to her in a vision advising her to go to court the next day in order to recover the house she had lost through calumny. That same night the judge also had a vision in which the saint warned, "Unless you do justice to this abandoned woman, you will incur the wrath of God [ira Dei] and will answer to the highest judge." The next day, both of them compared their visions and the woman's rights were restored. Here, such faith in divine intercession to restore equity is shared by both judge and judged.

The fourteenth-century miracle collections, which have thus far received little attention, suggest a reappearance of many of the conditions which had obtained in the early middle ages, demanding divine intercession in the resolution of conflict and the reduction of fear and anomie.[4] In the face of ever-present fears of injustice (despite the rationalization of law which had occurred during the central middle ages) appeal to the supernatural through oath, divination, and magic reasserted itself when neither kin-based law nor a weakened central authority were able to provide adequate evidence to settle troublesome cases. As Hoebel has pointed out, religion often steps in when such kin-based law ceases to function.[5] The use of sorcery and other supernatural means is most widespread when central authority is weak or absent.[6] In his classic study of the Azande, Evans-Pritchard has also demonstrated that the appeal to the supernatural could serve at the same time as an effective means of social control.[7]

A survey of miracles attributed to both long-recognized saints and to those who had only recently achieved cultic veneration reveals an increasing number of "rescue" miracles involving conflict and violence in comparison to the central and early middle ages, when thaumaturgic cures had predominated, although more recent saints such as Bernardino of Siena nevertheless continued to cure the diseased, lame, and paralyzed.[8] Studies by Vauchez and Sigal, which have focused on the twelfth and thirteenth centuries, further suggest a continuing change in favor of posthumous miracles, often performed at some distance from the site of the relics, in which the themes of deliverance and protection predominate.[9] The proliferation of icons, panels, frescoes, and predellas as foci for the performance of miracles, rather than the saint's relics, even achieved divine approval. For example, a Franciscan friar, so close to death that he had already received the last rites, experienced a vision of the recently deceased Pope Urban V, saying: "Vow yourself to the painted portrait of the person you have invoked, i.e. the figure [Urban V] which appears on the right [of a panel?], since another figure appears on the left. If you do this, you will not die of your malady, but will escape."[10]

But although such thaumaturgical cure of disease and lameness remained the focal point of many fourteenth-century miracle collections, an increasing proportion of reported miracles concerned persons rescued from the vagaries of a turbulent society torn by crime, warfare, civil unrest, or the damage wrought by nature. For the supernatural tends to intercede when human mechanisms, such as the state, prove unreliable or flawed, and the brutalization of human relations demands outside intervention to achieve equity. The oft-noted breakdown of the medieval consensus which accompanied the "terrors" of the fourteenth century and the decline of its characteristic institutions, such as the feudal system, the papal church, and the democratic commune, enhanced reliance on the mystical, irrational, magical, and miraculous. Cases of suicide, adultery, mental disorder, and family violence, for example, were especially amenable to such intercession, in order to avoid the infamy and obloquy that recourse to the state would entail. Instances in which divine intercession served to reduce the threat of violence, mediate disputes, and intervene on the side of innocent victims (which are the focus of the present inquiry) may fall into several broad categories: (1) the miraculous resolution of communal or factional strife in the absence of other reliable mediating agencies; (2) the settlement of family or domestic squabbles, often centering around sexual misconduct or other difficulties in the home or workplace; (3) relief from the distress and destruction of war; (4) protection of both victim and accused against the vagaries of an unjust judicial or social system; (5) the rescue of a victim from suicide or accident; and, (6) succor against the terrors of the natural world, such as shipwreck, pestilence, marauding animals, fire, and famine. Such "rescue" miracles, filled with colorful detail, may supplement the picture of a brutal and violent society portrayed in more conventional sources.

By the beginning of the fourteenth century, much of the economic and technological progress of the previous period had come to a halt, as Europe's substructure had fallen into decay and disrepair. Work-related accidents, drowning, ship disasters, and accidents due to fire and faulty construction thus became a common source of miraculous intercession. Those persons especially dependent on the forces of nature, such as sea folk and their families, whose livelihood demanded calm seas and clement weather, continued to seek the aid of a patron saint.[11] The peasantry in particular lived in a continual state of fear dominated by a struggle for survival in the face of hunger, severe winters, high infant mortality, incurable disease, marauding wolves, and fear of the dark forces of the Devil. Perhaps the most hapless victims of this deterioration in the quality of life were children, who were often portrayed in miracle collections as being saved from drowning, plague, or disease. Such distress engendered a faith in the protective presence of the supernatural, whose vengefulness could be tempered by grace and mercy.[12]

The destruction wrought by nature was compounded by the ravages of war. The many miraculous escapes experienced by all classes during the Hundred Years' War, the Italian communal wars, the dynastic struggles in the empire, and other local conflicts suggest the

deterioration of aristocratic, feudal warfare and the growing victimization of noncombatants. Among the inequities that divine miracle
could mitigate were: (1) the failure to honor safe-conducts; (2) the
plundering and confiscation of goods and chattel; (3) the ransoming
of defenseless captives; (4) the spread of games of chance by routiers
and freebooters; and (5) the use of inflated and counterfeit currency.
Case studies of the cults of Charles of Blois, Leonard of Inchenhofen,
and Martial of Limoges, for example, reveal the extent of reliance on
divine intercession in time of war. Such rescue miracles, in which the
victim seeks redress from the consequences of violence, have formed
the core of the present investigation. The majority of miracles, which
continued to deal with the thaumaturgical cure of disease, injury,
lameness, and so forth, have therefore not been considered. Such issues as the social structure of miracle and cult, or medical practice
versus folk medicine, for example, remain uninvestigated.[13] Further,
nearly all the miracles dealt with here were performed posthumously,
so that the difficult issue of whether the saint's healing power was
affected by his or her charisma, personal relationship to the victim,
or public reputation is avoided.

Clerical Control of the Miracle

Since the well-reported and edited miracle possessed certain common features designed to guarantee its credibility, such material
is receptive to comparative analysis, and suggests a nearly universal
acceptance among the learned of certain standards for judging cases
of miraculous intervention. In accordance with both systematic the-
ology and canon law, the natural philosophers, theologians, canonists, and notaries entrusted with investigating and recording claims
of supernatural intercession attempted to bridle the enthusiasm of
those who had witnessed or experienced a miracle, who formed a local community of the faithful. At the same time, there was a shared
consensus—apparently cutting across geographical and social
lines—concerning those instances which might lend themselves to
divine intercession and the means required to achieve its successful
application.

The extent of reliable documentation concerning alleged miraculous intervention in the normal processes of nature varies consider-

ably from cult to cult. The mere quantity of available material has necessarily required limiting this inquiry; and perhaps some representative or emblematic saintly intermediaries have been omitted. This book has been based on an examination of miracle stories connected with about one hundred fifty cults active in the fourteenth century; some refer to the relics or shrines identified with long-standing cults such as Sts. Agnes and John the Baptist, while others concern recent historical figures whose charisma endowed their relics with supernatural power such as Charles of Blois or Nicholas of Tolentino. Some of these reports appear within such standard hagiographical genres as the *inventio, translatio, vita et miracula,* or *processus.* Others may be found scattered in contemporary chronicles, sermons, or other literary sources, and are often difficult to reach in any systematic way.[14] Some miracles are attested by one eyewitness, like the hundreds recorded at the shrine of Leonard of Inchenhofen in Bavaria by three observers beginning in 1258; or those recorded by a local clerk around the time of the translation of the head of Martial of Limoges in 1388. Others are based on official inquiries conducted in accordance with a well-developed canonical procedure, such as the cults devoted to Yves Helory of Tréguier (Brittany, 1330), Gerard Cagnoli of Pisa (1347) and Pope Urban V (Avignon, 1374), in which each miracle may be attested by as many as five or six witnesses.

The documentary evidence suggests that theological speculation in the schools concerning the nature of miracle was not divorced from the need to establish uniform standards to distinguish false from true miracles. This coincided with the church's desire to exercise control over the haphazard, popular recognition of relics, saints, and new religious movements lacking canonical, papal approval.[15] As a consequence, the circumstantial detail demanded in order to guarantee conformity to higher standards of credibility provides us with the kind of microhistorical data necessary to reconstruct the mental structures of a wide segment of society. The clergy, aware of papal demands that inquiries must be made before a cult could be established, are thus often portrayed as being more cautious than the people. In 1344 the relics of the hospitaller St. Allucio (d. 1134?) were discovered in the parish of Pescia. The Bishop of Lucca, Guglielmo Dulcino of Monte Albano, consulted the clerks and rector of

the hospital of Sant' Allucio before empowering the Dominican lec-
tor in philosophy, Paolo Lapo, to make a thorough investigation into
their authenticity. After the report had been prepared and an old *Vita*
was discovered, the canons and rectors of the city were consulted.
Finally, the bishop granted an indulgence on 25 June 1344. Similar
consultations occurred prior to the translation of the relics of Sts.
Lucian, Marcian et al. at Vich in 1342.[16]

Nevertheless, warnings of caution were not always effective and
were later turned to the advantage of the putative saint. In the case
of Dauphine of Languedoc, in 1360 her body had been brought to
the church of Ste. Catherine and the people appeared in order to say
vigils and kiss the feet of the dead countess as though she were a
saint.[17] One Bertrand Gale, notary and squire to the bishop of Apt,
rebuked them for doing so. He suggested that this was idolatrous behavior as long as she had not been canonized. But even his wife argued with him, and asked him to allow her to attend vigils with two
neighbors. His reply was, "How can you call her a saint, since if she
should break a pitcher of wine in Paradise, it will fall apart outside."
He was punished with an eye ailment which ceased only after he
made a vow to Dauphine.

The Raw Material of Miracle and Cult

By the mid-thirteenth century, the ecclesiastics, canon lawyers,
notaries, and theologians who were charged with determining
the authenticity of miracles had begun to formulate a list of questions
to which witnesses testifying under oath were asked to respond. All
of the extant canonization reports are prefaced by such a formal list
of questions covering the putative saint's life, conduct, ministry, and
faith; the saint's public reputation; the cult surrounding his ministry;
and miracles, both in life and posthumously.[18] The learned investigators were asked to determine the number of alleged miracles performed and the evidence for their occurrence, to distinguish between
miracles above and against nature, the use of natural substances, incantations, or deceit, the invocation employed, and whether the miracle benefited the faith. The charge issued by Pope Clement V in
1307 to guide the panel of investigators (which included the promi-

nent theologian William Durand the Younger) appointed to look into the case of Bishop Thomas Cantilupe of Hereford (d. 1282) listed the questions posed to witnesses.[19] These queries appear in other papal canonization trials, which demanded a high standard of judicial accuracy in order to avoid any lingering doubts about the candidate's suitability for sainthood. It should be stressed that, by their very nature, the surviving miracle collections contain only the allegedly successful reports of supernatural assistance, although should the case achieve discussion in the curia, many of these claims might be rejected. Beginning with Clement V's canonization (1312) of Pope Celestine V the Avignonese papacy introduced the very precise citation of canonically confirmed miracles as a sine qua non of papal bulls of canonization.[20] Throughout the fourteenth century, miracles performed on women and children overwhelmingly predominate in such bulls of canonization.[21]

On the other hand, most of the surviving *miracula* are drawn from locally produced legendaries, notarial records, or chronicles, or are mere stenographic reports, which did not always include all the pertinent information. An examination of those miracle collections which were apparently not the result of a specific papal order, drawn from different regions and of different literary genres, suggests that those entrusted with the recording, collation, and publication of such reports were nevertheless aware of ecclesiastical expectations, whether dealing with a new saint or a long-standing cult. The following items, which assist in verification of the miracle, appear in the fullest such reports:

1. the date of the testimony
2. the name of the witness
3. the geographical origin of the witness
4. the witness's place of residence
5. the profession of the witness
6. the age of the witness at the time of testimony
7. the name of the person who had experienced the miracle
8. his or her age
9. his or her geographical origin
10. his or her place of residence

11. his or her profession

12. the amount of time which had elapsed since the alleged miracle had occurred

13. the date and time of the alleged miracle

14. the site of the miracle

15. the problem or injustice (disease, natural disaster, etc.) which had been miraculously resolved

16. the time the problem first occurred

17. the precise symptoms (if the subject was a miraculous cure) or causes of the difficulty or injustice

18. the natural means attempted to cure the disease (fracture, etc.) or solve the difficulty

19. the reputation of the miracle-worker or relics

20. the identity of the person making the vow

21. the conditional terms of the vow taken by the penitent, victim, or bystander

22. the vow itself

23. the results of the vow (the miraculous event per se)

24. a description of the vow's execution

25. a report of the offering made by the penitent

26. the names or identity of those who could corroborate the story

The dramatic focal point of this series of questions is item 23, which corresponds to item 19 in Vladimir Propp's classic study of the structure of the folktale. In the case of the miracle, the interlocutor reports the solution of the disaster, the end of a misfortune, or the removal of some physical disability or impediment which had plagued the victim.[22]

Notarial Procedure and Miracles

In addition to the aforementioned data, the fullest miracle collections would also provide the names of the notaries and other officers of the court present at the hearing.[23] The critical role of the notary as the principal official charged with recording and translating the testimony of witnesses has too often been overlooked. Such "men of law," like those who fashioned letters of remission, were well-schooled in forensics and legal rhetoric and had received early training in devotional and classical texts. They functioned much as English solicitors do today and had been trained to listen attentively and record accurately the words of their interlocutors. The presence of a professional notary could guarantee the avoidance of those errors which had delayed earlier processes. The testimony in support of Maurice of Carnoët, for example, had been rejected in 1225 since the witnesses had been examined in a group rather than singly; the first hearing concerning Hildegard of Bingen had likewise been rejected in 1233; while the 1252 case of the Franciscan Simon of Collazzone simply listed the names of the witnesses to each miracle without providing full testimony.[24] The capital importance of the notary is suggested in the case of Pope Celestine V, for example. Although a document labeled as the saint's autobiography containing several miracles (perhaps written by his disciples) had been circulated shortly after his death, none of these is included in the canonization process as it comes down to us; well-documented, notarized miracles were preferred.[25] While notaries had been charged with turning the depositions into a judicially acceptable form, the precision and variety of the accounts which remain nevertheless often allow us to detect the authentic voices of a wide spectrum of participants and witnesses to the miracle.[26]

The notarial art had been perfected in the thirteenth century and its practitioners had been organized into a guild (*societas tabellionum*), requiring a rigorous course of legal training which could grant a *doctor artis notariae*. The program was subsumed under the arts faculty of the university at Bologna in 1306, and other universities soon followed suit, although some continued to acquire their training through apprenticeship rather than at a *studium* or university. A series of treatises laying out the theoretical basis of the profession and providing formulas for the drawing up of documents appeared in the thirteenth and fourteenth centuries. The high social status of the notary, which would require that he both adhere to recognized professional standards and protect the state's reputation, is suggested in the protocol of Clare of Montefalco.[27] The notary Ciappo of Spoleto had served as notary to the *podestà* of Montefalco at the time of Clare's death, and was the chief witness called upon to describe the discovery of the cross and instruments of the passion found engraved on her heart.

He testified that he had been among the seven notables of the town (including the *podestà* and *prior*) who had conferred secretly concerning the initiation of an inquiry.

The *Summa notariae* (1289?) of John of Bologna listed the formulary oaths and procedures followed by witnesses appearing in ecclesiastical courts and allowed the notary both to record a summary statement and to pose specific questions.[28] The papal protocols clearly reflect this procedure, whereby the witness's testimony often appears in two forms: firstly, a full, uninterrupted statement; and secondly, replies to specific queries.[29] In the locally initiated processes, the notary's position was cardinal, since these and similar reports might soon reach the curia, which insisted on reliable eyewitness testimony.[30] The first report of a miracle attributed to the Mercedarian Mary of Cervellone, for example, concerned several members of the order who had nearly been shipwrecked off the coast of North Africa. Rescued by the saint, they presented a notarized statement of their experience at the general chapter of the order held at Lérida in 1291.[31] In the 1311 case of a child drowned at Achères (Seine-et-Oise), nine witnesses were noted, all reported by a notary.[32] The miracles attributed to Rayner Fasani at Borgo San Sepolcro, for example, were examined by a judge named Orlandino and recorded by an imperial notary named Cortonuzzio Bentivenga of Perugia at the order of the local *capitano*.[33] The brief preface, presumably composed by the notary with the judge's assistance, begins with an invocation of the Trinity, and notes that God reveals himself by performing miracles through the saints, whose virtues and grace renew the faithful. The sworn statements of witnesses which follow are no less detailed than those found in a papal inquiry.

A similar notarial protocol appears in the miracle collection of Simon of Todì, which was recorded at Bologna beginning on 20 April 1322 by the imperial notary Alberto Papazoni, who had been deputed by the vicar of the bishop of Bologna; the actual scribe was a second notary, Giovanni de Manellis, identified as a *doctor decretorum et notarius*; several other notaries were to take part in later hearings at Bologna, which may be regarded as the intellectual center of the notarial art.[34] Alberto's protocol begins with a detailed account of the public excitement surrounding Simon's death and the notary's deputation to record the miracles. The following briefly described miracle is reported:

> On 28 April [1322] a certain forty-five-year-old woman named Albarina, the daughter of master Bernardino de Argellata of the parish [*capella*] of Santa Maria the Greater, and wife of Master Prohenzalis Florini of *Terra di Argellata* in Bologna, said that for fifteen months or more she had been possessed by a demon. From the day it had happened, she would never look at the body of Our Lord Jesus Christ, and [the demon] would not allow her to take part in the sacred office. One day the enemy of God threw her into a well. While she was there she began to cry out; her daughter rushed to the well, and brought a large hook to her, and began to draw her out of the well with the hook. She had behaved in every way as demoniacs [customarily] do. Owing to the merits of the blessed Simon, she was freed. Her husband Master Prohenzalis, their son Bonaventura, and their daughter Ysabetta confirmed these things.

This notarial report contains all of the aforementioned essential elements of the miracle, although the precise vow and its fulfillment are lacking. The critical evidence concerning the symptoms of her disorder, its apparent causes (possession by the Devil) and consequences, and the natural methods employed to assist the victim, all appear.

Many of these incidents were reported in miracle collections by merely one witness testifying before a local notary (or cleric) responsible for documenting rumors of apparent supernatural intercession. Such reports are often rather sketchy, and are limited to the witness's name and the general circumstances of the reported miracle. For example, the miracles of Catherine of Fierbois, recorded over a hundred-year period (in French), provide the rudimentary elements of the miracle story, but are often corroborated by merely one witness, and did not undergo papal scrutiny.[35] Other reports, however, allow us to flesh out a more substantial description of the alleged event. The many cases found in the miracle collection (1347) of the Franciscan Gerard Cagnoli by Bartolomeo Albizi, for example, display a high degree of detail, allowing us to identify the very spots in Pisa or its *contado* where the incident occurred, the time, the names of the witnesses, and the reaction of the bystanders.[36]

Ecclesiastical Procedures

The fullest accounts appear as part of a large dossier prepared under episcopal or papal auspices in accordance with curial standards. Such ecclesiastically sanctioned inquiries often called as many as six witnesses to substantiate every alleged miracle. The processes of Pope Urban V, held from 1374 to 1376, questioned 659 witnesses.[37] The 1330 process of Yves of Tréguier lasted forty-three days and heard the testimony of seven or eight witnesses per day; 191 dealt with miracles and fifty-two with the putative saint's life.[38] One of the commissioners was the soon to be elected Pope Benedict XII (1334–42), Jacques Fournier, who had presided seven years earlier at the famous inquisition into heresy in the region of Pamiers. While such a formidable array of officials might well intimidate the callow witness, a conscientious attitude characterized the work of the notaries in this and other cases. In this case, four Breton dialects had to be translated into French and Latin; at least three notaries took part along with four translators. Some local terms in such inquiries of necessity remained untranslated: a vat known as a *buhot*; seaweed in coastal Brittany termed *goaymon*; a bolt or quarrel of a crossbow (*carellus*) called *enguengne*; a poisonous herb called *cavallina*; a vat filled with water, termed a *tina*.[39] Nevertheless, owing to the Hundred Years' War, Yves's canonization was much delayed, requiring the intervention of Charles of Blois, Duke of Brittany, and the appearance of the saint in a dream to Pope Clement VI.

Skeptical cardinals had been known to reject reports of miracles in which certain necessary evidence might be lacking, where the signs of death were inconclusive, or an insufficient number of corroborating witnesses had appeared. In the absence of a protocol of the curial discussions, the relatively small number of miracles eventually cited in the papal bulls of canonization suggests that few reported miracles were persuasive enough to stand up to learned scrutiny. Participants in the discussion of the miracles of Thomas of Hereford, for example, were concerned to show that the saint's miracles were confirmed by earlier acceptable precedents found in Scripture, Bede, Gregory, and Augustine; and in some cases, they cast doubt on either the reliability of the testimony, or the "scientific" evidence that a true miracle had occurred.[40] The care which was taken to insure that only irrefutable miracles received public recognition is indicated in the secret protocol of the discussions held in the papal consistory regarding Celestine V's miracles.[41] Cardinal Colonna reported that a small number of miracles had been selected "after many discussions and various debates, so that no doubtful cases should be recalled."[42] The cardinals were then polled in the presence of Pope Clement V; some miracles were rejected outright as lacking sufficient evidence; even some of those cases which were accepted by majority vote eventually failed to appear in the papal bull of canonization. The view was voiced that at least two witnesses were required, exclusive of the person experiencing the miracle. Among the most skeptical cardinals were Richard of Siena, Gaietano Stefaneschi, and the future Pope John XXII. Stefaneschi in his own *Ordo romanus* described the great care taken to verify, confirm, and discuss all the evidence following the initiation of a papal inquiry as a result of requests from prominent persons.[43]

In order to substantiate the witnesses' testimony, commissioners might visit the scene of the alleged miracle. Thus, those investigating the case of Charles of Blois visited the bridge at Angers where a man had fallen into the river Maine, but had been saved by divine intercession from certain death.[44] According to several witnesses, the site had in the past been the scene of the deaths of over one hundred persons and innumerable animals. This miracle represents one of the few examples in which the victim himself was allowed to explain at length why he believed he had been saved through supernatural power. The fifty-year-old Ralph Multoris[45] of the parish of St. Maurice in Angers reported that in 1368 along with other sailors, he had assisted a merchant in the portage by rope of a barge filled with wine to the mill at Angers. As they passed under a bridge on the banks of the Maine (called by one of the interlocutors the *Rue des chalons*), the heavy undertow caused him to fall into the river. In the amount of time that it "would take a horse to travel a quarter of a league" Ralph was dragged a distance of forty fathoms or arms-lengths. Nevertheless, he was saved by invoking Charles of Blois, and believed that this event could be attributed to miraculous causes for the following reasons: (1) he did not know how to swim; (2) he had never heard of anyone who had fallen into the river at the same spot and had survived; (3) he was of a relatively advanced age at the time (forty-seven, and therefore presumably not terribly fit); (4) he was fully clothed, wearing heavy boots, which would retain water; and (5) the merchant whom he had accompanied had already drowned. Other witnesses corroborated his testimony and provided detailed descriptions of the heavy work gear and boots Ralph had been wearing, which enhanced the likelihood of his sinking.[46] This episode illustrates the detail demanded by the professionals entrusted with the task of examining alleged miracles.

The Universal Appeal of the Saint

In addition to data about the miracle per se, those undertaking a canonization inquiry were also expected to inquire into the putative saint's public reputation (*de fama et communi voce et opinione*) and the cult (*devotio*) surrounding his or her relics.[47] The cult's supporters sought to emphasize the miracle as a public witness to the faith which bound the community together. Hagiographers claimed universality for their cults by portraying the active participation of all believers without regard to income, social class, age, or sex. Many of the best-documented miracles took place in public view of the crowds which had come to participate in the funeral of a recently dead saint, the invention and translation of his relics, or his feast day. The participants could thus reestablish their primal unity as members of the body of the faithful and overcome the boundaries of age, class, profession, sex, political persuasion, and education which separated them. The religious cult and its trappings had become one of the major expressions of social and political unity in the later middle ages. The reputation and relics of the miracle-worker were the foundation of the saint's cult, and much of the energy of the believers was focused on expressing their patriotism and membership in the Christian polity through participation in local cults. The desire to possess relics, to take part in the cultic procession, and to experience or witness a miracle were hallmarks of popular piety, particularly at a time when the wrath of God (*ira Dei*) had brought about such otherwise inexplicable calamities as the plague, endemic warfare, high mortality, and natural disasters characteristic of the age.

Witnesses to the miracles were asked how long the cult had been active and to identify its chief supporters, what kind of reputation they had, and whether they had some personal interest in its propagation. Such inquiries invariably suggest that a thriving cult had preceded the initiation of the papal process, which reflects the saint's "constituency." This proof of popular veneration was regarded by Hostiensis, for example, as the sina qua non of a canonization inquiry.[48] As Durand Curaterii, a citizen of Aix who had been taken hostage in Catalonia in 1289 and had served as steward in the household of Louis of Toulouse, said, "The citizens of Aix had already venerated and celebrated a feast in that year [1297, the year of Louis's death]; they honored him as a saint and, doing honor to God and Louis, established a confraternity whose membership grew in numbers."[49] The humanist archivist, hagiographer, and chancellor of Padua Sicco Polenton (1376–1447) in his lives of Anthony of Padua and Helen Enselmini was even to argue in favor of a kind of popular canonization paralleling papal authorization, saying, "Even if neither one has been approved by a judgment of the high pontiff, nevertheless, each one performed miracles and both may, in the opinion of the people [*populi opinione*] be placed among the blessed [*in ordine beatorum*]."[50]

While such inquiries allow us to view the public perception of sanctity and miracle and to determine the geographical and social boundaries of the cult, the *fama* or reputation of the saint had long been a standard hagiographical *topos*. The need to publicize miracles as a means of strengthening the faith, following ancient precedent, was therefore often voiced by contemporary hagiographers. Dorothy of Montau's biographer Johannes of Marienwerder argued that "just as the Jews had been instructed by God to recount to their children [during Passover] about the miracles [of the Exodus] from Egypt, the crossing of the Red Sea, the Judaean Desert, and [the conquest of] the Holy Land as a means of praising God through recollection of His deeds," so more recent miracles should be publicly exposed.[51] The

Benedictine chaplain Eberhard of Fürstenfeld (ca. 1346), who reported the miracles of St. Leonard of Inchenhofen, cited the words of the angel Raphael in Tobit 12.11 as justification for the publicity which should be accorded contemporary miracles: "A king's secret ought to be kept, but the works of God should be publicly honored." He suggested three further reasons: (1) to honor and glorify God and Leonard; (2) to satisfy his conscience, since God's works should not be hidden; and (3) to rectify evil, edify the good, and excite devotion and love.[52]

Each particular miracle created a hard kernel of followers whose allegiance to the cult was cemented through participation in a life-forming event. Nevertheless, in order to praise the saint and his relics, the hagiographer sought to stress the wide appeal of the cult through its miraculous effect on all classes and its geographical dispersion, even encompassing former foes. The grief displayed at the murder of the rector of Orvieto Peter Parenti by heretical "Patarenes," for example, was allegedly shared by "all the clergy, men, women and children"; so many were present at his funeral that disagreement arose over where to hold the service; the cathedral church was selected.[53] Other evidence concerning Peter's ministry, however, suggests that he was not universally loved. At the time of Elizabeth of Thuringia's canonization (1236) adherents allegedly flocked to Marburg from Germany, Bohemia, Hungary, and France, including persons of both sexes, drawn from every region, condition, and age group. The presence of Emperor Frederick II presumably strengthened Elizabeth's appeal. According to Pietro Cantinelli, the translation of the body of the Franciscan Tertiary Nevolo of Faenza on 27 July 1280 called forth the participation of "all the inhabitants of the city, men and women, urban and country folk"; and at the death of Clare Gambacorta of Rimini a multitude of persons "of every age, sex and condition" came to her tomb.[54]

Such claims of universal acceptance and participation in the cult may make reference to the social classes into which society was divided: for example, free and serf, or *magni* and *parvi*, which presumably refers to the two large classes of guild which divided the Italian commune.[55] An unusual list of participants appeared at the funeral of the Carmelite Peter Thomas at Famagusta: Greeks, Armenians, Georgians, Jacobites, Nestorians, Copts, and Maronites; while the procession he organized against the plague included Moslems and Jews.[56] An equally thorough list of participants is noted in the cult of Catherine of Siena, that is, persons of "every condition, age and status, secular, clergy and religious, monks, spiritual persons, poor and Jesuates, prelates and nobility, doctors, physicians, merchants, artisans, youth, children, and penitents of St. Dominic."[57] The very graphic description of persons stirred by the cult of William of Bourges noted that "men abandoned their rooms, and women their beds . . . villages were emptied, homes were left unguarded, servants and maids left their work; women still nursing babies came, some leaving the doors open and their children still in the cradle, so that they could attend the funeral service; children were left prey to beasts of field and forest."[58]

The theme of universal recognition, which may guarantee communal peace and concord, sometimes reflects a convergence of the thaumaturgical ministry of the saint or his relics with the kinds of persons who benefited. Wenceslas "freed some from prison, loosening their chains, snatching them from the sword, assisting different persons suffering many infirmities, aiding some in war and rescuing them from their enemies."[59] This was particularly the case in the strife-torn Italian communes. Venturino of Bergamo, who preached in 1334 and led over a thousand penitents to Rome, attracted persons of "every age of both sexes, every condition and social status [*conditio et gradus*], persons convicted of every kind of crime became penitent, peace was made between mortal enemies, demons were driven away."[60] Bartolomeo Albizi suggested that "inside and outside the city [of Pisa], in many families and homes, peace was achieved through the merits of St. Gerard [Cagnoli]."[61] Pietro Domenico of Baone (1380), writing about the festivities surrounding the cult of Henry of Treviso, said: "An endless number of persons who had been ensnared in crime miraculously would make confession of their sins, would repay the injuries they had inflicted; peace would reign between mortal enemies, both among citizens and villages; in short, such great peace and consolation would reign that year, and it subsequently so grew, that if

Homer had been present, he would scarcely be able to describe it."[62] One of the hoped-for consequences of the miracles of Bernardino of Siena was an end to the endemic warfare between Guelphs and Ghibellines in Aquileia.[63] All such descriptions of social peace and brotherhood as a consequence of the saint's charismatic power in fact contradict the known concentration of heretics and anticlerical groups in those very same areas where miracles took place.[64]

The Cultic Procession

The effort to mobilize support for the cult and to demonstrate its political and social powers focused on the ceremonial procession bearing the holy relics. This theatrical event occupied a central role in many of the protocols: it provides us with a tour of those spaces sanctified by the relics and summarizes the genres of miracle and the persons touched by supernatural intercession.[65] Participation in the ritual procession of the saint's relics reflected the social relationship between governed and governor, between church and state, between class, gender, and age cohorts. Ecclesiastical authorities attempted to maintain their monopoly over such festivities, which extended to both new cults and the revival of older cults, often initiated by a reburial service, when a wealthy donor was granted recognition for his benefactions to the church. In June 1342, for example, the relics of the martyrs Lucian, Marcian, and others were reburied at Vich in Catalonia thanks to the generosity of one Andrea Baratti. Following a sermon on the martyrs' lives and *passio* and a processional, the keys to the sepulchre were handed over to the authorities who regulated the extraordinary display of such relics during times of famine and plague.[66]

Considerable variation had characterized such processions. While the parish or quarter as a whole may be considered a sacred space by virtue of the saint after which it is named, a specially defined geography of the sacred found expression in the circuit followed by the religious procession. Certain persons, dates, places, and objects are "re-sanctified" in the course of the festivities, while others, given their secondary involvement, suffer exclusion or institutionalized disenfranchisement. The route of the procession may be of two kinds: either enclosed, that is, beginning and ending in the same place, generally the site of the relics, and encompassing major civic spaces, such as the church, cemetery, public square, or monastery; or linear, celebrated on one street or byway, joining the end points of the town or village. Topographical considerations may limit the routing of the procession. Geographically, the circumambulatory processional served to sanctify all quarters of the city, and to sanction a ritual assertion of the primitive unity which had once allegedly characterized the medieval commune.[67]

The procession bearing the relics of Gerard Cagnoli, described in great detail by Bartolomeo Albizi, began on 5 July 1346 with their arrival from Palermo and their placement in an alabaster reliquary at the Clarissian house of All Saints just outside of Pisa.[68] After a sermon at the church of San Giovanni, the procession commenced, consisting of a golden cross, many flags, candles, spears, four singers, and an orchestra, accompanied by church bells.[69] The celebrants criss-crossed the commune to the accompaniment of a series of miracles experienced by the chief town trumpeter, a local notary, a Franciscan friar, the wife of the communal sword-bearer, a knight's son, a woodcutter, a notary's wife, and the wife of the well-known artist Francesco Neri da Volterra, who was to be elected an *anziano* of Pisa in 1358.[70] The recipients of these miracles appear to have been members of the solid middle class. In the course of such a transit of relics, all quarters of the city were sanctified, special safe-conducts and indulgences were granted for attendance, arrests were halted, even for debt, and a special fair or trade day was declared.[71] The miracles which occurred in the course of such festivities or soon thereafter were the surest reminders of the divine favor with which the community had been blessed; those whose words or deeds threatened the withdrawal of such favor would be swiftly punished.

The drama and pageantry of the procession was not confined to Italy. A contemporary observer described the festivities that accompanied the display of the relics of Amalberga on the Thursday of Pentecost in the village of Temsche near Ghent. The entire population was expected to take part in the triumphal procession in which these and other sacred relics were carried about by the barefoot participants. Mimes, clowns, actors, organists, drummers, lyre, trumpet, hurdy-gurdy players, and other musicians took part. The people gathered together in the village of Avestone, accompanied by noblemen and women in covered carriages. The participants entered the church of St. Amalberga after a sermon and an account of her miracles were recited and the carriage bearing the saint's relics was held aloft. In 1322, a relatively small number of participants had taken part in the festivities and, as a result of the paucity of bearers, the carriage reached the altar with difficulty. A great hailstorm arose, which nearly destroyed the entire village. Since the storm did not extend beyond the borders of the village, which was regarded as Amalberga's sacred terrain, it was believed that God meant in this way to express wrath at the failure to honor the saint. Therefore, in 1323 everyone took part in the ceremony; and in 1331, Bishop William of Ghent granted an indulgence to those who visited the saint's tomb at St. Peter of Ghent.

Reports of miracles surrounding Amalberga's feast are a particularly rich reflection of social life in a village dominated by cloth-making. In 1327, a girl who had preferred to continue her spinning until nightfall rather than participate in the ceremonies was struck down; a councillor (*scabinus*) who doubted the exorcism of two persons became mute. Another woman had been prompted by devilish urging to steal twenty-one measures (*ulnas*) of linen cloth from a woman engaged in the cloth trade. The victim of the crime mistakenly accused a foreign young wool carder in her employ of the theft. The accused, making her way as a barefoot pilgrim to Temsche in order to secure Amalberga's aid, came upon the real thief trying to sequester her stolen goods in a pond. After the neighbors, including the local lord, had appeared, the criminal begged for Amalberga's pity, saying that the saint had urged her to reveal her crime, and was duly pardoned. All three women, reconciled, took part in the festivities and provide a fine illustration of the socially unifying role which its advocates attributed to the cult.

At the same time, a local prostitute, who had plied her trade for four years, renewed her plea to be freed of her hateful occupation (born of poverty) as the triumphal carriage bearing the saint's relics passed. On her way to Antwerp, near the well (marked by a cross) where Amalberga herself had once drawn water, she bent down and made an offering. Unable to move, she fell asleep, envisioning the saint accompanied by a great noise. Despite the efforts of lay and clergy to move her, she remained transfixed all night long, and the next day appeared as a penitent at Amalberga's shrine. Others so rescued in 1327 included a woman whose home had been spared during a general conflagration, a child saved from drowning, and several demoniacs.[72]

Scenes of mass enthusiasm were common in the course of the translation of relics, during the days surrounding a putative saint's funeral or on feast days. Ecclesiastical authorities often required the assistance of the civil arm to restore order. Such public displays of religious fervor, during which the precious relics might be torn to pieces by souvenir seekers, and persons jostling for a glimpse of the funeral cortege might be trampled underfoot by the mob (including pregnant women), were a commonplace of later medieval hagiography.[73] The most well-known such report concerned the relics of the charismatic Francis of Assisi, which were spirited away secretly in the dead of night lest the mob gain control of the situation. The local notary described the hysteria which erupted in the byways near the Augustinian church of San Jacopo at Bologna on 20–21 April 1322 during the funeral of Simon of Todi. The din was deafening, the crowd overwhelming, and the saint's clothes were dismembered. Civic authorities were called in to quell the near-riot.[74] The desire to possess the precious relics of Pope Celestine V after 1306, led to a conflict between the people of Ferentino, L'Aquila, and Anagni during which the monks of San Antonio tried to hide their "booty"; and the cities of Ferrara and Brona quarreled over the relics of Contardo of Este (d. 1342). When the people demanded the burial of Clare Gambacorta outside her cloister, the sisters refused, but were forced to provide a small opening above the altar through which spectators could view the funeral rites. In the case of Gandolph of Binasco, the brethren tried unsuccessfully to hide the relics.[75]

Although public excitement generally ensued immediately after the death of one who had gained a reputation as a miracle-worker, the establishment of a cult occasionally required some encouragement. A colorful story is found in the life (1335) of Joachim Piccolomini (d. 1305).[76] Despite the many miracles which had occurred during his lifetime, the first posthumous miracle occurred in 1310, only five years after his death:

> In the fifth year after his death many people had come in May because of the indulgence granted San Galgano [i.e., the monastery of San Galgano at Chiusdino, about twenty-two miles from Siena]. Gathered around a fire because it was a bit cold, they began to discuss the life and miracles of the blessed Ambrose of Siena [d. 1286] and Peter Pettinaio [d. 1289] and of other good, dead men whom they knew and who had lived in their lifetime. One of them began to praise the blessed Joachim, and in order to raise him above all the others, said that he was somewhat surprised that God had not performed miracles through him. A *conversus* of their order was seated with them and reported that he had a severe infection, called in the vernacular *inguinaria* [inflammation of the groin].

This narrative, which is followed by the report of a miraculous cure, suggests the competition between rival cults, which often masked political conflict and rivalry between religious orders and confraternities. It should be noted that while Ambrose of Siena came from one of the leading oligarchical Guelph families of Siena, Peter was probably a poor wool carder, whose supporters may have preferred the Ghibellines. Despite Joachim's long-awaited miracle, a more public display of the saint's power was required in order to stir up the necessary enthusiasm to create a new cult. A young girl was freed of an incubus following a sermon preached beside the saint's tomb in 1310. The demon declared that he had preferred to be expelled through Joachim's power rather than by his competitors.

The festivities surrounding the saint's cult and the circuit of the relics through the village or town were visible signs of the unity allegedly engendered by divine patronage. The popular enthusiasm was an effective means of restoring unity and social order to a fragmented and conflict-ridden society. Ritual has been defined as "rule-governed activity of a symbolic character which draws the attention of its participants to objects of thought and feeling which they hold to be of special significance."[77] Such rituals tend to communicate shared values in groups and to reduce internal dissension; new rituals will appear when the social institutions or traditions of society are under severe attack, often as a result of rapid social change. The ritual drama surrounding the cult of Corpus Christi or the cult of a local saint helped to reinforce society's self-image and to consolidate and integrate commonly held norms and values. Such rituals served as communal bonding systems which reduced intragroup violence.

The medieval consensus was founded on the principle that society was made up not of isolated individuals, but rather of persons united by God through the act of baptism. One's social role as a member of the body of Christ absorbed the individual, while anyone who was excluded by virtue of blasphemy, heresy, or deviance risked divine retribution.[78] The failure to participate actively in the cult, to fulfill a vow, to recognize a miraculous event when it occurred, or to deny the saint's power after one had enjoyed his or her patronage, were classified as acts of blasphemy and punished accordingly. In 1345, a youth of Pisa had been attacked by a malign spirit and was cured after a visit to the shrine of Gerard Cagnoli.[79] But although his health had returned and his parents had fulfilled their vow, be began to "condemn the relics of the saint." As a result he suffered an incurable relapse. Nearly every hagiographical source contains a rubric under which are subsumed such miracles in which those who blaspheme the saint or his relics or fail to honor a feast day are punished.[80] The public character of the cult and awareness of the punishment wrought against doubters encouraged believers to call on supernatural intercession in time of stress.

The image of the saint as an intercessor in time of distress appears in both learned sermon and popular belief. The supreme heavenly court of justice was populated by saints who could sue before God on behalf of their devotees. In an All Saints' Day sermon Jordan of Quedlinburg likened the Christ in majesty, the King of Heaven, to the source of light; Mary, the Queen of Heaven, to a lesser light; and the saints, the knights of the heavenly court, to the stars.[81] One preacher reported that a monk who had accidentally fallen off a bridge and was about to be taken by Satan, was defended by the Virgin, who said, "I will put my case before my son's tribunal so that he can pass judgment."[82] A French preacher argued that the kings of the earth have their prisons to punish evildoers and maintain justice, just as the King of Heaven has three prisons to incarcerate sinners, namely hell, purgatory, and limbo.[83] Such allusions were not limited to contemporary art or sermons, but reached the more popular level. For example, in 1347 one Neza Alliata of Pisa fasted on bread and water in hope of receiving a revelation concerning the fate of her sister, who had died suddenly from unknown causes.[84] After beseeching Gerard Cagnoli for assistance, she had a vision of her sister, who reported that she had died of natural causes and had been saved through invocation of Gerard at the time of her death. She reported that the saint himself was a resident in the court of heaven, where his requests were answered. Elsewhere, Gerard's Franciscan biographer described him as a heavenly knight whose arrival in heaven was treated by the King of Heaven and his consort Mary as befitted a new soldier recently admitted to the royal court.[85]

T W O

The Church as Mediator and Victim

A lthough the natural philosophers and canonists sought to define and limit the miracle, the distressing conditions prevalent in the fourteenth century encouraged such belief in the efficacy of the rescue miracle among all classes. The procession, confraternities, feast days, and other public activities connected to the cult served as the means of enforcing such uniformity of belief, and encouraged the suppliant to seek divine assistance from the local patron. In his classic account of the waning middle ages Johann Huizinga rightly spoke of the fourteenth century as a time of both excessive exhilaration and despair: "All things presenting themselves to the mind in violent contrasts and impressive forms, lent a tone of excitement and of passion to everyday life and tended to produce that perpetual oscillation between despair and distracted joy, between cruelty and pious tenderness which characterize life in the Middle Ages."[1] Such extremes of emotion and violence have been defined by Marc Bloch as the most distinguishing mark of a decaying feudal system and were aggravated during the destructive warfare of the fourteenth century, which hastened the brutalization of society.[2] The despair, violence, pessimism, and anxiety brought on by the traumas of the later medieval period have continued to be documented by historians.[3]

Even before the depredations of the Great Plague in 1348–9, the deteriorating social environment had been heightened after the onset of the Little Ice Age (ca. 1307). Protracted and destructive military conflicts like the Hundred Years' War, earthquakes, food shortages and hoarding, theft of grain from communal granaries, falsification of documents in order to obtain unjustified payments from the state, speculation, and smuggling were increasingly widespread.[4] As a woman of Kleinmüchen in Upper Austria said in 1359, "When the pestilence filled the world, men became accustomed to spreading great violence among us."[5] In 1364 one of those who recorded the miracles of Leonard of Inchenhofen (like his early medieval monastic predecessors) linked the plague, war, and exploitation of the poor together, saying, "After this on the vigils of St. Bernard [19 August], there came [a plague of] locust and grasshoppers, of which there were many; because of their great number they darkened the light of day and they devastated the land in a miraculous way [see Psalms 104.34] and destroyed much of the vegetation. In those days a great war and conflict raged between the Bavarians and Austrians in which monasteries and many poor folk suffered."[6]

The extremes of emotion noted by Huizinga were evident not only on the interpersonal level, but also in the public sphere. The catastrophic "terrors of history" were paradoxically accompanied by sumptuous parades and lavish festivals, often dedicated to local saints, and organized by both government and private benefactors. Such grandiose and conspicuous displays of wealth were noted by contemporary observers like Boccaccio as a characteristic feature of the plague period. The post-plague period, as Mireille Vincent-Cassy has noted, also witnessed a sharp increase in expressions of envy, and a growing resentment of the unjust hierarchical social structure.[7] The contemporary observer Jean de Venette spoke of an avaricious, covetous class which was born after the plague and reached maturity after 1370. Such envy was often regarded by moralists as a cause of the popular revolts which broke out in the 1370s and 1380s, during which the nobility, clergy, and urban oligarchy felt threatened by villeins and artisans. One such case of civil disorder is found in the protocol of Leonard of Inchenhofen. In 1404 a man of Kelheim in Lower Bavaria appeared at the shrine at the order of the consuls and principal judges of the city. Fearing that their lives and property were endangered by a movement (*conspiratio*) against them, they had sent a messenger to Inchenhofen bearing an iron ex-voto offering in the form of the place where justice is rendered. Their faith was rewarded, and the commotion died down.[8] Political changes in the city in 1404 may have been related to these events.

The plague, warfare, famine, and revolution which afflicted much of Europe after about 1330 served to weaken the sense of personal responsibility and to loosen social and institutional restraints. Violence had become a normative means of settling disputes, however petty, while extremes of emotional expression had become distinguishing marks of contemporary culture. Recent monographic studies have confirmed the macabre presence of death; demographers have suggested that after reaching a high point in the late thirteenth century, life span had begun to decline.[9] Public beatings for such crimes as adultery, sodomy, false witness, slander, and default were widespread. In the absence of any trustworthy agency of appeal, the victims of such injustice often sought divine assistance, and the miracle stories provide evidence of these conditions. Irrational, brutal, and impulsive behavior seems to have been the norm, demanding considerable attention on the part of the governing authorities, who were concerned with guaranteeing public safety.[10] Summarizing the genesis of violence in the eyes of contemporary moralists, David Herlihy has said, "The young, the unmarried, the spoiled rich, and the degenerate poor, those too much neglected by their fathers and pampered by their mothers identify as the chief perpetrators of violence and disorder."[11]

The Need for Divine Intercession

Four categories devised by J. R. Hale describe the violence during this period: (1) personal violence, such as assault, rape, and murder; (2) group violence, such as revolution, aimed at achieving political or economic ends; (3) organized illegitimate violence, like brigandage and sea piracy; and (4) organized, legitimized violence, carried out by armies, police forces, and so forth.[12] Prevailing conditions in the fourteenth century encouraged appeal to the supernatural in pursuit of relief in such cases. In the medieval, urban context, one may perhaps add the kind of psychological violence and humiliation through shaming which was to become an integral part of the festive calendar in the late thirteenth century. In the course of cathartic games, competitions, and processions, such marginal groups as the Jews, *ribaldi*, prostitutes, residents of conquered cities, the youth, and others, were subjected to ritual, public humiliation as a means of defining the consensus of respectability, and stressing the legal and social inferiority of such groups.[13] As Victor Turner has noted, such ritualization (even if it involves some violence) "reduces intra-group violence, serves as a communal bonding system, communicates shared values, underlines the exclusiveness of cultural events, [and] assigns emotional value to handed-down customs."[14]

In general, conflicts may fall under three broad categories: (1) disputes between parties of relative equality, (2) conflicts that cross lines of stratification, and (3) disputes caused by the ruler's efforts to govern and in which the ruler and his agents are directly involved. Bilateral negotiation, third-party arbitration, or resolution by an allegedly neutral party (such as a judge) are the most common institutionalized means of achieving adjudication of such disputes. And in order to guarantee compliance, the adjudicator must invariably be able to invoke coercive sanctions. However, resort to a supernatural agency, armed with the sanction of divine revenge, becomes more widespread in the resolution of conflict when: (1) the state or authorities appear to have lost control, are perceived as excessively partisan, or have themselves become the source of victimization; or (2) in a struggle between two unequal partners, the weaker party can no longer rely on the state as an arbitrator.[15] These conditions were often fulfilled in the fourteenth century, especially when the competence or even the willingness of human judicial authority to act was in doubt. A woman whose son had been detained for five weeks in 1315, and whose life was in danger, for example, justified the resort to divine intervention as a means of avoiding "the partiality of the commune."[16]

There had been many earlier precedents for the intervention of supernatural power or its surrogate agent, the institutional church, in the adjudication of disputes or the reduction of violence. In the early middle ages, for example, ordeals had reflected a generalized belief in a divine justice immanent in the world which would intervene in order to judge the guilty and free the innocent where alternate means of adjudication were lacking. In the central middle ages, however, reliance on immanent divine justice had given way to faith in human judicial competence and authority with the concurrence of both clergy and laity. Nevertheless, despite the efforts of theologians, canonists, and lawyers, belief in the possibility of appeal to the divine against injustice remained ingrained among much of the laity, as revealed in miracle stories. The institution of torture in the mid-thirteenth century suggests that even established authority maintained only a limited faith in reaching judgment by means of judicial standards of proof. A continuing faith in supernatural mediation was one means of insuring universally recognized infallible judgment, by bringing heavenly justice closer to earthly in order to achieve concord and peace.

In the fourth century the intervention of the church in the settlement of disputes had received imperial sanction with the official recognition of the decisions of episcopal courts. This involvement in the settlement of disputes—even in business matters—found support in 1 Corinthians 6.1–6 ("Dare any of you, having a matter against another, bring your case to be judged before the unjust and not before the saints? Do you not know that the saints will judge the world?").[17] This considerably enhanced the spiritual and political authority of the church; as early as 318 or 321 the constitutions of Constantine had provided for the inviolability of episcopal arbitration; in cases of conflict between church and state, the accused might exploit the precedent of sanctuary and the right of appeal to the bishop as a means of escaping imperial or royal justice.[18] Appeal to the bishop was to become an accepted means of receiving pardon. Clerical inspection of prisons, the release of prisoners, and the manumission of slaves were classified as acts of charity, based on Isaiah 61.1 ("The Lord hath anointed me . . . to proclaim liberty to captives and release those in prison") and Isaiah 63.7 ("The Lord hath called thee . . . to bring out the prisoners from prison, and they that sit in the darkness out of the prison-house"). Among the early bishops who freed prisoners from bondage were Sts. Aubin of Angers, Evermode of Ratzeburg, Gregory of Langres, and Lupus of Châlons. An early theme in Christian hagiography portrayed the saint miraculously freeing a suppliant from the gallows.[19] A report appears in the life of Hugh of Lincoln of a thief condemned to the gallows who appealed to the clergy. The secular judges allegedly admitted that English law recognized such a right, although it had fallen into disuse owing to the "tyranny of princes, and the apathy of modern bishops."[20] Although there was no uniform system of adjudication, by the thirteenth century Pope Gregory IX was to recognize Roman law as the basis of arbitration procedures in which the church was involved.[21]

The bishop thus became a major dispenser of justice and the episcopal patron saint traditionally used his charismatic power to bring about communal and national harmony. Furthermore, following pre-Christian tradition, the right of sanctuary within sacred precincts was recognized. Such intercessory rights were easily transferred to the saint himself, who patronized the church or monastery; and even the requested pardon of undeserving petitioners might warrant divine intervention. The bishop or the saint, as God's surrogate, could thus soften the rigors of the law and save a convicted criminal from execution. During the Carolingian period, the transfer of political power to the episcopate (particularly in the towns), strengthened such clerical intervention in secular law. Clerical involvement and presence in the sanctification of the marriage contract, the feudal oath, and trials by ordeal further erased the thin line between spiritual and secular authority. Such crimes as simony, heresy, apostasy, sacrilege, perjury, and transgression of a vow would by their nature necessarily be dealt with in ecclesiastical courts.[22] The tradition of the ordeal, along with the direct mediation of the local priest or bishop in the settlement of disputes, thus represented precedents for divine intervention in the reduction of violence.

Clerical and Divine Mediation

Aside from the intervention of the bishop or saint as mediator, another extralegal form of adjudication was the *assurement*, a contract between warring parties for the settlement of disputes without direct judicial involvement. In areas where family vendetta was common, the publication of such public instruments might be required as a means of freeing the imprisoned.[23] These peace pacts between rival clans were an effective means of arbitration in a period of endemic clan warfare and lack of central political authority. In Florence, for example, the communal statutes of 1322–5 attempted to enlist the aid of the court system in the promotion of such informal pacts, while procedures formerly limited to the nobility were now extended to include affluent peasants, *popolani*, and artisans.[24]

If violence, intimidation, or direct negotiation failed, resort to elected arbitrators or third-party mediators became necessary options for the settlement of conflict. This system of arbitration was introduced in France largely through clerical influence.[25] In the Italian cities, where communal violence was widespread, extraordinary tribunals to settle disputes were common. The defeat of the Ciompi at Florence, for example, led to the establishment of a special court on 2 September 1378.[26] Such arbitration was not confined merely to secular and common law, but canon law also encouraged such procedures, and monasteries and episcopal records abound in such cases, especially when the church's dependents demanded justice against the allegedly unjust exactions of the clergy. The chronicle of St. Albans sheds much light on quarrels over feudal rights. A very serious dispute which arose between the people and the abbey of St. Albans in the early fourteenth century required the appointment of twelve arbitrators to secure an agreement.[27] Such procedures traditionally began with a *compromissio*, which suggested a willingness on the part of the two parties to observe the decision of the arbitrators, including an expressed undertaking to pay a large sum of money if one failed to submit. It defined the arbitrator's powers, stated the form of arbitration, identified the issues of the case, and set forth the terms of its completion. This was followed by the *arbitrium*, that is, the final decision of the judges. Both of these stages were generally written down in formulaic terms. Because of the voluntary character of the *compromissio*, arbitration granted the participants greater freedom of choice and was cheaper than other forms of adjudication.[28]

The phases of this procedure in many ways recall the suppliant's vow made to a patron saint in return for miraculous assistance. Both the religious vow and the arbitration agreement included the following elements: (1) an implicit willingness to resort to an external agency for assistance, (2) a summary of the problem and its hoped-for solution, and (3) a conditional promise to provide an offering in the event that the problem was solved. In both cases, appeal from the final judgment was not permitted and the breach of contractual terms warranted severe reprisal. The failure to fulfill the conditions of such a vow was a mortal sin and entailed the kind of retributive punishment resulting from the failure to abide by the arbitration procedure.[29] And indeed, all miracle collections contain examples of individuals who had not fulfilled their vows and who suffered the revenge of the saint whom they had offended. Particularly in situations of fear and uncertainty, vows and ex-voto offerings were made on condition of obtaining one's demands. Such offerings were of two kinds: commemorative offerings were generally related to pilgrimage, procession, Jubilee, and so forth; and devotional offerings represented the continuing contact of the individual believer with his divine patron. The ex-voto offering served as a witness to the intermingling of the extraordinary, miraculous, or marvelous in everyday life.[30] The suppliant's relationship to a divine protector was characterized by both respect and reciprocity; a violation of this contractual relationship through failure to fulfill a vow could "naturally" entail divine revenge.[31] Thus, the appeal to divine intervention in order to rescue a helpless victim from the fearful grip of a life-threatening situation, which is the central theme of the rescue miracle, bears comparison to more traditional forms of mediation in which a human agency is present, whether clerical or secular; in the absence of such an agent, appeal is made to a saint in return for the fulfillment of a vow. The care taken to record the precise words of supplication uttered by the *miraculé* or his surrogate suggests the ritual nature of this relationship with the divine, which differs little from the formulas required in the secular court.[32]

In addition to the conclusion of a formal agreement between the two parties, should a criminal be found guilty of injuring another, in lieu of direct supernatural or clerical intervention, clemency could be granted by means of a royal pardon; and many of the pilgrims who appeared as witnesses in miracle collections may have been involved in one of the many expiatory pilgrimages peopled by heretics, murderers, and the like.[33] The institution of royal remission began to acquire definitive form in the fourteenth century, although the documentation is sparse. In some instances its issuance may have been prompted by a religious event, like the Holy Thursday 1362 general deliverance issued to prisoners at the Paris Châtelet. Most of the surviving letters of remission (largely from a later period) deal with cases of involuntary homicide, and were issued following an accord reached between the perpetrator and the victim's family, in which some indemnity was pledged. While the growing use of royal letters of remission seems to have paralleled a rise in the crime rate, the institution also served to enhance royal power. Although rarely stated in the miracle collections, many penitents may well have been fulfilling the provisions of such a letter, which required an expiatory pilgrimage.[34] Such a rare, explicitly stated remission is found in the collection of Catherine of Fierbois. Pierrot Contentin appeared at Catherine's shrine in late 1385 or early 1386 after having taken two women by force to sleep with him and a companion. He reported that a pilgrimage had been prescribed by King Charles VI and Queen Isabella in return for his freedom.[35] The protocol of Urban V also reports the imposition by the court of Nice of a fine of thirty-five crowns for an unspecified crime committed by one Antoine Bove; in lieu of payment, which he could not afford, he would be imprisoned. Following a vow to go as a penitent pilgrim to Urban's shrine with an offering of two lire of wax, and the intervention of his cousin Gaspar Aguilhon, a merchant of Nice, the seneschal granted remission of his punishment.[36]

The continuing role of the clergy as mediators in the reduction of communal conflict and assistance to persons in distress is made explicit in miracles drawn from various regions. In these cases, the clergy appear as benefactors. Blezvanna Gasqueder of Tréguier, for example, discovered in March 1312 or 1320 that all of her wealth had been stolen and promised to offer ten sous to the tomb of St. Yves and two deniers annually for the rest of her life should her goods be restored. Although she allegedly had no prior suspicions, she suddenly suspected that three malefactors might be the culprits, and asked the episcopal officers [servientes] to search their homes. Three-quarters of her lost property was immediately found in one of the criminals' homes. The third man, Yves Ponteur, had already fled to a village situated about a league from Tréguier, and was unexpectedly stricken with blindness. The perpetrator's wife consulted her brother-in-law, who suggested that the affliction was caused by his thieving ways. A third brother, a monk of Beauport in the diocese of Dol, was asked to accompany Blezvanna to a neutral spot where she could regain her stolen goods. Yves admitted that drunkenness had led to his thievery, and he promised to give two sous annually to St. Yves in return for the restoration of his sight, which occurred several hours later.[37] This same Blezvanna was the victim of a second theft in which clerical mediation also helped to retrieve her goods. During the feast of St. Nicholas (6 December), 1318, she had lost an elaborately decorated golden dish weighing (or valued at) one-and-a-half marks of Tréguier, which was restored to her in 1324. It had been found in the ruins of a burning house by a knight and a baker (termed the son of the *presbyter novus*), both of whom had searched the house at the urging of the local priest. Perhaps the perpetrator had revealed his theft in confession, and the priest could assist only after the conflagration.[38] In addition to confirming the impartial role played by the clergy, these episodes also suggest the existence of bands of thieves or "organized crime," which preyed on relatively affluent folk such as Blezvanna; and that as a local patron saint, Yves's benefactions could extend even to reformed criminals. The victim's repeated dependence on clerical assistance suggests, in the absence of supplementary evidence, that she was in some way a dependent of the church.

The presence of several parallel law codes—clerical, royal, seignorial—is a medieval commonplace and sometimes made it difficult to define jurisdiction clearly. The miracle stories provide many examples in which civil matters such as theft and imprisonment for debt might entail resort to clerical authority. One case suggests that in some areas the church continued to possess some residue of jurisdictional power. Hans Marolff had been sentenced to hang for murder sometime before 1370 on the island of Linden on Lake Constance, although he had acted in self-defense. The abbess and fourteen sisters of St. Mary had been present at the judgment. Although the town councillors were responsible for such cases, the women had succeeded in freeing Marolff, owing to the authority of Sts. Mary and Leonard.[39] In another case, a quarrel (*rixa*) had arisen at Die in October 1374 in the course of which Guillaume d'Urra, lord of Tauxières, was critically wounded. After the final rites had been administered, the *preceptor* of the hospitallers at Pouget invoked Urban V and suggested that the perpetrator, Jean Dalficus, offer ten gold florins to the saint's tomb; the man survived.[40]

Such clerical assistance sometimes extended to debtors in distress. A man of Schönau in Pomerania had been warned by his creditors; he vowed to Dorothy of Montau that he would undertake a penitent pilgrimage should the money to pay his debts be found. A local priest then lent him the money; after failing to fulfill his vow to the letter, he eventually brought his offering by foot, took communion, and confessed.[41] The saint's mediating assistance to the debtor following a vow also might call forth unanticipated assistance from lay persons. One man who had already been imprisoned for debt was led past the tomb of King Wenceslas. After pleading for the saint's aid, he was released. A man of Pisa who owed four hundred florins had fled for fear that the judgment might go against him and he would be imprisoned; his sister's vow led to sureties being supplied unexpectedly by some friends until he could raise the money himself.[42] Bridget of Sweden herself had reportedly suffered distress concerning debts during a stay at Rome. Following a vision that all would be well, she was aided by messengers from Sweden, who helped to settle her affairs.[43]

In some of the more detailed miracle reports, the existence of a formal arbitration agreement in which the church played a role is merely implicit, but appears to have required the fulfillment of a vow and the conclusion of a treaty of peace between the participants. Gerard Cagnoli's protocol reports that two young men, Gaddo and Francesco, who had quarreled on an earlier occasion as a result of Gaddo's anger, met two days later (on 11 January 1346 at about nine o'clock) on a street situated between the Ponte Vecchio and the Ponte Spina on the Arno River at Pisa. A duel ensued, and Francesco, whose sword-tip had broken off and who had no shield, tried to flee. Stumbling, he was pursued and caught by Gaddo, who grabbed him by the head and inflicted three deep wounds in his lower chest. The perpetrator fled, and the bystanders, taking Francesco for dead, took the youth to a nearby druggist; astonishingly, he began to breath, opened his eyes, and reported that a vow to Gerard at the moment of injury had saved his life. Gaddo was later to report having heard the vow being uttered. No torn garments or blood were to be seen. Hearing what had transpired, Gaddo made peace with his opponent and they both appeared at Gerard's tomb bearing an image of the saint and embracing in a kiss of peace, offering Francesco's shirt and Gaddo's sword to the saint.[44]

This report sounds very much like an account of the reckless activities of the *charivari*, those bands of youthful troublemakers so often noted in late medieval communal records. The patriotic appeal to a local mediator such as Gerard, whose Franciscan order had often brought peace to warring communal factions, was a means of bring-ing such factions together. The protocol of the Dominican Ambrose of Siena contains a similar report of two men, Cherubino de Francheris Caietani of Arezzo and Salimbergo de Rosellis, who had sworn to fight a duel. On the eve of the event, Cherubino, a devotee of Ambrose, had celebrated a mass and commended himself to God and the saint; wounded in the course of the duel, he again invoked God and Ambrose. Although he regained his strength and gained the upper hand, he expressed to Salimbergo a willingness to concede, and told his friends that he had seen a vision of Ambrose urging him to spare his enemy. The two embraced and were cured of their wounds.[45] In these two cases, both families may have been involved in the mediation of these quarrels, which could otherwise have led to further bloodshed. The solution required mutual acceptance by both parties of the saint's authority.

Both of these cases suggest that the saint and his relics, as local apotheoses of a higher power, could be invoked to restore communal peace. While these episodes merely imply the fulfillment of a treaty of peace between two warring clans, in which the *consorterie* of young men served as the shock troops, an episode at Siena explicitly refers to an *instrumentum* which concluded an agreement between warring families. A man of Tuscany had been attacked at night in his own home. The intended victim invoked Ambrose of Siena, and the as-sassin's sword struck the window, rather than his prey. The perpetra-tor asked forgiveness of God and St. Ambrose; the intended victim offered him peace, and a public instrument to maintain the peace between them was drawn up.[46]

The genesis of such conflicts was regarded as anger. Raymund of Penyaforte had listed the six progeny of anger (*ira*) as "brawling, an inflamed mind, contumely, outcry, indignation and blasphemy," all of which were amenable to the curative balm of divine intercession.[47] Among the "victims" of such anger, whose unfortunate consequences were overcome by a vow were: Bernard Vernet, who (as a student at Montpellier in 1367) had wounded a third party in the fracas during a quarrel with a companion; a man of Bruges who had injured a prominent citizen during a brawl in 1374 and feared life imprison-ment because he could not pay the two-hundred-franc fine; and a canon and acolyte of the canons regular in Rebdof (Franconia), who had been jailed for injuring a subdeacon.[48]

The above examples merely intimate that the failure to settle a dispute could have damaging implications beyond the warring parties themselves. Several other episodes reveal that what had begun as a private disagreement could involve an entire community and endanger the public welfare, and that, despite widespread efforts to curb private war, only supernatural intercession could restore concord. In a case reported in Bridget of Sweden's protocol, attempts to restore peace between rival clans required mediation by many parties: a friend who was devoted to Bridget, a monk, Pope Urban V, Joanna I of Naples, the King of Hungary, and the saint herself.[49] In the end, only the fear of dying unreconciled and suffering damnation (at least as the clerical reporters saw it) led to a reconciliation. Andriolo Morismolo (d. 1393), a knight of Naples, was seneschal or major domo and lord of Castelnuovo in 1388. According to his sister, he had decided to sell all of his landed property (*bona sua stabilia*) in the course of a mortal struggle (*lis et briga mortalis*) then being waged between his clan and the Costanzii (one of whose members, Cristoforo di Costanzo, had served as vice-seneschal to Joanna of Naples). Andriolo's aim was to prevent the royal authorities from confiscating or selling his goods. After the intervention of Pope Urban V, Joanna of Naples, and the King of Hungary had failed, Andriolo and his followers were incarcerated at the queen's order in order to bring peace between the clans and keep him from selling his property. After Andriolo fell ill, he was warned by a monk that if he was not reconciled with his foes, he could not be saved. A friend named Antonio de Carleto, who had been acquainted with Bridget, gave him a small crucifix which had once belonged to the saint, along with other relics; and Andriolo commended himself to her. In his illness he envisioned a demon warning him, "You are damned, because you have not voluntarily made your testament, but were forced to do so." Bridget also appeared, saying, "You are damned because you have made peace with your enemies with your mouth, but not in your heart." He then called his kinfolk and friends together, saying, "So that I may not perish, and so that I may remit my sins, I want to make a firm and lasting peace between you and the Costanzii. In mouth, heart and deed I

accede to you in everything, and you should make peace with them."
After the peace was concluded, Andriolo had an image of Bridget
painted at the church of Santa Maria de Carmelo at Naples. It appears in this case that members of Andriolo's own family had been
instrumental in intervening to settle the dispute in order to insure
their inheritance. Bridget's long stay in Italy, where she had died,
and her continuing support for return of the papacy to Rome, had
considerably enhanced her reputation in the south.[50] A similar feud
(*rixa*) had embroiled the Augustinian nuns of San Marco (situated a
stone's throw from the gates of Pisa) from 1343 to 1347.[51] The intervention of archbishops, bishops, and the commune of the Pisa, along
with other ecclesiastical and lay persons, had failed to bring peace.
"The dissension grew daily, so that the archbishop's *familia*, and the
neighbors were forced to occupy themselves with settling the rum-
pus." The rancor was so great that the sisters could neither take communion nor even eat together. The posthumous appearance of Gerard Cagnoli restored concord to the divided house.

In this and all of the preceding conflicts several common features
appear: (1) the documentation is largely Mediterranean, particularly
Italian; (2) young men appear to have been the principal disturbers
of the peace; (3) the perpetrators often appear to have had the active
backing of some organized group such as a clan or fellowship; (3) the
solution of conflict required a supplication for aid from the saint on
the part of one of the participants and precise fulfillment of the vow
so as to avoid revenge; (4) the interceding saint had already gained
a local reputation as a peacemaker; and (5) some kind of treaty of
peace between the warring parties appears to have concluded the establishment of peace. Thus, in these intractable cases (which sometimes aroused the entire community), what was perceived as direct
divine intervention replaced the more formal agencies of ordeal,
compurgation, trial, or ecclesiastical or government intervention;
and such intercession appears to have been the only effective means
of restoring order.

Clerical Victims

Despite their privileged position and service as mediators between
sinful humanity and a merciful God, the clergy were no less the

victims of crime. On the one hand, since all of our documents are of clerical origin, the clergy may have been given disproportionate attention in the miracle tales. On the other hand, the breakdown of central authority, the Babylonian Captivity and the Great Schism, along with increasing expressions of envy and anger at clerical wealth (which were widely reported by contemporary moralists) made the clergy ready objects of criminal activity. Sometimes, they themselves were thieves, like the legendary Friar Tuck. At the Benedictine monastery of Montmajour in Avignon (one of Urban V's favored abbeys), a plate valued at twenty-seven gold marks had been stolen in August 1375 along with other valuables. The wrongly accused priest of Canigou in the diocese of Nîmes, Arnold of Prades, made a vow, and the true culprit was revealed to be a monk.[52] But the clergy were more often victims of theft. Thomas à Kempis reported that in 1408 that money had been stolen from his cell through an open window and was restored after a prayer to St. Agnes, the patroness of the monastery.[53] As another example, a priest of San Grado at Pisa was robbed of a horse in August 1346, which was then sold to another priest in Tuscany or Piedmont; an innocent man unjustly accused of the crime escaped after pleading to Gerard of Pisa for help.[54]

Sometimes clergy were victimized in the course of performing their duties. Jean, the Franciscan guardian of St. Jean d'Angelé, had gone to Aunay for three days in 1386 to preach; in his absence, a coat and other property were stolen from him. The malefactors admitted their crime a month later, following his vow to Catherine of Fierbois.[55] A whole cast of characters appears in the following story, which provided excellent propaganda in support of the cult of Pope Urban V.[56] Robericus Johannis of Óbidos (in the diocese of Lisbon), a thirty-six-year-old student of canon law, reported that in January 1376 he had accompanied the Cistercian abbot Martin of Alcobatia, to Montpellier. The abbot had in his possession a sizeable sum of money which he had divided among members of his retinue, among them a monk who had been given seventy gold pieces in a leather pouch for safekeeping. This monk had then given the pouch to the abbot's sexton (*cubicularius*), who had hidden it under a mattress at the inn in which they were lodged. After leaving the city, the monk inquired about the money, and the embarrassed sexton, who had forgotten the money at the inn, denied having received it altogether. An altercation ensued, in the course of which the abbot understood that the money had been inadvertently left behind at the inn, and was in all likelihood lost. Inquiries revealed that, according to the innkeeper and his wife, soldiers had occupied the room after the abbot's departure, and that no money was to be found in the bed. A month passed, and when the abbot still had no word of the lost pouch, at Robericus's advice he beseeched God, the Virgin, and Urban V. He then ordered both the precentor of Coimbra Alphonse Stephani and said sexton to return to Montpellier and undertake a new investigation of the matter. It turned out that the innkeeper's wife had stolen the money; in thanksgiving, the abbot offered an orphrey and some silken cloth valued at fourteen florins to Urban's shrine.

The large number of persons and the amount of money they were carrying suggest that the abbot and his retinue were on their way to Avignon in order to conduct official business. Urban V's protocol in particular is peopled with clerics caught in frustrating and costly litigation, sometimes the victims of the deliberate Avignonese policy of exploiting the papal right of *reservatio* as a means of enriching papal coffers. Urban had a reputation for restraining the greed of the papal lawyers and procurers and opposing the unwarranted accumulation of benefices.[57] Such victims of delay and unjust expense thus sought divine aid in order to achieve just settlement of their claims. Three illustrative cases may be highlighted. In the first case, Pierre de la Garde, prior of St. Stephen of Franquevaux (diocese of Mende) had litigated at the curia in Avignon in a case involving the sum of 300 francs. After long delay, he finally acquired enough money to pursue the case further; but he foolishly entrusted the money to a friend, who then denied having received anything. After a vow to Urban, the case was adjudicated and his adversary was forced to pay.[58] In the second case, an official of Auch and licentiate in canon law named Guillaume of Les Barthès had petitioned Pope Gregory XI at Avignon in 1376 in order to acquire a benefice. Although the pope had promised to sign the necessary document, because of a long delay the petitioner had been forced to depart Avignon for Marseilles; his case was dealt with only after a vow to Urban V.[59] In a similar case, a certain Arnold, who had a benefice at de Batsoa, feared that since his predecessor had died and the procurator of the bishopric of Auch (in accordance with episcopal law) was holding the benefice until Pope Gregory XI could deal with the matter, he would surely lose his petition.[60] Fifteen days after he made a vow, the property was restored to him. These delays in handing out benefices in the diocese of Auch may well be the result of curial efforts to increase the relatively low revenues reported from that diocese.[61]

The clergy thus found themselves very much at the center of a society torn by crime and social conflict. On occasion, following earlier precedent, the church used its good offices to bring peace to warring clans or assist those in economic need. At the same time, churchmen themselves appear in the miracle collections also as the unwilling victims of crime. In the case of patrons such as Urban V, they might even expect special assistance for their own peculiar difficulties. Rescue by means of divine intercession bears resemblance to secular forms of mediation in which the injured parties were drawn together through contractual ties.

T H R E E
Crime and Punishment

The growing interest in medieval court records among historians has produced a considerable number of studies dealing with crime in the fourteenth century.[1] Much of the evidence drawn from such judicial sources is corroborated by the miracle collections, which often contain detailed reports of victims of crime who appealed to divine justice against what they perceived as government inaction or lack of equity. Those miracles dealing with crime and punishment confirm the findings of legal and social historians. In rural areas (which also appear to account for most of those rescues from injustice recorded in the miracle collections) crime and violence tended to follow the agricultural calendar, reaching a high point from March to August; miracles of rescue from violence are similarly concentrated in the spring and summer months. The social and work activities during these seasons, the competition for food, the difficulties of planting and harvesting, arguments over debts, and land trespasses heightened communal and familial conflict. Hanawalt has noted that Sunday was the most murder-filled day of the week; that the hours from vespers to midnight were the most danger-ridden time of the day; that the vast majority of both offenders and victims were men, particularly aged eighteen to twenty-five (although women might serve as accomplices); and that much of the crime was directed against neighbors and friends. In both court records and *miracula* women appear more often as intermediaries appealing before God for mercy on behalf of their husbands, children, or other family members who were either perpetrators or victims of crime.

Bribery, violence, and corruption were common means of settling disputes. Even the relatively impartial abbey court of Aurillac, studied by Roger Grand for the period prior to 1350, elicited brutal punishments which seem to have been backed by popular sentiment.[2] The noble class and the rural peasantry seem to have shared a particular penchant for violent behavior, which found ample room for expression during the endemic warfare of the period. Urban folk and the clergy appear often in the *miracula* as victims, the nobility and country folk as perpetrators. The high rates of crime did not spare the cities, in which crowded streets and alleys, poverty, public drunkenness, class differences, and political conflict were some of the contributory factors; and much communal legislation was taken up with attempts to preserve the peace which was threatened by rival clans, which were often held liable for the crimes of their members. Much of the urban violence was out in the open, often beginning at home or in a public tavern, and continuing into the streets in the presence of neighbors, family, and passersby. The lines between social revolution, crime, and family vendetta are not always clear, and some of the miracle stories may mask deeper social divisions.

The employment of violence as a means of dealing with conflict, however petty, had become a widely learned cultural trait.[3] The widespread availability of weapons (including agricultural tools), the apparently high consumption of alcohol, the absence of effective police power, the decline of traditional familial restraints, the high likelihood of escaping punishment, and an ethos of violence which infected the noble and peasant classes in particular, were some of the factors which contributed to the brutalization of society.[4] Even a friendly ball game among neighbors could become an occasion for violent confrontation.[5] On the other hand, the relative absence of intrafamilial disputes in lay courts suggests either that the family had remained an effective tool for the control of social deviance, or that resort to clerical or divine intervention was preferred; vendetta, family solidarity, and private warfare against royal officials and enemy clans continued, despite attempts to curb such activity.[6] Since cases were generally heard only when a litigant was willing to make a claim (or *clamor*), it may be assumed that much crime went undetected or unpunished. Good-neighborliness and custom were often the only viable means of settling disputes, and informal bargaining between parties was the rule. As the earlier laws of Henry I of England had argued, "Agreement prevails over law and love over judgement."[7]

The miracles provide much complementary material concerning the solution of such conflicts at the more informal level of the family.

The participants were generally well-known to each other, and the acts of violence often followed a ritualized form, entailing the utterance of insults, blows to the face (a form of degradation of the whole body), the raising of a clamor, and the involvement of the spectators.[8] The fourteenth century also witnessed the multiplication of public festivities, such as the Easter carnivals, the Feast of the Innocents, and the series of feast days following the 6 December Feast of St. Nicholas, which included Christmas and Epiphany, during which bands of uncontrolled youths played a central role. Such events might often turn into occasions for the violent expression of pent-up emotions and the commission of crime.[9]

Theft and Brigandage

As protectors of the cult and objects of considerable animosity, the clergy had appeared as major actors in all the miracle collections. Nevertheless, most of the victims remained simpler lay folk (whose social status cannot always be determined). In light of the brutal character of late medieval society and the chronic lack of confidence in human agencies of justice, it is not surprising that divine intercession was often the only means of restoring equity and righting the wrongs caused by roving brigands, an unjust state, or covetous neighbors. This was particularly true in cases of theft (which occupy a central position among the crimes cataloged in the miracle collections), when the victim's livelihood and savings had been taken. The term used for thieves is invariably *latrones* (rather than *fures*), which suggests the commission of acts of violence, and often also refers to persons who hide in the forest and prey on travelers; it was thought that such perpetrators should be made to suffer.[10] Among the reported sums of money and items stolen which were recovered only through divine intervention were: sums as large as a hundred scudi, seventy gold pieces, or thirty-five gold florins;[11] garments, gold plates, and measures of cloth.[12] The house of one penitent apothecary had been looted following a fire, thus endangering his livelihood.[13]

The most frequently mentioned theft was that of beasts of burden—horses, oxen, and mules.[14] By the fourteenth century, the horse in particular had often replaced the ox as an all-purpose beast for haulage, ploughing, and transportation, to say nothing of its military role; a horse-oriented husbandry had become widespread.[15] A frequent hagiographical theme therefore dealt with injury, disease, loss, or theft of such animals, which could endanger a family's livelihood.[16] The poor shepherdess Giovanna, who performed miracles in the region between Signa and Empoli, "showed the power [of God] not only in the elements, but even in animals."[17] Theft of a horse could be a capital offense, since in a subsistence economy, a family's meager income could depend upon this one animal. So dependent were rural folk on their horses that a poor man whose horse could no longer pull his wagon to the mill feared that "he could as a result no longer earn the necessities of life."[18] Another poor old woman feared that a chicken (*gallina*) whose "eggs . . . had sustained her for half of her life" was about to die; while a man was distressed over the snatching by wolves of the horse by which he subsisted.[19] One man had reported being taken by brigands during harvest time from Monticelli to the area of Iesi along with twelve head of cattle. When he managed to escape and lead the militia to the thieves' lair, they were forced to pay forty *solidi* for the head of cattle they had already eaten.[20] The surest confirmation of economic dependence on such beasts of burden was the desperation often voiced in miracle stories by persons who could thus no longer support themselves because their animals had been struck with murrain.

Not all of the presumed thievery was real. A common hagiographical *topos* concerned the lost object, feared stolen, which is recovered following a vow and a thorough search. A notary of Les Ollieux (in the diocese of Toulouse), for example, had lost documents worth a hundred fifty gold florins; having searched through his cartularies for two years, he discovered the documents after a vow in August 1376.[21] A mule that had disappeared from an inn at Avignon was discovered by the guards roaming about the city.[22] Large sums of money were often misplaced or hidden away for safekeeping, and then subsequently found.[23]

Brigandage was a particularly intractable problem in the fourteenth century. Highwaymen, bands of routiers, and the unemployed roamed the countryside, and pirates sailed the seas, threatening all who traveled the roads or sea lanes unprotected. Particularly in

France, demobilized soldiers tarried about wreaking destruction as they waited for their next "commission." Such brigands were no re-specters of class, gender, or privilege, and their victims came from all regions and backgrounds. All of the miracle collections confirm the collective fear of brutal malefactors throughout Europe, particularly in strife-torn regions of France during the Hundred Years' War, Italy during the intercommunal wars, and Germany in the course of the dynastic struggles; while seafarers and merchants who plied the trade route between Corsica and Pisa, for example, were victimized by pirates.[24] Nor were pilgrims, women, or other defenseless persons spared.[25] The victims included several women in a forested area of the diocese of Lund nearly drowned by their predators; a pilgrim stabbed, robbed, nearly strangled, and left half dead on the way to the tomb of Stanislas of Cracow; a pilgrim from Papenberg on the way to visit the Holy Blood at St. Giles in Braunschweig; a poor farmer manacled and taken with his cattle to Petini near San Severino; a couple from Papenheim captured at Eger in the Bohemian forest; a merchant stabbed and robbed in Staffordshire; and two merchants of Steyer.

These roving bands rarely honored the traditional rights of unarmed merchants, pilgrims, clerics, and other persons protected by a safe-conduct.[26] Such cases are found throughout Europe involving all classes, and sometimes suggest a clear intention on the part of the brigands to rape or murder their prey after robbing them.[27] Those so attacked and threatened included the wife of a mercer dwelling in Marseilles returning from the Holy Land in 1375 and waylaid in a dense wood; a merchant of Catculne in Staffordshire; a man attacked at Thann near Trent; a priest of Mehring and the *plebanus* of Öttingen-an-der-Ries taken near Wörnitz by thieves bent on killing them; a man captured at Jourdain near Aix, by thieves who had already killed a priest; three pilgrims visiting the tomb of Stanislas at Cracow, attacked in the Pregina forest; a man of Urbino seized in 1337 near a remotely situated mill, waylaid by brigands intent on ransoming him; and a *rusticus* of Sermognano on his way to the shrine of Peter Parenti. Victims of such brigandage report having been housed in remote, presumably abandoned mills and huts.[28]

Some of these bands may well have been law enforcement officers in the employ of local "tyrants" or the congenitally warring communes and nobility whose armies beleaguered Europe throughout most of the period.[29] The term "tyrant" is applied by either the recorder of miracles or the witnesses themselves against those who have broken the law or violated traditional rights. A widow of Sulzberg near the Bodensee named Ursula Swärtzerinne, for example, was seized by the tyrant Hermann of Sulzberg, who tried to force her to remove her children from the monastery of St. Gallen to which she was attached.[30] Here, Hermann may have been within his legal rights. The communal and familial conflict endemic to Italy is likewise sometimes couched as a struggle against bands of hoodlums. The better documented cases do, however, suggest that the victims of abduction were persons of higher station whom it was expected could afford to pay the ransom; and that such activity may have been one aspect of the continuing interurban warfare which plagued the Italian communes. Count Gunifazzio de la Suuera(?) was waylaid and wounded by six of his enemies while one his servants was killed in the melee.[31] Adcursus, a doctor of laws and appellate judge and syndic at Florence, also reported that when he was a student at Siena, a fellow student (later a criminal judge at Todì) had been traveling from Montemilione to Todì. He was seized by two officers of Perugia who had a claim (*represalia*) against the men of Montemilione for a great sum of money. Held in a country house situated in the *contado* of Perugia, he was robbed of his horses, clothes, and five florins. Since he could not pay the ransom, he pleaded to Nicholas of Tolentino for aid; he and his men escaped, found the stable, and rode back to Todì uninjured.[32] Nicholas's protocol also reports the reprisals undertaken by the people of Recanati in the course of their rebellion against the church, when merchants were attacked at sea in 1325 and nearly robbed; Urban V's protocol reports reprisals by enemies of the church near Viterbo.[33] A man of Poggibonsi sequestered at the monastery of Turri at Siena specifically described such abductors as members of a *società*.[34] Such reprisal raids were not, however, restricted to Italy. The son of a *rusticus* of Ickelsheim near Uffenheim in central Franconia was taken in 1401 along with sheep, horses, and cows by five knights of Schwartzbach whose town was in conflict with the people of Rothenburg.[35]

Unprotected sea lanes represented another danger point, particularly for persons of higher economic and social rank. In many instances, it is unclear whether the highwaymen or pirates were motivated by more than mere greed. A large number of merchants from Middleburg in Zealand were seized by officers of the king of Naples; northern fishermen driven into pagan territory were captured and threatened with death; sea travelers were attacked by "thieves" while seeking refuge in a bay during a storm; and the *ministerialis* of the counts of Lütz was imprisoned by the Venetians. All of these persons may have been the victims of political or military conflict, rather than of freelance rogues and cutthroats, as their interlocutors suggest.[36]

Being found in the company of such malefactors could often impugn one's innocence. It was reported that a youth named Pietro of the parish of San Paolo all'Orto of Pisa had been captured with a companion in August 1345 by Ser Antonio of Florence and was taken to San Gondo.[37] He was apprehended with some of the band by law enforcement officials (that is, the *conservator*) of San Miniato and sentenced to death. After preparations for the execution had been made and they had been brought to the pillory, a Pisan in the crowd who saw what was going on asked the priors to release the innocent youths, since peace reigned between the two cities. Despite the priors' unwillingness, some of the crowd heard the discussion and cried out, "Let the Pisans go, lest peace perish." This presumably refers to the peace treaty that had been signed in October 1342 between Florence and Pisa. Only the evildoer was hung, and a two-hundred-lire fine levied against the youth was canceled. Pietro visited the shrine of Gerard of Pisa, to whom he had pleaded for aid.

Imprisonment

Once apprehended, the accused could be subjected to torture and harsh imprisonment. Such legally condoned torture had become a common means of eliciting confession; furthermore, penitential floggings, most notably popularized by the Flagellants, were an accepted form of religious expression; and the young were often exposed to the torture and dismemberment of saints through contemporary art and sermon.[38] The influence of James of Voragine's *Legenda aurea* in both the preaching and illustration of the tortures under-gone by the martyrs cannot be ignored. The suffering of such widely venerated saints as the Holy Innocents and St. Sebastian inured the public to such cruelties.[39] Despite its often moderating influence, the church also condoned the use of torture in such cases as heresy. The growing use of torture as a means of forcing a confession from the accused suggests residual doubt concerning human judicial competence and authority and the partial breakdown of the mechanisms of justice so painstakingly constructed in the central middle ages. In the absence of at least two reliable witnesses and a sworn confession, judges had difficulty in achieving conviction. Thus, in doubtful cases, the application of torture by local magistrates became more wide-spread and routinized in the mid-thirteenth century as a means of eliciting a forced confession and thereby arriving at the truth; and its use was particularly common in time of war.

The extremes of punishment exacted by the law are confirmed in the many reports of preventive detention, torture, unhealthy confinement in irons for long periods of time, confiscation of goods, life imprisonment, and hanging found in the protocols. Again, such draconic treatment is found throughout Europe for a variety of crimes. Preventive detention (binding in irons for eighteen weeks) was applied to a *colonus* imprisoned by the provost of the abbey of St. Magnus at Regensburg after his land had been unjustly taken away and given to another. It was feared that the man would injure the corrupt provost, whom he accused of having succumbed to bribery.[40] An appellate judge and syndic of Florence told of how a man had been held at the notorious Stinche prison for fear that he would flee before paying a fine of four gold florins levied against him. Claiming innocence, he preferred to appeal, and his case was delayed (along with his release) by the attack by Lucca on Prato in 1323.[41] Another innocent man, Bernardo Nuctii of Montemilione, had been charged in 1323 with the murder of one Matthew Boniscambi and, as a result, was arrested by the marquis and the officers of the *castro*, confined, and was about to be tortured (*per violentiam fecit ipsum ligari ad tormentum*). In despair, he admitted that said Matthew had been beaten many times and died of his wounds, although he himself claimed innocence. Sentenced to death, he vowed to Nicholas of Tolentino and St. Venantio to repent and cease all sin. Despite being watched by seven guards, he escaped. Encountering a band of two hundred armed men led by his foe, he lied that a Guelph army was in the vicinity, eluded their grasp, and came to an aqueduct; although impassable, he managed to cross the river and escape.[42]

The application of torture by means of the rack finds ample confirmation in miracle stories, which report its use in cases of homicide, espionage, treason, theft, forgery, illegal trading in salt, bribery, and collusion by public officials.[43] The accused were often held for prolonged periods and repeatedly subjected to the rack; some reported having undergone such suffering that, although innocent, they preferred death to continued torture.[44] Finuccio de Marti, for example, had been tortured four times by officials of the excise office (*gabella*) for the illegal sale of salt, before being freed by the judge; and a druggist of Toulouse resident at Vauvert in 1376 had been imprisoned for seven months and was put to the rack three times as a suspected counterfeiter before being freed.[45] Two brothers of Osimo had been mistakenly charged with murder at L'Aquila; they likewise preferred execution to torture, and admitted to a crime they had not committed.[46]

The close prison conditions were often described in the greatest detail in order to instill sympathy among those who heard reports of the rescue and to enhance its dramatic character (especially in the case of war prisoners): an accused homicide of Alsace, for example, reported confinement in a dark cell with a window four digits high.[47] A large number of these cases were persons accused of homicide, which could entail confiscation of all one's goods and, ultimately, capital punishment.[48] The witnesses rarely admitted to their crimes, although one penitent confessed to justifiable (*causaliter*) homicide.[49] While all manner of quarreling appears in the record, the shedding of blood could entail serious punishment. These fears of temporal punishment were often voiced as the reason for making a vow. A Pole of Ladekopp in Pomerania, taken in chains to Osterode in 1402, feared lest his arm be cut off for injuring an adversary; he thus vowed to undertake a pilgrimage to the holy places.[50] A goldsmith of Roche-Derrien (near Tréguier), having seriously wounded an enemy in a quarrel (*controversia*), fled to the forest. He heard that, since the man had died, the local people were calling for his head; a vow to Charles of Blois revived the victim.[51] In 1309 another man of Spoleto had been detained for aggravated assault; since he would be executed should the victim die, his family considered breaking into the prison and freeing him. After his wife's plea to Clare of Montefalco, he was released by the court, although the victim died three days later.[52] In the same protocol, it is reported that in 1311 the family and friends of a man accused of *maleficium*, a capital offense, also planned to break into the prison at Spoleto in order to prevent his execution.[53]

Execution

De Gaiffier has already cataloged forty-two cases up to the seventeenth century of persons miraculously saved from hanging (sometimes after hanging from a tree up to four days).[54] At least a quarter of these cases date from the fourteenth century; this list may be expanded to include at least another seven fourteenth-century cases (not including those persons who had already been sentenced to hang, but were nevertheless freed prior to reaching the execution site). These reports may be divided into two broad categories: those sentenced for crimes in time of war, and those in peacetime. Bartolomeo Albizi thus described the preparations for an execution at San Miniato: "Black garments were prepared to be worn, sticks to cover the eyes, an ass to be ridden, and he was sentenced to the gallows." The following graphic description of an abortive hanging from the process of Charles of Blois (not recorded by de Gaiffier) may be taken as representative of the rescue tales found in the miracle collections. The speaker is André de Boulogne, the provost of Le Mans, who described the attempted execution of one Guillaume Breton.[55] Guillaume had been sentenced at Baudeoncourt for consorting with the enemies of France, who had occupied Château Gontier and Silli-en-Goufern in the Maine region in the late 1360s. Held for seventeen weeks or six months (there is conflicting testimony) the accused was finally taken to the gallows:

> On a certain day during Lent . . . two years ago [1369] . . . Guillaume Breton was imprisoned at the tower of Le Mans and had

been sentenced to hang. He was taken from the tower, tied to the thong of a horse, to be dragged or drawn through a certain street, and from there led to the gibbet. He had a large and strong halter around his neck; he was tied to a rope made of hemp which was used for hanging. The executioner made him ascend the step of the gallows ladder, and when he had reached the top, tied him to the gallows. After this, the witness [André de Boulogne] said to Guillaume that if he had anything more to say or confess, he should do so; that he was to suffer the punishment of hanging; and may God have mercy on him. Guillaume then beseeched and invoked the lord Charles in these or similar words, saying, "Holy lord Charles, I ask you, if you have the power before God, intercede for me before Him, so that I might not die such a vile death." After he had said this, the witness told the executioner to execute Guillaume, since night was approaching ... The executioner then pushed Guillaume from the ladder, and thus hung him; at that moment, the large halter broke, and he fell down to the ground alive.

Further attempts to hang Guillaume were made, but all were unsuccessful. After a double noose was prepared, it broke again. Since it was agreed that a miracle had occurred, Guillaume was taken to the Leuce bridge and put in a carriage, whose wheel then broke. Returned to prison, he died; but the attending physician determined that he had expired from injuries inflicted falling from the gibbet and the carriage, rather than the hanging per se, since there were no wounds on his neck.

This theme of the defective rope or ladder is a common cause of such failed execution attempts. At Die in 1390, for example, a man accused of the theft of some oxen and collusion with the bishop's enemies was saved when the ladder broke and the horses fled in the ensuing excitement; during a second trial he was freed.[56] A man of Lincoln condemned in December 1291 was first saved by a broken rope; the second time he escaped death when the traverse bar of the pillory broke in the middle; in the course of the third attempt, he was hung from the highest post of the pillory in the presence of many spectators; but when his friends came to remove the body, he was found to be alive, in answer to a vow to Thomas of Hereford.[57]

In a case reported at the shrine of Leonard of Inchenhofen on the feast of St. Giles in 1384, a fisherman of Weil in Upper Bavaria reported that he had been sentenced to hang for forgery; tied hand and foot, he was hung from the bridge at Lansberg, the Lechsbrücke. Although his body was seen hanging by three hundred spectators, he fell into the water and managed to swim to Inchenhofen. Taken into custody a second time, he was freed by Stephen II of Bavaria (d. 1375).[58] This man, like many of the other victims in miracle stories, did not clearly deny his guilt, but he nevertheless escaped the perils of the gibbet after making a vow. Among such victims were four men accused of extortion; a man of Swansea accused of killing thirteen persons in 1291, who had a vision of the Virgin, and was rescued by Thomas of Hereford; a man of Périgord sentenced to hang as a thief; and a man of Châteauneuf in the diocese of Sarlat accused at St. Nazare of espionage.[59] On the other hand, in another well-documented case, the victim claimed to have been condemned for a crime he had not committed. In 1300 one Checco Andreae de Tesis had met a man named Martin on the road to Capua with an ass, and both had then proceeded to the market in order to sell it and earn some money. They were captured in the piazza of Capua and accused of having stolen the animal from a man of Sulmona. After being harshly imprisoned for seven days, Martin admitted his guilt, while Checco persisted in his protestations of innocence. But after being tortured, both of them confessed and were sentenced by the *podestà* to hang. At the end of February they were led to the gallows by two guards, and hung. Checco, however, survived after making a vow to Zita of Lucca, and on 25 March made a pilgrimage to her shrine.[60]

Those cases in which the accused were saved between sentencing and the date of execution differ little from the previous cases. An executioner of Danzig had been falsely accused of killing a child, and was judged twice. In accordance with local custom in capital cases, he was tried a third time, and since he had no witnesses to support his case, he vowed to Dorothy of Montau that he would change his profession should he be judged not guilty; the witnesses brought to prove his guilt unexpectedly exonerated him.[61]

The following tale (ca. 1335) graphically conveys the sense of inequity which finds voice in such contemporary execution miracles:

In the city of Massa Maritima [ca. 45 km from Grosseto] there was a man who had been unjustly imprisoned. After false testimony had been given against him, he was sentenced to be beheaded. As he sat sadly in prison considering that he had been unjustly judged, the blessed Joachim [Piccolomini] came to mind because of the many things he had heard about him in Siena, when he had once been at the hospice of Borgo San Maurizio in Siena [situated near the Servite church] during the feast of Joachim. Recalling the miracles about which he had heard, he devotedly vowed that, should he be saved from such a death and from prison by the blessed Joachim, he would go by foot in shackles to the altar and have a waxen offering made in the form of a prison with himself inside. Behold, in the evening the guards fell soundly asleep, leaving the prison open, having fallen asleep at God's behest. The captives saw that they could flee without any effort; not only him, but all the others. He then came barefoot to Siena in shackles with hands raised, to the [Servite] friary, in the middle of the city; and as he had vowed had a little prison made [as an offering].[62]

This miracle contains the central elements of the rescue miracle: (1) a sense of outrage and despair at having been wrongly judged by an unfair legal system, (2) an awareness of the saint's reputation as a redeemer of hopeless cases, (3) a vow to benefit the saint in return for his assistance, (4) a belief that the conditions for the victim's successful escape had been ordained by God, (5) exploitation of the optimal moment for the rectification of injustice, and (6) public acceptance of the possibility of divine intervention in capital offenses.

The survival of the miracle as a supplementary extralegal form of judgment may be contrasted with the declining fortunes of the ordeal, the chief precedent for the intervention of supernatural power or its surrogate agent, the institutional church, in the resolution of disputes or the reduction of violence. It has been cogently argued that the use of the ordeal as a means of resolving intractable cases, in which neither the accused has confessed nor sufficient evidence exists to provide a judgment of guilt, rests upon faith in the immanence of God in the world as a dispenser of divine justice.[63] Such a dispensation presumes the existence of God, his ability to transform the natural properties of the physical world, and his willingness to intervene in the course of a "manipulative ritual" in order to provide judgment.

The community consensus that had been offered by the ordeal as a means of resolving difficult cases may be defined as a kind of "controlled miracle," which was used to provide a solution to cases of homicide, arson, and theft. The liturgical blessing of the clergy had served to Christianize an institution which predated the spread of Christianity. By the late twelfth century, ecclesiastics had begun to censure the ordeal as an uncanonical effort to test God. Thomas Aquinas argued that "ordeal by hot iron or water is illicit because a miraculous effect is required by God."[64] The clergy further sought to clarify the distinction between sin and crime; one was dealt with through the institutions of ritual, penance, and confession; the other through the rational agencies of the law. The disappearance of the ordeal by the thirteenth century and its replacement by the standards of proof demanded in law or the employment of torture in order to elicit an admission of guilt, had been partly the result of such clerical pressure to clarify the distinction between the natural, sacramental, and miraculous.

The end of the ordeal accompanied the shift in law from consensus to coercive authority based on a social hierarchy and the use of such agencies of religious conformity as the Inquisition. This did not, however, eliminate the need for community consensus in the resolution of difficult cases which did not lend themselves to compurgation, or in which, despite the imposition of torture, the accused refused to confess guilt. The replacement of ordeal by torture as a means of resolving cases lacking sufficient evidence to convict, particularly prevalent in time of war, did not weaken faith in the possibility of divine intercession to rescue those in distress. If the scholastics and canonists sought to minimize the intervention of Providence in the daily life of humanity and to sharpen the distinction between the sacred and profane, the believers remained attached to a more fluid view of the universe, in which God's merciful grace would respond to the vow and supplications of the faithful. The miracle offered the laity more direct means of divine intercession. Canonists sought to reduce the number of phenomena properly labeled miraculous and preferred to achieve justice through confession. Nevertheless, miraculous intercession to assist persons who regarded themselves as the victims of injustice was a widely documented means of achieving the equity which so often eluded late medieval society. Theft, homicide, torture, prevention detention in unsanitary and unsafe conditions, brigandage, and communal conflict are some of the grim conditions that appeal to the supernatural could ameliorate when human agencies failed.

The hagiographical sources provide more graphic, personal evidence of the breakdown of faith in the equity of law and the impartiality of justice and judicial institutions in the waning middle ages. The innocent victim turned to the supernatural when the unbearable suffering of unfair accusations, repeated torture, and long detention without hope of escape could no longer be ameliorated by divine intervention through the ordeal and when the institutions of justice no longer seemed to provide relief, but were themselves the source of injustice. The conditions suffered by those seeking miraculous aid are voiced by the victims themselves. Regarding the partiality of justice, one man of Bruges, Jean Gabbaet, reported that after injuring a well-placed burgher, he was "caught and led to the prison of the lord duke of Flanders, bound by his feet for a year or more. As a result of the injury inflicted against said burgher, because of his great power, they asked said John to pay a fine of two hundred gold francs; since he could neither pay that sum, nor even a lesser fine, he feared that he would never leave the prison alive."[65] Another man of Berry "was incarcerated and held for four months, although no one had testified against him."[66] The harshness of incarceration, which led to despair and even thoughts of suicide, despite the innocence of the accused, was voiced by Jean de Mondolio of Châteauneuf in the diocese of Sarlat. He reported that:

> while traveling from Saint James in Galicia [de Compostella] and St. Anthony at Vienne, he passed through St. Nazare in the diocese of Valence, where he was captured and arrested as an alleged spy; he was placed in the castle of St. Nazare for treason, and put into a very dark tower, where he remained for five weeks in the worst conditions [in maxima miseria]. When questioned by the court, he confessed nothing, because he knew nothing. As a result he was brought four times to the torture and forcibly confessed what they asked; he was returned to the prison, where he experi-

enced such devilish temptations that he wanted to kill himself, believing he could not evade death.[67]

The loss of hope which such conditions engendered is further reported by Bertrand Garneri, who had been falsely accused of homicide and "remained bound in a very dark prison for eight months. Since he could produce no witnesses, he was condemned to be tortured, and a weight was attached to his feet so that he would confess to the murder; he nevertheless denied that he had carried out the homicide; but when his body was totally lacking in strength, he preferred to die rather than live."[68] Thus, victimization by petty tyrants, brigands, and an unjust state, along with the unbearable imprisonment and torture illustrated above, represented suitable conditions for appeal to the supernatural.

F O U R

The Vagaries of Family Life

O ne of the potentially most destructive sources of social and communal instability was disorder within the family, which was regarded as the foundation of a stable social order. In the thirteenth century, the maintenance of the Christian ideals of family purity, sacramental marriage, affection, and monastic celibacy had been central themes of hagiography.[1] The stress laid on sexuality in the Christian mission of penance and the imposition of Christianized ideals of family life have made hagiography, when critically handled, an important source of information concerning such themes as child rearing, the position of women, the mutual obligations of family members, and the differing structures (nuclear, stem, or extended) of the medieval family.[2]

Christian Marriage, Sexuality, and Social Stability

O ne of the themes that finds voice in the miracle collections is the conflict among members of the family, often the result of sexual disorder or misdemeanor. According to Augustinian Catholicism, as a consequence of human disobedience and the Fall from Eden, the bodily members, particularly the generative organs, have ceased being subservient to the will. "Wherein could be found a more fitting demonstration of the just depravation of human nature by reason of its disobedience, than in the disobedience of those parts whence nature herself derives subsistence by succession," wrote Augustine.[3] Carnal concupiscence is seen as a violation of the order of nature and the shame of sexuality is a consequence of the soul's shame at the fact that the body, which by its nature is inferior and subject to it, resists its authority. The inherent shame of the body was regarded by Augustine as the common heritage of humanity, and if children feel no such shame, it must be instilled in them in accordance with contemporary theories of child rearing. The following miracle story is from the *Vita et miracula* of Giovanna of Signa.[4] It illustrates the concern of parents to insure such a sense of shame:

> A man named Duccio Aringhi, who lived at Signa, had a daughter named Laurentia, who as an infant had been taken out of her cradle by her mother. When the swaddling clothes had been removed, the girl always put her hands on her lower frontal area and near her groin, indicating in her own body an unnatural vice [*vitium non modicum naturale*]. Much distressed by this, the father commended her to the blessed Giovanna, vowing that if she should be freed, he would take her to the tomb of the blessed Giovanna with a candle worth five *solidi*. Wonder of wonders! It happened that in the morning, when the girl was untied by her mother, she put her hands behind her back as other healthy girls do. The father fulfilled his vow, profusely thanking God and the blessed Giovanna. Her father reported all of these things to me.

The infant Laurentia's parents were thus concerned to insure that their offspring conform at the earliest age to the strictures of the Christian sexual ethic, which requires "regaining" control of the libido.[5] The Devil would not hesitate even to possess children in order to achieve his ends. Thus, on 3 September 1346, twelve Corsican children (*pueri*) placed a waxen image of Gerard Cagnoli before a picture of the saint, saying, "A ten-year-old boy was recently gripped by the Devil in Corsica. The boy's mother, having heard or seen so many of St. Gerard's miracles, came to friar Paul and had the sign made over the boy with Gerard's relics, and he was immediately freed. We have come here to present this image to the saint, since he [the boy] in his poverty asked for this, in order to humbly give thanks."[6]

Those who are capable of controlling their bodily desires and in whom reason dominates passion, may opt for celibacy; the more perfect among them, the saints, may immediately attain Paradise, where our natures cease to be conflicted. Others are satisfied with the marriage vow, which possesses several compensatory goods: (1) it is the ordained means of procreation; (2) it serves chastity by providing a remedy for sin and a means of restraining lust; and (3) it creates a sacramental bond between the participants. Conjugal intercourse purely for the sake of carnal satisfaction may be sinful, and thus the only permissible form of sexual expression is that which encourages the procreation of children. The married saints of the later middle ages, such as Hedwig of Silesia, Dauphine of Languedoc, and Dorothy of Montau were praised for the purity of their marriages, which were motivated by "faith, fertility, and sacrament" rather than lust; such marriages were often portrayed as the result of parental pressure and were characterized by chaste fulfillment of the marital debt.[7] The ideal Christian marriage was monogamous and indissoluble (unless there is some impediment to procreation). The exigencies of medieval social life further demanded the maintenance of family solidarity, the recognition of legitimate heirs, and the exclusive rights of men over their wives and progeny. Adultery and rape, for example, which compromised these aims, were prohibited.

Given the sacramental character of marriage and the role of the church in the control of sexual behavior, the violation of the sexual and familial code was amenable to religious, and even supernatural, intercession. Both Roman and barbarian legislation had recognized the public nature of the marital bond; sexual misdemeanors were subject to public prosecution, and adulterous wives might even be killed by their spouses.[8] Christianized medieval law added divine sanction to such involvement in private sexual behavior, and much late medieval communal legislation, in particular, dealt with the control of the libido by imposing draconian penalties for rape, sodomy, adultery, and consanguinity. Nevertheless, it is surprising how little litigation is found in contemporary judicial records (unless property is involved) dealing with these themes. Kirshner has suggested three possible explanations: (1) the sources themselves contain large lacunae; (2) the severe penalties acted as a deterrent; or (3) solutions were found within the family or through voluntary arbitration procedures.[9] The miracle collections suggest that recourse to the mechanisms of faith under certain circumstances was a legitimate means of dealing with the intractable consequences of prohibited sexual behavior and family conflict.

The involvement of the supernatural in the adjudication of such conflicts reflected a faith in divine Providence which through firm belief and the fulfillment of a vow would intercede in order to restore order to the family. In many respects, interaction with the divine was modeled after human forms of interaction, and the earthly order was taken to reflect divine order. Resort to the mediating role of the divine became most common in situations of fear and uncertainty, when the competence or willingness of duly constituted human judicial authority to act is in doubt, as in cases of family conflict.[10] The dislocating crises of the fourteenth century had created a more violent and brutal society, in which the efficacy of law enforcement was brought into question; this crisis of confidence engendered a renewed dependence on local agencies of law enforcement and the ties of faith and family as more effective means of insuring social stability. The quantity and quality of social relations depended to a large degree on the close-knit nature of community and family life and the control of social behavior, which was often sanctioned by religion.[11] Collective ideals and traditional communal behavior helped to maintain the fabric of society in a state of equilibrium, which could be destroyed as a result of intrafamilial conflict or sexual disorder.

While officialdom and state law had attempted to serve as agencies of stability, the maintenance of kin-related standards of behavior, which were enforced at the local or even family level, particularly in rural society, remained essential to social order. The breaking of these communal ties through internal conflict or sexual misdemeanor was to be avoided.[12] Family and collective honor in particular, which rested partially on the purity of blood guaranteed through the exclusive rights of men over their wives and of parents over their children, was violated in the event of illicit sexuality. Such honor could be restored either through violent reprisal or by means of the grace which is endowed by God and his saints.[13] Grace was obtainable through the kind of oral contractual vow of continuing allegiance and benefaction to the patron saint found in the miracle collections.

If the restoration and maintenance of civil order required the protection of the Deity and his agents, so the preservation of order and concord within the family often required such divine intercession in order to guarantee the maintenance of the values of obedience, loyalty, continence, and the generation of progeny upon which the family rested. And one was dependent upon the other, for both sexual disorder (generally classified under the multiple "sins against nature") and blasphemy could bring disaster upon the state and society by arousing the wrath of God, as witnessed by the destruction of Sodom, the plagues wrought upon Egypt, and the other catastrophes suffered by those peoples mired in sin.[14] Secular law was thus enlisted in the service of religious and sexual order and received its sanction from above. The Italian commune, in particular, viewed itself as a reflection of Paradise, and feared the consequences of sexual disorder within its precincts. The laws of Asti regarding sexual misdemeanors, for example, were prefaced with the following justification: "It is a grave sin and punished by divine law. Because of man's corruption many men cannot abstain from carnal temptations. Lest men fall into such great evils, and the republic be harmed, adultery and sins against nature should be prohibited in human law."[15] In the law of the *podestà* of Florence (1325), moral legislation was justified by the fear that "God may be offended and the honor of the city disparaged" through the presence of prostitutes within the city limits.[16] The breaking of such laws could call forth divine retribution. At Brescia, "the reverence and honor of God and His servants [Sts.] Stephan and Martin" were invoked; and at Modena prostitutes were expelled "in order to honor God, the Virgin Mary and all of the saints."[17] In some communes, physicians were enlisted in the service of religion and were required to enjoin their patients to visit a priest and confess.[18] This suggests that should conventional medicine fail in the cure of disease, "lovesickness," or bewitchment, physicians might direct their charges to the cures offered by the faith. At Naples, four physicians who had charged two hundred ducats in order to aid a man injured during a battle refused their fee, testifying that prayers to Peter of Luxemburg had been more effective.[19]

As many of the witnesses to the miracles themselves admit, the public scandal and infamy attendant upon the prosecution of cases of concubinage, adultery, or fratricide were so unbearable that suppliants had preferred to find a more "informal" solution through the agency of the saint or his or her relics.[20] The dishonor brought upon the family or clan by such acts may partially explain the relative absence of cases involving intrafamilial violence, infanticide, and sexual misdemeanor in the surviving documents of contemporary secular law courts, despite the severe punishments that the law allegedly meted out, and the frequent, sometimes obsessive condemnation of the church. It would appear that such injustices were more often handled through the informal agencies of religion.

Thirteenth-century hagiography had been characterized by proto-typical reports of forced marriage, loss of inheritance, conflict with parents over career, and ministry to widows and orphans in the lives of the putative saints themselves. By the late thirteenth century, as Vauchez's survey has shown, many miracle collections (which come from various parts of Europe) contain increasing reports of infertility, infant mortality, childhood disease, and accident.[21] A substantial number also report cases of possession and dementia—which presumably had important repercussions within the life of the family—such as the collections of Charles of Blois, the Franciscan Gerard Cagnoli, Leonard of Inchenhofen, and Yves of Tréguier.

The Saints and the Solution of Family Woes

Despite their differing provenance, these miracle stories suggest that a very similar culture of family life bound all of preindustrial Europe, whether rural or urban, Mediterranean or transalpine. They often contain examples of divine intercession in the solution of familial woes and the correction of sexual misdemeanors. This may perhaps be a consequence of the saints' reputations as peacemakers and ministers to the wayward and as devotees of the Christian ideal of chastity during their lifetimes. Yves of Tréguier, for example, had acquired a name as an honest broker, an "advocate of the poor" who was willing to defend the interests of the poor without a fee. This special power was manifested by his service as an amicable mediator in a dispute between one Ralph and his mother and stepfather concerning some property. It was reported that after the saint had said a mass in the presence of the disputants, the stepfather's intractability lessened and the case was brought to a satisfactory conclusion.[22] Those who testified about Yves's character noted that he was the progeny of a legitimate Catholic marriage; that he was chaste in word and deed, and had brought many women to religion with arguments in favor of chastity. Despite suffering verbal abuse, he defended a woman in her just suit to marry an unwilling young man.[23] As a result of these precedents, Yves's canonization process included several cases in which the saint's posthumous intercession brought an end to rancorous family quarrels.

A second contemporary saint whose posthumous miracles were much concerned with problems of sexual disorder, pregnancy, and family conflict was the Pisan Gerard Cagnoli. His own life contains some of the hagiographical themes common to the later middle ages. After the death of his father, he devoted himself to his ailing mother for the next ten years (until he was twenty-three or twenty-four). Described as a "robust and strong youth," he was urged by his relatives and friends to marry lest his paternal line die out. Instead he preferred to abandon the world.[24] The patrilineal family was a major factor in Italian communal life, and it was incumbent upon such an heir to fulfill his responsibility to continue the line.[25] Paradoxically, many of those saints who had themselves rejected sexuality and marriage devoted much of their ministry to easing the pains of childbirth, guaranteeing the birth of children (particularly male) to barren couples, and protecting the sanctity of the family. The desired result of such intervention, in the case of sexual miscreants, was penance, which was a central theme of contemporary hagiography and preaching.[26] Among the more recent saints, Philip Benizi, founder of the Servite order, which was patronized by the Virgin Mary, reportedly assisted local prostitutes to become penitent.[27] Two prostitutes whom he had met plying their trade suggested that they could not give it up lest they be unable to support themselves. He gave them some money in return for a promise not to entertain men for three days. When the three days had elapsed, they had repented and became hermits at Porcaria, about fifteen miles from Todì, where they spent the rest of their lives.

Bridget of Sweden was credited with successfully combatting both the witchcraft and sexual disorder that were still endemic in her region, which had been evangelized relatively recently and bordered pagan territory. Her canonization record tells of a parish priest who had allegedly been tempted by a woman employing witchcraft:

> The witness heard from mistress Bridget and from a certain good
> priest in Sweden named John that when he was a parish priest at

Rinna in the diocese of Lincöpen, as a priest he was so bewitched by a sorceress that he burned with carnal temptation like a fire, so that he could think of nothing except foul carnal thoughts; nor could he pray according to custom. After he had been driven out of his senses, but not wanting to lose the continence and chastity he had preserved so long, he asked mistress Bridget (who was then residing at the monastery of Alvastra) to be freed of such evil temptation and to beseech God to grant him his goodness. After mistress Bridget had prayed for him, Christ said to her, "You know that the sorceress possesses three things which are used in her incantations, namely lack of faith [*infidelitas*], an obdurate heart, and avarice [*cupiditas*]. The Devil therefore dominates he who drinks from the excrement of his bitterness; and you know that her tongue will be her end, and her hand her death, and the demon the author of her testament." All of this actually happened, since just as the witness said, on the third night the sorceress bit her own tongue, took a knife and cut her own groin with it and shouted to all who were listening, "Come, my Devil, and follow me." And thus with such a horrible cry she put an end to her life in a wretched way. The aforesaid priest, freed of temptation, immediately entered the Dominican order, in which until the end of his life he returned the fruit of divine grace, as the witness said.

This report contains many of the elements which characterized the medieval attitude toward sexuality.[28] The woman appears as a temptress serving the Devil, and her identification as a sorceress (*incantrix*) suggests the employment of love potions, abortifacients, or other artificial means to affect sexuality and procreation. Such practices were prohibited by the church (although apparently widely practiced) and were associated with disbelief and heresy.[29] Divine intervention through prayer and the assistance of a saint or his or her relics may defeat the Devil. The description of the burning fire of carnal temptation which consumed the priest conforms to the medieval view that heat represented the chief characteristic of masculinity and of sperm, which was considered the formative agent in generation. When the heart (the seat of passion) has been inflamed by the heat of desire, one's reason is lost and one might even fail to perform the simplest functions. Thus, the priest admitted to both his obsession and his consequent failure to carry out his responsibilities.[30] Following the woman's suicide, he joined a religious order.

The same penitential aim is found in reports of miracles attributed to more veteran saints and their shrines. During the feast of the translation of Bernward of Hildesheim's relics, for example, a certain prostitute visited the saint's tomb at Hildesheim after dinner and was motivated to reconsider her life. That night she had a vision in which she was advised to depart the city for a place to which she would be directed by God. She passed through Lübeck on the way to visiting her brother, whose counsel she sought. Near Flensberg, she met a rich farmer, whom she married. She was later to wed a younger man, keeping the secret of her past life from both her husbands, and revealing the truth only to her confessor in 1431.[31]

Infamy and Sexuality

Divine intervention in the adjudication of family disputes arising out of sexual disorder could be justified as a means of avoiding public prosecution and obloquy. The badge of infamy, which hung over persons guilty of illicit marriage, adultery, incest, rape, and abduction, among the sexual misdemeanors, could entail the loss of all civil rights and exclusion from the community; many would prefer flight and exile to such a fate.[32] One of the domestic woes that occasionally required intervention was concubinage, which could heap scandal upon the family and posed a threat to familial and social stability. The complainant whose petition led to the miraculous restoration of a man to his lawful wife was almost invariably a mother or wife, so that the offending woman was generally termed a whore, whatever her occupational status might have been. The fullest testimony comes from a woman who had sought the help of the recently deceased Franciscan Gerard Cagnoli at Pisa. In September 1345 she gave the following testimony:

> I have a son in the village [castro] in which we live who is twenty-one years old. He has been bewitched and taken away by a woman who has been unfaithful to her husband, and for the past two years my son has commingled with her. When the affair became publicly known in the town, her husband became very indignant, and we, his father and mother, were much distressed by our son's great devi-

ation. As a result we summoned him, and began to warn him; but our interference wasn't the least bit effective. Our son and this woman, preoccupied with evil, seeing this, thought of fleeing, and of continuing to sin together. Learning of this, I began to cry about the danger to my son. Since we could find no remedy for the situation, I turned to Gerard, whose fame had grown greatly, as my patron. One evening, totally preoccupied with my son's misdeed, I vowed to St. Gerard to go barefoot to him at Pisa and offer a waxen candle and three *librae*, and another one should he succeed through his grace, and should God free my son from such snares of the Devil, returning to the authority of his father and mother. For he had become totally rebellious and insolent toward us in everything. All night long I tearfully invoked St. Gerard, asking mercy for my son. In the morning, having secured virtue from the saint, this branch of rebellion turned into an obedient son.[33]

Although the general penalty for voluntary adultery here reported was the imposition of a high fine on the accomplices (dependent upon social *statuus*), it might occasionally be judged a capital offense.[34] For even the plague of darkness in Egypt was regarded as a consequence of the sin of adultery.[35] Despite this penalty, in the environment of the small village, the mother's concern was more for her son's rebelliousness. Although his sexual imbroglio had begun at the age of nineteen, he was still under parental control. For adulthood was not a purely legal condition, but was dependent on such factors as marital and economic status. Adolescence (*adolescentia*), which traditionally lasted until the age of twenty-one, was universally regarded as a time of intemperance, gullibility, sexual awakening, stubbornness, and tempestuousness. Such contemporary guides to family planning as Bellino Bissolo noted that the malleability, naivete, and weakness of the young demand that the selection of a suitable spouse should remain under parental control as a means of bridling youthful passion.[36]

A theme that finds voice in this Pisan miracle is the "bewitchment" of this young man by his lover as the explanation offered for his disobedience. Having been gripped by devilish temptation, he could be purged only through the exorcismic "white magic" of divine intervention. This is an entirely pragmatic approach, a practical resort to supernatural assistance when human agencies have failed. The destructive results of sexual disorder are clearly stated by the youth's mother. These include: (1) the indignation of the wronged husband, (2) the public scandal, (3) the son's disobedience and insolence, and (4) his planned flight from the village. The same miracle collection also contains the report of a young, recently married couple of Pisa (the bride was thirteen at the time) who quarrelled because they could not have sexual relations. Believing themselves bewitched by devilish incantations, they sought the aid of a Franciscan of Pisa, who advised seeking Gerard's help.[37] Here, the perhaps prepubescent age of the couple may well have mitigated against connubial ties, which became possible after both the dissipation of anxiety and the passage of time.

The intimate link between the sins of *luxuria* and the practice of witchcraft here voiced by the erring youth's mother reflects contemporary learning. Thomas Aquinas had eloquently argued that "because the first corruption of sin through which humankind became a servant of the Devil comes to us by means of the generative act, the power of bewitchment is therefore granted by God to the Devil in this act more than in any other. In the same way the 'virtue' of bewitchment is displayed more in serpents than in other animals because the Devil tempted womankind by means of a serpent."[38] Aquinas further argued that because the Devil cannot himself bear children, in the form of a succubus or incubus he may attempt to steal his victim's seed so that it may become the medium of copulation.

Much of the scholastic discussion of the relationship between witchcraft and sexuality is found in commentaries on Peter the Lombard's (ca. 1100–60) *Sententiae*, which noted that (unlike frigidity, which is inherent) the impotence that postdates a marriage may not render the marriage illicit if it has been caused by witchcraft and is therefore reversible. Since such impotence may be selective, that is, affecting a man with respect to a particular mate, it may be subject to remedy. The same caveat applies to the insanity which manifests itself only after marriage. The confession of one's sins to a priest, the giving of satisfaction to God (through acts of penance, tears, prayers, and fasts), and finally exorcism, may be effective countermeasures against the wiles of Satan.[39] It was widely believed that the Devil possessed enhanced powers over marriage and sexuality and that the substances employed by practitioners of witchcraft could prevent the organs of generation from acting properly, that is, assisting in procreation, which is the essential aim of marriage. This led to the growing use of various versions of the prayer over the bedchamber (i.e., the *benedictio thalami*), which was uttered by a priest in order to drive away evil from the bridal couch.[40] Aquinas further argued that since concupiscence and sensuality are natural human characteristics and nature can be transformed only by supernatural means, such corruption demanded supernatural intervention in order to effect its removal. Bonaventure (ca. 1217–74) had even likened the practice of witchcraft to the performance of a miracle; although miracles are generated through faith, and witchcraft involves disbelief, idolatry, and disobedience.[41]

In the miracle collections the consequences of sexual transgression included mental illness, melancholia, anger, and even homicide.[42] The wife of a distinguished citizen of Pisa, for example, fell into melancholy because of her husband's gallivanting about in public with a prostitute as though she were his true wife. A man of Grundelfingen in Bavaria (1408) "captivated by the love of a concubine" took his wife out into the forest in order to kill her. A woman of Wurzbach (1428) in Upper Bavaria was driven to a life of seclusion (perhaps out of shame) by her husband's adulterous ways. He accused her of insanity and, in her version of the story, tried to bribe the bishop of Wurzburg in order to have her permanently committed. A young girl of Obermairin-aus-Gesseltzhausen, seduced by a certain knave or "camp-follower" (*ribaldus*) about five weeks after her marriage, abandoned her family, fleeing to Nuremberg (as reported in 1432).

The most serious consequence of concubinage and sexual disorder according to secular law could be imprisonment or even beheading. This was the sentence to be exacted from Jacob Astaur of Pavia by the *podestà*.[43] While languishing in prison, he heard that others had asked Urban V for aid, and he vowed to visit the late pope's tomb should he be saved. Along with other prisoners, Jacob was freed in a general amnesty. In 1393, a wealthy citizen of Dinkelsbühl, a town with a considerable Jewish population, was imprisoned for twenty-four days for having slept with a baptized Jewess.[44] When he rejected the pleas of both his fellow citizens and the town council to marry the woman, he was imprisoned and his goods, valued at one thousand shillings (*solidi*), were confiscated. Canon law conformed to secular law in demanding that he marry the woman he had violated. That night, he was freed along with two other prisoners and they all fled to Nordlingen, later visiting the shrine of St. Leonard at Inchenhofen, crediting the saint with enabling their escape. Such adultery had also led to a sentence of imprisonment and public humiliation exacted against Jeanette, daughter of Jean Barram. Her prayers and those of her friends to Peter of Luxemburg led to her release and the cancellation of the sentence of infamy.[45]

The ceremony of public ridicule and violence to which Jeanette was to be subjected was widely applied to the infamous, public enemies, and other marginal groups in southern Europe.[46] In all of the preceding instances, the human instigator of vice is a person occupying the margins of society—a prostitute, a *ribaldus*, a baptized Jewess—who may have been aided by black magic in order to seduce his or her prey. A vow to the saint, occasionally accompanied by the salutary use of a relic or other means, could counteract such evil. Albizi tells the following tale of a youth tempted into adultery:

> There was a well-known secular youth who had a brother in the order of St. Francis. In 1344 he was so occupied with an accursed woman that he wasn't strong enough to cease his adultery. His brother invoked St. Gerard, fasted and placed a candle [in the image?] of the saint at the head [of the bed] where the youth slept. Wonder of wonders! The youth's lust [*libido*] eased, he expelled the accursed woman, and began to reform both his house and family.[47]

Adultery and other sexual misdemeanors are seen in this and the previous examples as born of devilish interference, and its purification restores family unity; the victim's brother demonstrates family solidarity by undertaking the necessary penitential act (fasting) in order to insure his brother's liberation; his membership in the Franciscan order presumably insured a more favorable hearing from the Franciscan Gerard Cagnoli.

In another case, one of the few instances of rape that appears in the sources, a widowed noblewoman was raped in 1345, and soon felt all the signs of pregnancy: "Grieved by both the violence of the sin which had been committed, and by the shame of the conception which was beginning to appear, and the subsequent birth," she turned to Gerard for aid. As a result of her supplication, "she felt a change in her body, and the signs of conception and the pregnancy to follow, ceased entirely."[48] The danger which a blasphemer or doubter could pose to the welfare of a monastic *familia* is also graphically recalled in a miracle reported by Bartolomeo Albizi. In 1343 a quarrel had arisen among the Augustinian nuns of San Marco just outside Pisa, which engaged the energies of the archbishop, bishop, commune, and clergy of Pisa.[49] Despite the intervention of many parties, conditions in the nunnery reached such a pass that the sisters could no longer hold divine service together. During Lent 1347 Mistress Gheccha of Pisa, whose niece was cloistered at San Marco, told the prioress about the postmortem miracles which Gerard had performed in the region. During communion, the prioress Neze heard a voice instructing her to invoke Gerard Cagnoli in order to restore peace to the monastery. After making a suitable vow, an unidentified holy man appeared, first alone, and then accompanied by a friend (St. Gerard?). He gathered the warring factions together and secured a peace.

Male Anger and Violence

The most widely cited cause of sexual and familial disorder, aside from bewitchment, was male violence and anger, which also appear in contemporary secular court records as a significant cause of crime, and could threaten a family with catastrophe. The protocol concerning Charles of Blois suggests that such anger, which led to the physical abuse of spouse and children, often had an economic basis.[50] A forty-five-year-old citizen of Angers, one Matthieu le Ferron had litigated in the royal parliament for nine and a half years, and was much angered by the effort and money he had expended, having lost half his goods. As a result, he lost his senses (*alienatus fuit a sensu*), and during Christmas 1367, he began to beat his wife and tried to throw his children out the window; he was therefore manacled at home for half a year, until St. Bartholomew's feast [24 August]

1368, when a vow to Charles of Blois returned him to his senses. In another case taken from Charles's process, Jeanne, wife of Godfrey Vaillant of Guincamp, had placed a box containing fifty or sixty gold pieces under the bed; when it disappeared, her husband blamed the woman.[51] After she made her vow, a local priest, who had retrieved the box from the real thief, returned the missing item. In a third case, a thirty-year-old man in the parish of Ste.-Marie de Guincamp who, it was said, customarily entertained many guests, threatened his wife because she had supposedly lost or misplaced a valuable goblet. A vow to Charles of Blois led to its restoration.[52] Since all of these cases coincide with the Hundred Years' War, they may reflect the familial consequences of the lawlessness and theft which accompanied hostilities.

The protocol of Yves of Tréguier also provides such evidence of the fear of male fury, apparently a consequence of economic pressure, as the trigger of divine intercession.[53] A sixty-year-old widow of Ploeneyt told how in 1314 (the story was reported in 1330) during the feast of St. Giles [1 September] she had taken a horse laden with grain to the mill. In the presence of the miller and his assistant, the horse fell into the Lan river, and remained completely submerged from morning until night. The woman was so fearful of her husband's angry reaction that she turned to St. Yves for assistance, saying (in Breton), "Oh Saint Yves, I vow my horse to you, because I won't go to my husband's home without it. I promise to give you a candle [equal in length to the horse]." After making her vow, the horse's ears appeared, and it stepped out of the water unharmed.

Disputes over property could sometimes degenerate into bloodshed or even fratricide, continuing an old hagiographical topos. A rather fantastic tale is found in the miracles attributed to Lucchesio of Poggibonsi by Bartolomeo Tolomei.[54] He reports that a man of Recanati had killed his brother in a conflict over the division of their goods and was sentenced to death, while his brother was buried at the Franciscan cemetery at Recanati. Their maternal aunt, who was herself from Poggibonsi, recalled the saint's benefactions, and after she beseeched Lucchesio's help, the dead brother was brought back to life. In the notarized miracles of the Dominican Ambrose of Siena, a woman of Siena was threatened with death by her dead husband's family when she refused to give up her dowry. In the course of an attack in which his disgruntled kin entered her house in order to take her life, she pleaded for Ambrose's aid and was saved.[55] This miracle echoes the widely known tale of Landgravina Elizabeth of Thuringia (d. 1231), who lost her dowry and all other means of support to her husband's greedy kinfolk and was forced to roam about nearly penniless after the death of her spouse.[56]

Fraternal violence also appears in such testimony.[57] In August 1324, Francesco Andrioli of Macerata quarreled with his brother Napoleone. Francesco's thumb was severed, and was flung a distance of fifteen feet. He picked it up and cried out, "O blessed Nicholas of Tolentino, you well know how often and how many letters I wrote on your behalf to the Roman curia in support of your canonization. I beg and beseech you to demonstrate your virtue, so that I won't lose my hand and this finger, because I promise to go to Tolentino and to visit your tomb in order to offer a wax candle and to continually fast on the vigils of your feast day [10 September] and to continue to write on your behalf without being paid whenever I do so." When Andrioli came to Tolentino in order to fulfill his vow, blood oozed out of his dry finger onto the tomb; after fifteen days he recovered, left with only a small scar. In addition to illustrating the kind of family violence which divine help could ease, this tale suggests that some of the lobbying for a saint's canonization depended very much on the exchange of money, and a quid pro quo was expected.

Divine intercession might be necessary in order to forestall the unwanted involvement of state authorities. This justifiable fear of outside intervention was partly the result of the growing inefficiency, partiality, and costliness of justice which was endemic in the fourteenth century. Such fears appear throughout Europe, and are attested in cases drawn from different regions. In 1345, a young girl of Pisa was beaten by her husband and driven out of their home.[58] "Her family [parentela]," it was reported, "was disturbed by this act, and no small scandal threatened. The girl, who grieved more about the imminent scandal than about her expulsion [from home], piously invoked St. Gerard, asking him to bring about peace in this matter." As a result, the man realized his error, relations between the two were resolved, and the family was pacified. In another case, in 1367 a certain Grelet, who had found refuge in the Augustinian house at Albo near Bourges during the Hundred Years' War, "moved to anger against his wife," attempted to strike her with a spinning rod while she was holding their one-and-a-half-year-old daughter.[59] The child's head was fractured. Fearing her dead, Grelet fled to a cave, lest he hang for the crime, and spent three and a half days in hiding. The child's head was bandaged in strips dipped in egg white. Although she appeared dead, her feet remained warm. Prepared for burial, she awoke, asked her mother for the breast to be fed, crying, "La tête, la tête." Grelet returned, and reported that at the very moment of the child's resuscitation, he had in fact asked the aid of Charles of Blois. The girl survived two and a half years longer. In a well-documented case from the 1307 file of Thomas of Hereford, a man whose son had suffered what appeared to be a fatal accident was afraid to call for help or have the event publicized, for fear that he would be arrested by the coroner as a suspected homicide.[60]

Possession by the Devil and Mental Disorder

In addition to such sexual misdemeanors as adultery, one of the most troubling sources of domestic violence and conflict was emotional distress, which was often characterized as possession by the Devil. While many saints gained reputations for sexual purity, assistance to widows and orphans, and mediation in the solution of family squabbles, so also did the exorcism of demons and the calming of troubled souls have a long pedigree among miracle-workers. The 1301 exorcism by Yves of Tréguier of a demon which had possessed a young man is described in detail by several eyewitnesses.[61] After hearing the youth's confession and conversing with the demon, Yves lay the youth down in his own bed and sprinkled the house and bed with holy water. He kept an all-night vigil, reciting the Evangel of St. John and other prayers, as the youth lay there. The next morning, after having suffered for three years, the young man reported that he had not slept so well in years and that the demon had departed. Yves suggested continuing a Christian life as the best antidote to possession by the Devil. As a result of this precedent, Yves's canonization process included several cases in which the saint's posthumous intercession brought an end to possession by the Devil.

In the case of Joachim Piccolimini such a posthumous exorcism was decisive in reviving a moribund cult. His cult had lacked sufficient miracles, but received special impetus when an incubus was publicly ejected after contact with his relics in the presence of many spectators. The hagiographer reported:

> On Pentecost [7 June 1310], when friar Nicholas of Siena was preaching in the [Servite] cloister after nones [3:00 p.m.], a woman possessed by a demon was led in. When the preacher had reported the aforementioned miracle, the demon began to cry out and speak through her mouth saying, "The time has now come for me to exit, and for Christiannella's liberation." After the sermon had concluded, a large number of persons poured in, since the demoniac was very well known. When the brethren had urged said spirit to say why the other saints had not expelled him, the demoniac approached [Joachim's] tomb, saying, "Because God has reserved this miracle for this saint."[62]

This is followed by an account of the public exorcism of the incubus, which provided just the kind of dramatic visual demonstration needed to arouse support for a new cult. In neither of the two preceding cases was the exorcism entirely spontaneous. Both confirm that faith is a necessary prerequisite for the exorcism. The young man had confessed, while the woman had taken part in a service prior to the successful exorcism. Engelbert of Admont had argued in his treatise on miracles that since diseases of both the mind and the spirit are consequences of lack of faith, the touch of the saint (or his relics) could reactivate the seeds of health which lay dormant.[63]

The miracle collections confirm that it was widely believed that the lustful, confused longings of youth made young women and girls (like Christiannella) particularly susceptible to possession by a succubus or incubus. The most systematic account of the Devil's machinations is Bartolomeo Albizi's protocol of Gerard's miracles, which contains a chapter entitled "On Liberation from Persecutors and the Power of the Devil," in which the hand of a well-trained exorcist is evident. Twenty-four cases of exorcism and possession are cited, eighteen female and eight male, which had been relieved through contact with relics; of those whose age is given, ten are under twenty-one, while several others had been obsessed so long that the first

possession may have occurred in their youth.[64] In this chapter Bartolomeo also provides a useful summary of the symptoms of Devil-
possession. The victim: (1) claimed to possess the soul of a certain
dead neighbor; (2) might refuse to honor God or the saint in word
or genuflection; (3) refused to make the sign of the cross; (4) refused
to receive or look at holy water; and (5) might babble or barely get a
word out. Some of the sufferers might also refuse to hear a sermon,
gaze at the Eucharist, or complete a Paternoster. The Devil appeared
variously as a recently deceased neighbor, a man recently executed,
an ass with pawlike arms, and a girl's mother. The laity, on the other
hand, possessed a less discerning eye, and apparently inexplicable
violence (demanding the manacling of the victim) was often the
clearest symptom of such possession. A demoniac in the process of
Yves of Tréguier, for example, verbally abused her family, tore her
clothes, broke dishes, and had to be held and tied down by four
men.[65]

Insanity

Much violence and sexual disorder was attributed to temporary
insanity, regarded as possession by the Devil, which could be
dealt with through the application of the curative power of the saint
or his or her relics. The typical thaumaturgical miracle had contained
an etiological explanation of the initial causes, the symptoms, and
the natural means undertaken to cure the disease before resort to the
supernatural through a vow. In the same way, the family conflict and
sexual disorder found in miracles had almost invariably suggested Satanic intervention and alleged that the tempter had made use of the
wiles of witchcraft, or that the victim was possessed by a succubus or
incubus. Such alleged possession heightened the victim's emotional
state and was treated in much the same way as other diseases. A servant at the monastery of Alvastra which housed Bridget of Sweden,
for example, had been separated from her husband by the bishop as
a result of affinity.[66] Grieved and embittered by her divorce, while
the *Dialogues* of Gregory were being read aloud, she asked Bridget for
help. As all the bystanders prayed for the distracted maidservant, she
visualized a foul-smelling Ethiopian rise up from the cleavage between her breasts. His dank odor and image had recurred to her

whenever she thought or heard about her former spouse. Here, the complex imagery suggests that the woman had been possessed by a devilish incubus which brought about her supercharged emotional state. The Devil took the visual form of a black Ethiopian, an identification found in the earliest Christian descriptions of Satan. And his expulsion via her cleavage possesses blatant sexual overtones. Again, as in the case of the young man near Pisa bewitched by a supposed whore, the kind of exorcism undertaken by the saint—or his or her surrogate—led to the expulsion of the demon. It is also reported that the woman was "half asleep" when the demon was expelled.[67] This miracle suggests a more complex relationship between the woman and her former husband, but the evidence is too sparse to draw any further conclusions.

The symptoms of such mental disorder (which lasted several months, and may have been the result of the ingestion of some hallucinogenic substance by the nuns involved) gripped an entire *familia,* the Cistercian nunnery of Santa Lucia in Pian de Peca, and is graphically described.[68] Succumbing to demons between 1320 and 1323, the nuns sang foul songs, shouted abuse, laughed uncontrollably, gesticulated while walking, suffered memory loss, shrieked night and day, invoked the Devil and other dead evildoers, rolled their eyes, bit their tongues, twisted their mouths out of shape, and generally behaved "worse than whores," believing that they were being pursued by certain knights and dead criminals. Resort to the saint's relics by members of the nuns' families and those of the convent who were not so afflicted restored order. One of the women, named Philippuccia, had called out to the demon Belial for assistance against a horde of dead murderers and other scoundrels (some of whom are named) by whom she was pursued. She had also managed to stand an egg upright on the edge of a wall without its falling, allegedly with Satan's assistance. The fact that traditional means of expelling the Devil were not always effective when an entire convent was infected in this way is attested by Alvaro Pelayo in his *De planctu ecclesiae* (ca. 1332).[69] He wrote: "Some women give themselves over to a demon who has been transformed into an incubus. In the same way, in a certain convent of nuns, after many acts of penance, discussions, and sermons, the demoniacal difficulty [*vexatio*] can in no way be expelled from them." Nevertheless, the climate of witch-hunting, in the course of which women were accused of sexual congress with the Devil, had not yet gripped Europe. A deviant sex act did not necessarily create a permanent stigma, since the application of penance could restore a person to spiritual health. The apparent compact between the nuns of Santa Lucia in Pian de Peca, therefore, was amenable to correction by means of exorcism, vows, or other forms of penance.

One of the best-documented such cases of a *furiosus*, in which the stated cause of the man's disorder was a family argument, is found in the canonization process of Yves of Tréguier ordered by Pope John XXII and held in the summer of 1330.[70] The witnesses reported that a twenty-year-old youth named Yves Andree from the Breton village of Penguennan had been stricken in May 1329 in the late afternoon after his mother had shouted at him, "Was it you who have defamed me, and should you have said what you said before?" She allegedly withdrew her breasts from beneath her blouse and shouted, "I give you my curse and the curse of my breasts which suckled you, and the curse of my loins which bore you. Whatever I may possess of you legally and can have, I utterly relinquish and give to the Devil." The young man immediately became possessed, and had to be held down by several bystanders. That night, in his delirium he saw two towering goatlike demons who cried out, "You belong to us. You belong to us because your mother has given you to us." After asking for St. Yves to assist him, the saint agreed to help because the young man had visited his shrine several days earlier, and because, as the saint's apparition said, "your mother can't give you to the Devil because she legally possesses nothing which belongs to you except a sack in which grain is taken to the mill." The next day, his mother relented and commended the stricken youth to St. Yves. He was then taken by his father to the saint's tomb at Tréguier, where the curse was removed.

This miracle story contains many of the standard elements of conflict between God and Satan found in the earliest biblical miracle tales, beginning with the confrontation between Moses and Pharaoh's magicians, and Elijah and the prophets of Baal. In this case, the cosmic struggle is worked out within the life of a peasant family. The participants, including the already dead St. Yves himself, do not doubt the mischievous power of the Devil and his minions. They simply employ a kind of countermagic, which is made effective through: (1) the victim's identification with his saintly namesake by having participated several days earlier in ceremonies on his feast-day, even prior to Yves's official canonization; (2) the requisite utterance of a vow; (3) a reconciliation with his mother the next day; and (4) a salutary visit to the shrine of St. Yves in fulfillment of the vow.

The appearance of the demons as black goats is a feature found almost exclusively among French adherents of popular witchcraft; a delirious man, also of Tréguier, had in 1369 described two black, horned demons threatening to take a man's soul away to hell because of an unconfessed sin committed in 1362. After the man invoked Charles of Blois, the saint appeared to drive away the demons.[71] The possession of an object belonging to one's intended victim as a means of doing him injury is an almost universal feature of witchcraft. As Kieckhefer, Peters, and others have emphasized, although Pope John XXII (under whom the canonization process of Yves of Tréguier had taken place) was especially concerned about the power of the Devil, until the fifteenth century, trials for witchcraft and the use of magic were almost invariably directed against dangerous political foes like Bishop Hugh Geraud of Cahors, Archbishop Robert Mauvoisin of Aix, and Galeazzo Visconti of Milan. "Crones" such as Yves of Penguennan's mother—who herself commended her son Yves to the saint and thus suggested that her invocation of the Devil was a momentary lapse—were largely spared, particularly in a region like Brittany, with its strong Celtic heritage.[72]

Despair and Suicide

One of the vices which could have the most malevolent effects upon the family was *desperatio*, that is, despair or loss of hope, whereby the victim is seized by the Devil and doubts the possibility of divine mercy and salvation. It is frequently cited as the cause of suicide. In court records, the stated cause of suicide was primarily insanity, and secondarily illness, loneliness, a death in the family, poverty, hunger, jealousy, imprisonment, and the ruination engendered by war. Since the majority of the judicial cases of attempted suicide are urban and artisan-centered, it may be that the nobility could avoid punishment and the peasantry detection. The preferred means of suicide was hanging, followed by drowning. It may well be that many of the *furiosi* described in hagiographical sources, who were cured through thaumaturgical intervention, were bound and restrained by family and friends because they had already attempted suicide or might harm not merely themselves, but also others.[73]

Since the body of a suicide could not be buried in consecrated ground, but was cast out into a pit or river, his family was subject to shame and infamy.[74] Pontius Pilate and Judas Iscariot were regarded as emblems of the suicide.[75] Thomas Aquinas dealt with suicide as a form of homicide, relying on Scripture, Aristotle, Augustine, and the lives of the saints in his argument.[76] A mortal sin, it is contrary to human nature and to the virtue of charity, which demands self-love and protection. Further, since we are by nature members of a community, it is damaging to the interests of society. Life is a gift of God, and only God can take it away (Deuteronomy 32.39); the commandment not to kill applies not simply to others, but also to oneself. Since no one may be the judge of one's own case, one cannot kill oneself in order to pass into a more blessed state; or conversely, in order to escape misery, since, as Aristotle has said, death itself is the most fearful evil of life. By committing suicide, one deprives oneself of the opportunity to perform penance, and even victims of attempted rape were advised not to commit suicide. As St. Lucy had said, when threatened by such violent persecution for her faith, "The body is not spoiled except by the consent of the mind." Since the ends do not justify the means, one may not commit evil in order to achieve some good or avoid evil. Aquinas rejected the suicide of Razias (2 Maccabees 14.41ff.), who killed himself rather than fall into the hands of sinners, since rather than true courage, he displayed softness of spirit, that is, the inability to suffer punishment. Nevertheless, he noted two cases of suicide that may be praiseworthy: Samson's suicide (Hebrews 11.32, Judges 16.30) may be excusable because the Spirit secretly ordered him to do so; and in a second case the suicide of a holy woman during the persecutions had been justified by Augustine, since the event was used to perform a miracle.

As in Aquinas, Italian communal legislation appears to have dealt with suicide as a form of homicide, and would minimally demand a high fine, although the confiscation of the attempted suicide's goods might not be required.[77] I have found four cases of suicide in contemporary hagiographical sources, namely the Swedish witch noted above who had failed in her attempt to bewitch a priest successfully, and three other cases of Italian provenance. All were reportedly instigated by the Devil and were thus amenable to the consolation of miracle. A 1316 Genoese case from the miracles of Peter Martyr deals with a woman who, "in a state of despair at the Devil's instigation," shut her front door and hanged herself.[78] Her neighbors looked for her through the transom and found her hanging from a crossbeam. An old woman who was present had, in her youth, once made confession to Peter. Recalling his miracles, she suggested that he might be of assistance. She brought a piece of the saint's cap or hood which she had kept as a relic, and placed it on the woman's throat. All of those present invoked the saint, and when the victim revived, she said that she had never felt such sweetness in her throat as she had just experienced. In the second case, on 13 June 1317, shortly after the translation of the relics of the Servite founder Philip Benizi, a woman was suffering from a demonic compulsion to take some instrument and hang herself.[79] Because this demon had been urging her to do so for six years, her parents had kept her under constant watch. Then she was taken to Philip's tomb, where she fell into a deep sleep. She had a vision of Philip who said, "Confide in me, daughter, because I will restore your sanity, and will free you from the power of the demon and his evil will. May the Holy Spirit be with you." When she awoke, she was free of her long obsession.

The best-documented case of attempted suicide appears in the process of the Augustinian friar Nicholas of Tolentino held between 7 July and 28 September 1325 at Tolentino, San Ginesio, Camerino, San Severino, and Macerata.[80] The witnesses included: the victim himself, Jacopuzzo Fatteboni of Belforte-sul-Chienti in the Marche, aged about fifty-five at the time of the attempted suicide; his daughter Pianucia, aged about twenty-five at the time of the suicide and wife of Andrea Francesco; and two neighbor women. A relatively detailed reconstruction of the events is possible. On the morning of Thursday, 24 April 1320, a day before the feast of St. Mark, Jacopuzzo's wife Bionda (who had since died) had gone to the weekly market held in

Tolentino. While she was out, his daughter by a previous marriage, Pianucia, who lived nearby, visited her father's home, where she left him sitting on a bench. When Bionda returned, Jacopuzzo ordered her to bring grain to the communal bakery in order to bake *calzone* to feed their children and her brothers (it is unclear whether the reference is to Bionda's or Pianucia's brothers), who would return from work in the evening.

While she was at the bakery, which was situated six houses away from the Fatteboni home, Jacopuzzo hung himself with some stable rope (of the kind used during executions) from a crossbeam supporting the arched ceiling, about twelve feet from the ground. When Bionda returned and discovered the suicide, she cried out, and some local women rushed in to help her take him down and lay him on the bed. He appeared dead, since his body was black and swollen, and gave off an awful odor; and his blackened tongue stuck out stiffly from between his teeth. Jacopuzzo's overwrought wife rent her clothes, tore her hair out, lacerated her cheeks, and cried out; and at the urging of one of the women, sought the aid of Nicholas of Tolentino, who had already gained a local reputation as a miracle-worker. She begged the saint to ask God to revive him, at least in order to do penance, lest he lose his immortal soul and the family be subject to shame and scandal, since he would be thrown into a pit rather than buried in consecrated ground. Bionda tearfully vowed to bring an oxload of grain as an offering to Nicholas's tomb should her husband be revived. Jacopuzzo was restored to life at vespers, that is, about 5:00 p. m., and the next day the vow was fulfilled.

Jacopuzzo himself admitted to remembering almost nothing of the event, including the suicide attempt itself; by his own admission, almost all of his testimony rested on what others had told him. On the other hand, his daughter admitted that she was so upset at the time, she could scarcely identify those who were present. Nevertheless, she was very precise about the date and time, her stepmother's vow, her father's physical condition, and how she was informed about his suicide. A less than sensitive neighbor had asked what she would do now that her father was dead, even before she had known about the unfortunate event. Pianucia said that she was much saddened by his death; her stepmother Bionda, on the other hand (according to another witness), was more concerned about the public scandal. Several witnesses viewed Jacopuzzo's behavior as the Devil's mischief, and Pianucia stated that he had always been a foolish man (*fatuus*), not of very good sense (*non boni sensus*), and subject to illusions (*fantasticus*).

This final characterization suggested that demonic temptation lay at the root of Jacopuzzo's condition. Another witness described him as a man of melancholic temperament. This provides a biological etiology for his state of mind, since an excess of bile was regarded as a destabilizing factor. Melancholics suffered from an absence of warmth and wetness, which are the major constituent elements of life. They experience despair, impotence, poor judgment, sloth, and longing. Such weakness of character (*acedia*) provides an opening for the fantastic illusions wrought by Satan.[81] Albertus Magnus noted that evil angels (i.e., demons) may bring such phantasms at any time. Citing Hugh of St. Victor, he defined such temptation as "the impulse to do the prohibited." Medieval medicine regarded melancholia as a particular vice of persons aged forty-nine to fifty-six (like Jacopuzzo), who are mired in timidity and hesitancy; the condition may be accompanied by epilepsy, skin rash, tremors, and weakened reasoning.[82]

The miracle collections thus contain much evidence concerning continuing belief in the efficacy of supernatural intervention in pursuit of the Christian goals of monogamy, purity, procreation, emotional stability, peace, and order within the family. Since the Fall the damaging expression of human lust and anger has required the controls of state and church in order to guide humanity toward salvation. The saints in their lives had epitomized the ideals of chastity and Christian marriage and had intervened in order to bring sexual miscreants to penance, drive away the terrors of mental anguish, and restore unity to the family. By means of their relics and the community of believers supporting their cults, they posthumously continued to provide the divine grace required to cure the ills of sexuality and family conflict and to counteract the wiles of Satan, who exploited the corrupting influence of human lust and anger. Although the state intrusively demanded conformity to a specifically Christian sexual ethic and feared the consequences of disorder, believers often resorted to the patron saint as a means of restoring unity and imposing a moral consensus on recalcitrants, thus avoiding public scandal, infamy, and loss of honor.

All of these tales likewise highlight the conditional nature of belief in the supernatural. The postulant strikes a bargain with his or her patron, which is to be fulfilled only should a satisfactory solution be found. It was not concern for the eternal suffering awaiting the sinner that moved the petitioner, but rather a wish to avoid the public scandal to which the family or community would be exposed. This principle is illustrated in the affair of the nunnery of St. Projecti, Helis de Monte Peiroso, which constituted a legal *familia* which replaced the traditional family.[83] The convent had been thrown into great distress as a result of the pregnancy of one of the nuns, who accused a dead priest, the prioress's nephew, of paternity. Knowing that her dead nephew in fact had no testicles (!), the prioress despaired of ever getting at the truth and vowed one gold florin to the tomb of Urban V if he should help provide a solution. The erring nun soon admitted that another man had been responsible, thus clearing the priest's name.

Although in each of the above cases, the personal circumstances were clearly different, nevertheless, all of these episodes, including those of attempted suicide, mental illness, sexual disorder, and family conflict, were understood to have a similar etiology. They were often linked with the practice of witchcraft, usually by a woman (although the stereotypical linkage of women and Satan-worship occurs more commonly after the fifteenth century). Fear of the Devil and his minions had become an increasingly intrusive feature of late medieval culture, and its invasion into the more intimate regions of private life demanded the countervailing intervention of divine Providence. The feared consequences of sexual misconduct, suicide and unresolved family conflict included: (1) public prosecution, ridicule, and imprisonment; (2) the label of shame and infamy, which could entail ostracism not only of the offender, but also of his family, from the community; (3) emotional and mental disorder; (4) violence, which could involve murder, child abuse, or other civil crimes; and (5) eternal damnation. The suppliant—either the victim himself or a family member—often preferred to resolve these difficulties and forestall public scandal through resort to the unofficial agencies of religion. The malevolent results of bewitchment could be overcome only through the performance of a miracle and the fulfillment of a vow to a saint who undertook to do battle against the forces of Satan.

FIVE

Children as Victims

Scholars have observed the greater attention given to the infancy, childhood, and adolescence of the saint beginning in
the thirteenth century and have noted the large number of
miracles performed on children which are to be found in miracle collections of the period.[1] The uncertain conditions prevalent in the
fourteenth century appear to have enhanced concern for the safety
of children in the face of the dangers lurking in the natural world,
the perils of war, the high mortality rate of the plague years (particularly among minors), and the disrepair of Europe's physical substructure. The sharp drop in population further heightened the desire to
insure the survival of endangered infants and children. Some demographers have argued that the period 1250–1360 witnessed a catastrophic drop from about 3.5 to about 1.9 children per family.[2] The
selective replacement rate (that is, the number of children who survive the death of one or another parent) seems to have remained
negative well into the late fifteenth century, following a very high
positive rate in the central middle ages. This was compounded by an
apparent drop in life expectancy. Anxiety over the vulnerability of
children, coupled with a belief in their innocence and purity, led to
their prominent placement in religious processions, a growing number of visions of the Infant Jesus and of visions credited to children,
and the celebration of the Feast of the Innocents.[3]

Not only do such saints as Elizabeth of Thuringia and Sperandea
of Cingoli, whose own ministries were directed toward women and
children in distress, indicate a special concern for children suffering
from plague, accidents, lameness, or other difficulties.[4] While earlier
saints such as Thomas Becket had been credited with helping the
young, such miracles now also constituted a substantial proportion of
those cited in papal bulls, which suggests that concern for the welfare
of children had become public policy. Nearly all the cases noted by

Pope John XXII in the 1320 canonization of Thomas of Hereford, for example, deal with children; and a majority with childhood accidents.[5] In a sermon of 18 May 1347, *Exsulta et lauda habitatio Sion* (Isaiah 12.6), Pope Clement VI cited thirteen proven miracles in the case of Yves of Tréguier; seven of these dealt with children, and five of these with childhood accidents, largely falls.[6] The pride which a community felt when one of its younger members was touched by the sacred is evident in the name given a girl who had survived an apparent drowning, "Joan the daughter of Adam the sheriff, whom St. Thomas had revived."[7]

Even up to a third of the miracles attributed to Martial of Limoges, Leonard of Inchenhofen, or Charles of Blois, who are generally regarded as patrons of soldiers in distress, pertain to children; while nearly all of the fourteenth-century miracles of the Dominican Peter Martyr, whose reputation had been made as an inquisitor against the Cathars in northern Italy, deal with the difficulties of childbirth, infant mortality, and childhood disease.[8] The biographer of William of Bourges, enthusiastically praising the saint's thaumaturgical reputation, notes that on his feast day, parishioners flocked to the saint's shrine, abandoning babies in their cribs and children who fell prey to beasts of field and forest. But owing to the saint's protection, despite this parental neglect, the children were safe. Nevertheless, addressing the genres of miracle performed by the saint on children, he said, "some fell into wells, others into rivers, and were submerged in deep water, some were injured by broken walls, others, having fallen from a height, invoking St. William's name, experienced not the slightest injury."[9] Bartolomeo Albizi in his report of the miracles of Gerard Cagnoli included a full chapter devoted to "those tied together in the great gift of matrimony, and those not bound together; those suffering sterility, and those whose fecundity had been regained; those aided or saved during childbirth; and those men and women blessed miraculously by God with children."[10] One of the most thorough witnesses at a canonization trial was the notary Berardo Appillaterre in 1325; he describes nine cases, six dealing with children, some of them his own.[11]

The Survival of Infants

This concern for the vagaries of pregnancy, childbirth, infancy, and childhood may be attributed to several causes: (1) the special interest of the newly established mendicant orders in the innocence of childhood and the formative years as the critical period for the inculcation of Christian belief, which find their most dramatic expression in the cults of the Infant Jesus and the Holy Innocents; (2) the proliferation of charitable institutions, especially in the cities, concerned with the care of orphaned and indigent children; (3) a striking demographic drop in the fourteenth century, partly attributable to the depredations of the plague, which struck the young with greater force; and (4) a decline in the quality of life, which inevitably led to a fall in hygienic standards and a breakdown of Europe's material substructure, thus endangering the life of the young.[12] The miracle collections provide numerous examples of the desire to insure the survival of at least one legitimate offspring, the revival of a seemingly dead infant in time to guarantee baptism, and the birth of at least one son in order to guarantee inheritance and to support the parents in their dotage.[13]

The failure to bear at least one surviving child, exacerbated by a high rate of infant mortality, could lead to severe animosity directed at the offending woman.[14] Albizi reports such a case in which he served as an intermediary for supernatural intercession:[15]

> Mistress Melducia, wife of Cegne of Colle Val'Elsa [?], the nephew of the honored Pisan citizen Ser Cellini of Colle, had been married for many years and has already often conceived, but could never bear a live creature. In the year 1345, feeling that she was pregnant, she came to me seeking counsel concerning the mercy of St. Gerard regarding the birth of her child. I had her confess and gave her a candle with the relics of St. Gerard, prepared in a manner described above, which she was to keep on her person day and night, often making the sign of the cross over the creature in her womb; after the sign of the cross had been made on her with the relics of St. Gerard, I left in peace. When she had faithfully done all of this, she gave birth successfully, I believe, in the month of May, 1346. For on May 16 she sent a living offspring to our church,

along with an offering of four pounds of wax presented to St. Gerard. Afterward, during the coming June, when the child was suffering from gout and his arms, hands, shins, legs and whole body
were paralyzed, he would eat nothing for five days. The physicians
feared that he would die, so they made a vow to St. Gerard. He
immediately began to suckle at the breast and stretched his limbs
so strongly that, within a few days, he returned to perfect health.[16]

This report indicates that parents were distressed not simply by the
difficulties of childbirth, but also by such postnatal complications as
infant disease, paralysis, and loss of appetite, so that the continuing
protection of the saint was required. The formulary use of relics as a
kind of good-luck charm is also perilously similar to the prescriptions
offered by the magician.

The notary Berardo Appillaterre (aged about fifty) reported in
1325 that his late wife Margarita had borne many children, most of
whom had died, and that in desperation he had asked Nicholas of
Tolentino's help.[17] Albizi also tells of the wife of a spice dealer of Pisa
who had already borne three sons, all of whom had died of childhood
gout shortly after their birth. She promised to name her next son
after Gerard; but when he was born healthy, considered calling him
Niccolo or Agostino. When this child also showed signs of gout, she
remembered her earlier vow, beseeched Gerard's help, gave the infant
its originally intended name, and it survived.[18] In a similar case at
Metz, a woman had reportedly borne seven children, none of whom
had survived baptism. When she was again pregnant, she became
fearful and depressed at the prospect of losing another child. She
therefore sought the advice of a Dominican relative, who advised her
that (1) should a son be born, he ought to be named after Peter Martyr; (2) every year she should bring offerings to his shrine; (3) she
should conscientiously celebrate his feast day; and (4) she should attend the office and sermon devoted to Peter. Her spirits rose, the
child survived, was duly baptized Peter, and other women began to
follow her lead.[19]

The absence of heirs was an especially acute problem during the
plague period, which continued in waves for many years following
the initial outbreak of 1347–9. In 1375, a judge at Aix bemoaned the
loss of all his children to the disease. When his eight-year-old son

was also threatened and two physicians confirmed the grim prognosis, the posthumous intervention of Urban V saved the day.[20] Urban's records are particularly graphic concerning the suffering wrought by the plague upon human and beast in 1373–4 in southern France. As one of the witnesses from Arles reported, the epidemic or pest was so severe that "children and youths" (*infantes et juvenes*) especially perished, including one of his own brothers.[21] When the plague broke out at Perpignan and its environs between November 1384 and March 1385, eight thousand inhabitants allegedly died; the peril ceased only after the display of the relics of Gauderic of Agricola.[22] The high mortality rates were aggravated by food shortages, among other things. A *praepositus* and canon of Majorca (and brother of the count of Rodas) testified that the outbreak at Majorca during Lent 1375 was compounded by famine, so that he doubted whether his family of eight could survive. In return for assistance, he made a gold offering and the promise of a perpetual mass in honor of Urban V.[23]

The clear desire for a specifically male child figures prominently among all social classes. This is illustrated in examples dealing with children of a king, notary, and mason. In the protocol of Gerard Cagnoli, the ability to prophesy the birth of a son or to ease miraculously the pangs of birth was an integral part of the saint's ministry in life. It is reported that while visiting Palermo, Queen Elizabeth, wife of Peter II of Aragon, bemoaned having borne seven daughters and no sons; Gerard foretold the birth of a son and heir, the future King Louis of Sicily (1342–55), born 4 February 1337.[24] Ser Nocchi, a notary of Calcinaia in the region of Pisa, already had six daughters, but no sons. He and his wife first asked St. Louis (probably of Toulouse), promising to name their first son Louis. In 1345, when this child fell ill, and they feared he might die, they made their petition before the relics of Gerard Cagnoli, and the child was cured.[25] This desire for at least one male survivor in the family may have been based not merely upon the wish to insure that the inheritance remain in the family's hands, or that the family name continue. The protocol of William of Bourges recalls a father whose son was crushed by a wall his father had been building. The grief-stricken mother beseeched the saint to restore their son so that he could support them in their old age; the child was saved.[26]

The considerable concern to ensure at least the briefest revival of still-born children in order to permit their baptism finds confirmation in such collections; such revival would allow the child to join the mystic body of Christ in heaven, and sanctuaries which could assist such revival have been active until very recent times.[27] A woman of Felletin (Creuse) had, for example, given birth to a still-born child, and was preparing the shroud for its burial in unconsecrated ground. "She cried out tearfully, concerned about the damnation of her progeny, since it had not been baptized, and [disturbed] by the opprobrium that would be directed at its soul by the neighboring women." She therefore sought the aid of Martial of Limoges.[28] This same protocol tells of a first-born son who appeared to be on the verge of death. It is reported that his father "was less concerned about the death of his child, than by the fact that he would not be baptized."[29]

The high rate of child mortality finds confirmation in such documents. To cite one well-documented case, in the summer of 1369, fraternal twins were born to a woman at St. Jean-sur-Croison (?) in the diocese of Redon.[30] The infant girl survived, while the boy showed no vital signs, and many members of the house (*domus*) were called in to confirm whether the child was dead, including the chief witness, a squire (*armiger*) named Gaufrid Chesnel, who had recently returned from Roquette in Normandy. He suggested invoking the aid of Charles of Blois. While the little girl was wrapped up and taken to the parish church to receive baptism (such a hasty attempt at baptism suggests that she was also less than healthy), the squire wrapped the infant boy up in his mantle, invoked the saint, and took him to the church. The local priest, although he had already baptized the girl, refused to baptize her brother, fearing that the infant was dead. Gaufrid again asked the saint at least to provide the infant with the breath of life so that he could be baptized. The boy was reportedly dead "for as long as it would take [to walk] about a league." The child revived, and was still alive in 1371 at the time of Charles's canonization trial. The birth of twins could also endanger a mother's life. For example, at Spoleto in June 1314 or 1316 a woman gave birth to one daughter, while the second daughter had remained lodged in her womb. Despairing of the woman's life, her family invoked Clare of

Montefalco, promising to give silver thread to the shrine, and the dead body came out. The mother's life was saved.[31]

The miraculous rescue of an endangered child illuminates the ways in which children might become the means whereby a community of believers reaffirmed its unity. Since only the cases of apparent miraculous intervention are reported, it may be assumed that the dangers of infancy and childhood occupied a central place in the contemporary pantheon of fear. The mere quantity of such reports suggests that infancy and childhood were perilous times of life and that the rural child in particular was exposed to considerable danger from accidental drowning or falls. Finucane has estimated that between one-half and three-quarters of the accidents involving children in miracle collections refer to near-drownings (especially prevalent in northern Europe), and of these, boys outnumber girls by a ratio of about two to one, a figure which closely parallels more recent statistics.[32] The dangers cited include wells, ponds, lakes, ditches, marshes, streams, pits, cesspools, dams, springs, vats of wine, beer, and water, threshing pits, canals, sewers, baths, and floods.[33] Children could be mortally burned by ovens, boiling oil or porridge, hearths, fires, and lightning storms.[34] They were much prone to falls from overturned boats, towers, benches, steps, ladders, bridges, and open windows.[35] Among other common sources of injury were falling trees, knives, falling bricks, collapsing walls, spindles, runaway carriages, and mill machinery.[36]

The forests and countryside were the source of dangers peculiar to rural folk: poisonous roots, dog bites, marauding wolves, snakes, spiders, and horses.[37] The criminal behavior spawned by war did not spare the young, who were victimized by thieves and taken for ransom by criminals, freebooters, and soldiers. The widely acknowledged deterioration of standards of conduct in fourteenth-century warfare had entailed the victimization of noncombatants unparalleled in the central middle ages, including children, who were taken for ransom, or injured and killed by marauders.[38] The most common form of injury reported in the home was suffocation in bed; the most unusual such case entailed a child who was accidentally suffocated in 1396 by a drunken man who lay down in bed over the child during festivities.[39] All of these dangers must be added to the congenital deformities, injuries of childbirth, undernourishment, possession by the Devil, mental illness, plague, and other diseases which afflicted an even larger number of children.

These reports suggest that the progeny of poverty-stricken parents might be even further endangered by being forced to work at a premature age, abandoned, or neglected by parents who lacked the means to support their families. Two cases of differing provenance may suffice to illustrate this condition. A poor woman of Montemurlo near Florence who lacked milk could not afford to hire a woman to feed her child.[40] In the end, her sixty-year-old mother through devotion to Zita of Lucca produced enough milk to feed not only her granddaughter, but also many others. In another well-documented case, villagers at a beer tavern in April 1288 at Wisteston near Hereford mistakenly believed that the body of a child found drowned in a fishpond was the daughter of a local beggarwoman. They assumed she had thrown her child into the pond out of despair over her wretched, poverty-stricken condition.[41]

Childhood Drowning

Some of the fullest dossiers deal with accidental drownings, which occurred beside every conceivable kind of body of water: including ponds, rivers, ditches, lakes, seas, lagoons, bays, springs, moats, canals, wells, cesspools, brooks, and swamps. The reports may include the following information:

1. the identity, age, profession, and origin of the witness
2. the age of the victim at the time of the accident
3. the name and origin of the victim, along with those of his or her parents
4. the site of the drowning
5. the date and hour of the event, including when the child was injured, and the amount of time elapsed since it occurred
6. the identity of other witnesses to the event
7. the nature of the accident
8. the depth of water in which the child was submerged

9. how long he or she remained submerged until extracted from the water

10. the means undertaken to extract the child

11. the length of time he or she remained unconscious before resuscitation

12. the precise signs of death

13. the measures taken to revive him or her

14. the identity of the miracle-worker and his or her reputation

15. the identity of the person or persons making the vow

16. the vow and invocation

17. the results of the vow

18. the vital signs of life

19. the site of the revival

20. the fulfillment of the vow, and

21. any other circumstantial evidence to corroborate the report

The answers to these queries allow us to catch a closer glimpse at such related themes as the sense of time and distance, medical knowledge, work schedule, family structure, and the religious faith of rural and urban members of the laboring classes.

Four forms of evidence were universally demanded to prove death: (1) the amount of time the child was (a) submerged underwater and (b) unconscious after being taken out of the water; (2) the stiffness of the body; (3) the coldness of the body; and (4) its coloration.[42] As one witness described the signs of death of a drowned child: "his body was cold, stiff and white, his eyes were closed and he did not breath." A mother described her dead son as "completely stiff, and lacking in color, and his neck was hanging down, as is usual among the dead." A man whose neighbor's son had drowned defined "whiteness, coldness, an immobile body, and black lips" as evidence of death; and a one-and-a-half-year-old boy who fell into a spring possessed "a black face, totally stiff and cold, except for his neck, which appeared broken, and other signs of death." One woman checked the condition of her ten-and-a-half-month-old child by placing a feather near his mouth and nose.[43]

The resort to professional medical assistance as the first means of dealing with the apparent death or injury is found far more often in urban areas, particularly the Italian towns, where such medical care was more readily available. The sketchier reports make no mention of such natural means. In the cases of children who were the victims of a fall into a river, lake, pond, canal, or mill, the means undertaken to extricate the child are usually described in great detail. A fishing rod or crook, catapult or furnace stoker could be used to reach the child and extricate him from the water.[44] If this was unsuccessful, a bystander might leap or wade in.[45] If the child had been caught in a mill wheel, the mill could be turned off and the child freed by the water released from one of the canals.[46] If possible, the child was wrapped in warm clothes and taken to a nearby hearth to be warmed.[47] Several reports note that not all the witnesses could swim, and thus the rescue was very much delayed.[48] At the Leguer bay near the Breton coastal village of Lanyon in 1306, several children were bathing, while two of them swam further out to sea.[49] One drowned, and he was retrieved by a third boy, apparently a better swimmer, who had to dive three times into the sea before locating his friend. He then took him to the victim's father's house, but left before being thanked, fearing the father's wrath (apparently the boys should not have been swimming in such deep water).

The following report, which employs the aforementioned scheme, is taken from the miracles (1388) of Martial of Limoges.[50] Owing to the minimum amount of detail, it would have surely been rejected by the papal curia:

> A five-year-old boy from Aixe-sur-Vienne (Haute-Vienne) in the diocese of Limoges, while crossing the Vienne river, which passes that place, accidentally fell into the mill-stone and was dragged or borne by the water the distance of the shot of an arrow. He was pursued by the men of that place with a great clamor, and when found, his mouth was forcibly opened with a sword; after a large amount of water was expelled, his eyes remained closed, and he displayed no sign of the breath of life [spiritus vitae]. His mother and father, aware of the miracles which God had carried out to the crowds of people venerating the blessed Martial, and especially during the course of the blessed display of the saint's head, cried out with a great wail to the glorious apostle Martial so that with

his holy prayers he might restore their only son to them. After the vow had been uttered, the boy immediately revived and spoke. The mother and father immediately journeyed to the blessed Martial as joyous pilgrims, giving thanks to God and his blessed disciple, devotedly fulfilling their vow.

This simple narrative, which contains many of the aforementioned elements of the *miraculum* and was presumably suitable for inclusion in a collection of *exempla*, nevertheless lacks some of the essential data: the names and identities of both the victim and the witnesses; the length of time the child had remained underwater; the precise signs of death; the time which had elapsed between extraction and revival; the natural means employed to revive the child; and the time and date of the event. Nevertheless, this sparse report suggests that all of the bystanders participated in the effort to rescue the endangered boy.

A fuller report, from the canonization record (1307) of Clare of Montefalco, corroborated by other witnesses, contains a good deal of graphic local color and provides considerable evidence concerning the life of the rural child.[51] Petruccio Benvenuti of Villa Vayani in the district of Montefalco reported that in October 1305, Gninluctia, the six- or seven-year-old daughter of one Ufreduccio Bartholomei (from the same region) had fallen into a nearby spring, the *fonte di Puccie*. The witness had been working in a nearby field when a little boy reported what had happened. He found the girl with her head submerged the depth of the spring and her feet one arm's-length in the water, although sticking out; because of the extent of the pond, he could not even reach her; but after wading in, he dragged her out feetfirst. Although she appeared dead, having been submerged (he estimated) for "the amount of time it would take for a man to walk one and a half times the distance covered by an arrow shot from its bow," Petruccio lifted her out so that water could be expelled from her body. At the same time he called upon both Clare of Montefalco and the Virgin to help the child. Once these words were uttered, although formerly she did not breath or move, she began to cry, moving her mouth and head. Others present included his own children, Vannello and Vannella (twins?); Genteluccio, the son of Thomas Iacobi; and mistress Benedicta, mother of said Genteluccio. As the

major actor in this drama, Petruccio was able to provide details concerning the signs of death, the site, witnesses, time, and distance elements of the miracle. But since the witness's own narrative did not
contain all the material needed to confirm the miraculous nature of
the event, the commission was forced to question the witness a second time so that eighteen of the twenty-one aforementioned points
had been covered. Nevertheless, one essential issue is lacking which
could cast doubt on the occurrence of a miracle—namely the natural
measures, if any, undertaken to revive the victim.

Many of these victims were clearly injured in the course of doing
the kind of work reserved to children, including gathering herbs in
the forest, fishing, drawing water, pasturing animals, spinning, washing clothes, or accompanying their parents or employers with stocks
of produce or grain to market.[52] While the first witnesses to such accidents were usually either their playmates or other children to whose
care they had been entrusted, some of the children were in fact the
victims of an accidental push by their playmates, which had ended
in tragedy. In other cases, the servant who may have been responsible
for childcare is the first to report the accident; one infant had been
accidently dropped into a pot of water by his mother.[53] The protocols
often mention members of the family who had discovered the body,
made a vow which revived the child, or provided testimony concerning the events, although often passersby discovered the body before
local villagers and family.[54] Comparing miracles drawn from southern
and northern Europe, Finucane has detected some evidence of the
extended family in the south, while unrelated neighbors and friends
were more involved in the north.[55]

A delinquent maid or nurse who has left the children alone occasionally appears in such reports. The dangers of abandoning one's
child to the care of a nurse are evident in the reports of children
who were found dead, presumably from strangulation, or were left
unattended and drowned.[56] Medieval child-rearing manuals were
aware of the dangers of child-minding. Mother's milk was considered
superior. Since several children might be cared for by the same person
for a fee, some neglect was inevitable.[57] A three-year-old girl of Wun-
siedl in Franconia, whose mother had died, for example, was left
alone by her nurse and fell into a basin. Her father promised to un-

dertake pilgrimages to Inchenhofen, Bogen, and Our Lady of Lautenbach in order to effect a cure.[58] A similar case of a child at Engelsberg near Bratislava who nearly died when left in a bath by his mother was reported among the miracles of Dorothy of Montau.[59] The two-year-old son of the castellan of Olesno had drowned in the Oder near Othmant when his tutor had gone into the river to cool off, and had forgotten his charge.[60] The most detailed case of such negligence appears in the protocol of Thomas of Hereford.[61] Here, Gervase (cook to lord William de Cycons, a knight and constable of Conway castle) had been attending an evening service at the church of the Blessed Mary situated near Castle Conway on the Welsh border. He was joined by his wife Dionysia and an older servant woman named Wenthliana. Three children, including a toddler named Roger, aged two years and three months, and two daughters aged about three and five had remained at home. When the father returned, he discovered that Roger was gone. A search failed to reveal the child's whereabouts, until the child was found at dawn the next morning in a ditch beside the bridge leading into the castle.

In several cases, it is noted that the local citizenry was torn between the desire to assist the victim and the demands of secular law that the body not be moved until a coroner had been called. For example, a nine-year-old girl had been washing clothes on the Vigils of Ascension [15 May] in 1366 in the Sarthe river above the Chevrier mill near Le Mans.[62] She fell into the river in the course of trying to retrieve a fallen garment and, drawn by the rushing water, was caught beneath the wooden dam or dike (*retenaculum*) of the mill. After the child had been extracted, the locals feared moving the body without license from the secular authorities. Nevertheless, the bystanders wrapped her in warm clothes and carried her to a hearth to be warmed, although she still appeared dead. The initiative to move and attempt to revive the child came from the female rather than the male bystanders, who were more concerned about the reaction of the authorities. The same canonization trial (devoted to Charles of Blois) also reports the willingness of a mother grieving over her drowned eight-year-old daughter to establish a chapel in Charles's honor should she be saved.[63] This woman did in fact contribute a chapel adorned with an equestrian statue of Charles of Blois in the pose of St. George to the Augustinian canonry at Ste. Marie de Borgomedio near Blois. In another case of a little girl drowned in a fishpond at Wisteston in Herefordshire in 1288, the locals' fear of being accused of homicide should the coroner be asked to examine the body suggests an unexpectedly wide understanding of the law regarding homicide among the local peasantry.[64] In the aforementioned case at Castle Conway in Wales in 1303 it was impossible to hide the event, and the child Roger was immediately pronounced dead by the coroner.[65] This recognition of the need to await a coroner's investigation also appears in the miracles of John of Bridlington. After being killed by a rival, a dead man remained unburied for three days because there was no royal official present. The man eventually revived after his murderer had made a vow.[66]

The fullest reports provide graphic details of the circumstances preceding a near-fatal accident and attempt to explain why the child was in danger. In nearly all of these cases, one may lay some responsibility on the parents for misjudging the child's physical ability or for parental neglect. In one case, a little boy named Nicholas, aged about nine or ten, son of John of How Caple, had been pasturing a white-spotted cow which invariably trampled on the grain.[67] The father therefore asked the boy to fetch a stick which had been left in their small boat out on the river in order to make a hobble to hinder the cow's movements. When Nicholas went to get the stick, he fell into the water. In the Wisteston case, the family had been visiting a beer tavern one Sunday afternoon while the children frolicked out back near the fish pond, throwing pebbles into the water.[68] In the course of their game one of the little boys accidentally pushed a little girl into the pond (his own mother was the girl's godmother). When he told his father what had happened, they quickly left for home lest the child be accused of homicide. In other cases, a child had apparently strangled in a crib when, left in the care of an older child, his mother had gone out to shear a sheep; one child fell off a donkey laden with wine and bread being taken to the market; and another was buried under a large amount of chaff.[69] One very full report, attested by several witnesses, tells how in August 1304 at the great Breton hospice of Ploelouan, a boy had gone to have bread baked along with others of the village.[70] As they tarried in the mill eating, the boy wandered off and decided to cool himself off because of the heat of the furnace, and fell into the nearby pond. One of the women, when the accident was discovered by an old woman (*nanna*), cried out, "Oh Saint Yves, I commend him to you, since I am guilty of this for having brought him here, and I wanted to remain inside." The victim himself was able to testify in this case, and he provided considerable evidence concerning the symptoms and circumstances of his near-fatal drowning.

Our knowledge of the ages of the victims depends on the completeness of the reports, which varies with the amount of time which has elapsed between the inquiry and the alleged miracle, and with the number of corroborating witnesses who have testified. Those children who had survived the perils of infancy (perhaps no more than 50 percent) appear to have been sufficiently well treated to avoid the dangers of falling and drowning. Nevertheless, parental neglect or even abuse could severely damage the child's chances of survival. The danger of drowning became more likely after the child was free to move about, and almost all such accidents are concentrated between the ages of one-and-a-half and seven. If the precise age is not stated, the more general terms *puer*, *infans*, or *puella* are used, which traditionally refer to children prior to age seven, endowed with the virtues of innocence and malleability.[71]

Time, distance, and depth of the water play a central role in the evidence required to prove the occurrence of a miracle. Only those protocols which were conducted under papal auspices, however, succeed in providing accurate, reliable information concerning the time and date of the event, the amount of time the child had remained submerged, how long he was dead after being extracted, and the depth of the water in which he had drowned.[72] The witnesses would be satisfied with such expressions as "at the time when people scorch the tips of the grain in the field and eat grain rubbed between their hands," "during harvest time," "when people go on pilgrimage to St. Milburga," and "at the time when the laborers return from work at the end of the day" as indications of the time when these accidents had occurred. Only the repeated questions of the lawyers and clerics who took part in such trials resulted in greater precision in conformity with "learned" demands.

The events described were generally dated with reference to a feast day rather than the civil calendar. Some of the reports cite the days dedicated to local saints, such as Sts. Kenelm, John Beverly, Milburga, and Ethelbert in the trial of Thomas of Hereford.[73] The vast majority of such accidents occurred during spring and summer, from late March to early October, when children were presumably endangered by proximity to mills, lakes, and rivers in the course of the labor and outdoor activities associated with those seasons. The earlier part of the week (Sunday to Wednesday) and the late afternoon after three o'clock appear to have been more dangerous times, just as scholars have found Sundays, feast days, spring, and dusk to be the times when crime was most rampant.[74]

Despite the wide geographical region, the terms for measuring time and distance were uniform, although in England and Germany the mile is noted, in Germany cubits are also employed, and in the south the league is the standard unit of measurement.[75] The speakers in all regions, both north and south, prefer to measure depth according to arm's lengths. The amount of time a child had remained in the water, or until he was revived, is measured in terms of either the amount of time it would take a man to walk at "normal speed" (*commune passu*) such and such a distance, or the amount of time it would take an arrow or stone to complete its path.[76] Less often, other means of measuring time were suggested: for example, a child had remained dead, "as long as it takes to say a small mass."[77] More precise measurements of depth are less common. In one case, however, the owner of the pond was called to testify and could provide the most exact measurements of the length, width, and depth of the pond in which a little girl had drowned.[78] In another case, a woman admitted to knowing the depth of a pool (*puteum*) to be seven fathoms, since a man had once drowned at the same spot.[79] In a third case, a man knew that the pole used to extract his daughter was eighteen feet in length.[80] The amount of water expelled by a child on the way to recovery was also occasionally estimated by onlookers: one or two gallons; ten large cups of water; or a bottleful.[81]

The *topos* of the child saved from drowning may be regarded as emblematic of the dangers of violent death faced by children due to the vagaries of nature, child labor, dangerous or poorly maintained equipment, and perhaps even parental neglect. While this theme contains certain standard motifs, the sheer variety and quantity of the cases one encounters in the fourteenth century allow us to flesh out our understanding of later medieval social life, particularly among the laboring classes. A concern for the welfare, or at least the survival, of the child, combined with the growing ecclesiastical interest in the confirmation of cults, provide us with much material regarding the daily concerns and mentality of the commonfolk. Such themes as the treatment of the young, notions of time and distance, labor and the family, and the signs of mortality are revealed. In such miracles, the child was transformed into the focus of family and community concern, and the apparently miraculous rescue from the danger of death became a means whereby the immanence of the supernatural in daily life was renewed.

S I X

The Violence of Nature

Many of the accidents experienced by children suggest that they had fallen victim to the gradual deterioration of the physical substructure of medieval Europe. The economic, technological, and demographic progress of the central middle ages had done much to bring the forces of nature under human control. Swamps had been drained, inhospitable forests had been cleared or reduced in size; rivers were made fordable and canals constructed through a massive effort at engineering and bridge-building. By the thirteenth century, the deforestation of Europe had become so severe that some animals had become extinct, such as the aurochs, bison, and ibex.[1] The sea had likewise become the friendly agent of economic and cultural development as a result of the reduction of piracy, the enactment of international shipping regulations, and the construction of more efficient and stronger vessels. Observers are largely unanimous about the unprecedented rise in population experienced throughout Europe between about 1150 and 1300. At the same time, an optimistic cosmology was disseminated by scholastic thinkers, who viewed humanity as a *habitator omnium*, arguing that all things in heaven and earth were created for its enjoyment. Humankind was regarded as a microcosmic reflection of the universe, possessing a unique blend of divine and earthly, rational and animalistic qualities, which are absent among the other creatures. Peter Comestor argued that man was made to serve God and the world to serve man.[2] The Christian conception of the cosmos led to the consequent desacralization of nature and permitted its exploitation in order to serve human needs.[3]

Fear of Nature

Despite this optimism, the series of natural catastrophes that struck Europe beginning in the early fourteenth century led to a loss of equilibrium between population and subsistence and suggested that the cosmos was wreaking its revenge on human pride. Thus, many of the themes found in early medieval culture prior to the conquest of nature by human ingenuity received renewed impetus. With the onset of the "Little Ice Age," heralded by the freezing of the Baltic Sea in 1303 and 1306–7, the rhythm of the seasons appears to have become more dramatic. Fear of tornadoes, drought, and flooding grew.[4] In southern France, for example, beginning in 1307–8, disastrous floods led to the destruction of crops, bridges, and people fairly regularly.[5] Periodic frosts led to the freezing of rivers and the loss of vines and animals. In 1355 there were, for example, twenty days of snow at Avignon and in 1397 thirty nights of freezing temperatures. Such bitter winters raised the continuing specter of poor harvests, famine, and consequent government efforts to supply grain to the poor and needy.[6]

The violence of nature and a brutalized humanity created an atmosphere of fear and uncertainty, which has been regarded as one of the hallmarks of late medieval society.[7] The hobgoblins of fear often found refuge in the primeval natural world, as the sea, forest, rivers, mountains, and lakes were considered sources of danger, threatening to return humanity to primitive chaos, where the infernal, earthly, and heavenly are joined. In myth and legend, the forest, lake, river, and sea, much as they had in the pagan past, often served as a danger-filled abyss separating the civilized from the savage, the earthly from the infernal. An illustration of the perils of the inferno found in a mid-fourteenth-century Cistercian encyclopedia includes a soul being stabbed by a wolflike creature, while another seeks shelter in a forestlike background.[8] Hagiographical sources often continued the time-honored tradition of employing animals as prototypical symbols of the vices and virtues.[9] Christiana of Santa Croce herself had a vision of a forest demon sent to bar her path at Altopascio near Lucca, where she met a rabbit who led her to safety.[10]

The saints through their perseverance could serve as living exemplars against such extreme vicissitudes of nature. Hedwig Repshliger, a widow of Danzig, had doubted reports that Dorothy of Montau had lain in a bath of frozen water during the winter and had emerged unscathed.[11] While navigating the Wistula in 1385 and thinking of this alleged miracle, Hedwig's boat entered some deep water and three men fell into the river. Two were rescued by the passengers, but the third had apparently drowned. After he had disappeared for about an hour, she and the others invoked Dorothy's help, vowing never to doubt her sanctity should the man be rescued. He appeared floating on the water in the form of a cross; was taken ashore and, when the bystanders tried to revive him with some warm beer, he protested that he was fine.

The inclement weather reported in contemporary chronicles is confirmed in miracles that describe how travelers were trapped on impassible roads, like the Franciscan brethren who found themselves stranded on the mountainous road between Florence and Alvernia, exhausted, hungry, and drenched from the rain. Finding shelter in an abandoned shack, the next morning they were confronted with snow and feared for their lives; in another case, several members of a group of more than twenty pilgrims trapped in a snowstorm were saved by Urban V.[12] The employment of relics as an antidote against inclement weather or the depredations of nature is often portrayed as spontaneous. On a day in May during in the early fourteenth century, for example, a terrible storm destroyed the grain and vineyards at Todi. The Servite brethren draped the scapula of Philip Benizi over a cross and undertook a procession, crying out, "Take pity on us, Lord, who wants no one to perish. Free your servants who have faith in you through the merits of your faithful servant the blessed Philip, and grant peace to your devoted people."[13] The air was forthwith stilled.

At the same time in many areas the reencroachment of the forest and the abandonment of villages, roads, and bridges in need of repair resulted in virtually irreparable damage to the physical substructure of the European economy. It has been convincingly argued in Malthusian terms that the loss of equilibrium between population and subsistence (caused by Europe's inability to support an ever-increasing population base) set the stage for the plague, depopulation, and general gloom which pervaded fourteenth-century Europe. Nature took revenge on human efforts to control the environment.[14] The crisis was perhaps most severe in the cities, which suffered food shortages, crowding, and high death rates.

It may not be possible to establish a clear correlation between mental structures and such factors as demographic change, family structure, or climatic and economic dislocations. Nevertheless, the rise of macabre themes in art, the obsession with death, and the sense of solitude, "orphanization," abandonment, and melancholy so often observed by historians during this period suggest a traumatic change in consciousness.[15] When technology could no longer master the elements, calls to the supernatural for assistance seemed the only alternative. An oft-repeated theme of medieval hagiography was the mastery of the divine over the natural and animal world. Tomasso Caffarini's (1417) biography of Catherine of Siena notes that "even inanimate objects showed obedience" to the saint.[16] Giovanna of Signa's biographer wrote: "Not only in the elements, but also in the animals does God demonstrate the power of the blessed Giovanna."[17] The apocryphal *Autobiografia* attributed to Celestine V, while praising the virtues of eremitical isolation, at the same time demonstrated the saint's mastery over the forest fire, drought, wild beasts, snakes, hunger, and cold, which were the lot of those who secreted themselves in the remote mountains of the Abruzzi.[18] Such stress on the domination of the saint over the perils of nature appears elsewhere. John of San Gemignano suggested that Seraphina had "snatched the incarcerated out of prison, led those injured by drowning out of the water, navigated the shipwrecked to a safe port, and stanched the searing flames of fire."[19] Perhaps the most concise catalog of such miracles of rescue from the forces of nature is found in the testimony of the minister-general of the Teutonic Knights, Conrad of Jungingen, in support of Dorothy of Montau. He reported that she had rescued him "at sea, on an island, in a castle and in the forest" in the course of his campaigns against the Lithuanians near Vilna in 1394.[20]

Fear of the dangers lurking in the forest, sea, lake, and desert was fed by those preachers who spiced their graphic sermons with vivid narrative accounts of the demons which populate the peripheral and nether regions. On the one hand, preachers employed images drawn from nature as a ready source of their didactic messages; on the other hand, appeal to the saints and their relics was portrayed as one means of surviving the perils of nature and trained the audience to call on the supernatural for salvation in time of danger. Armed with the illustrative weapons of the *exempla* and the saint's life, the late medieval preacher exploited the primeval subconscious fears of his audience, who were well-acquainted with the dangers of the natural world. He could employ a large catalog of tales in which these human anxieties became the means of stirring the listener.[21] Penance and piety were generally stressed as the surest bulwarks against the dangers of nature.

Johannes Herolt's *Sermo in dominica duodecima* contains exempla dealing largely with nature's revenge against those who do not fear God and fail to invoke him against inclement weather, poor harvests, stormy seas, and so forth.[22] Such descriptions of desperate situations caused by natural disasters (the products of divine anger) represented an opportunity to encourage his flock to invoke divine assistance. The miracle was invariably to be presented as a means of directing his listeners to the transcendent power of God; in a sermon on Peter Martyr he quotes William of Lyons [Auvergne?] to the effect that no other faith or sect besides Christianity is confirmed by miracles.[23] To illustrate how one should fearfully invoke God's help and seek mercy upon hearing the bells that warn of a coming storm, Herolt tells of three sleeping youths awakened by a tempest at night. One got up to pray, while the others derided him. They were forthwith struck dead by lightning.[24] In another example, he reported visiting England when an abundant grain harvest was approaching. But owing to a plague of flies caused by God's ire, hardly any grain could be found. In a third case, he cited the example of two religious who had prayed for rain, one with serenity, the other without. The land of the first was blessed with abundance, while the other was sterile. Of all the miracles which had been attributed to Nicholas, Herolt chose to stress not the cases of therapeutic healing, but rather the kinds of drowning, theft, and false imprisonment which had become dominant themes in contemporary miracle collections: (1) sailors saved from a tempest by invoking Nicholas; (2) a boy saved from drowning in return for the promise of a waxen offering equal to the child's weight; (3) a man who had been robbed and tied to a tree by thieves; and (4) a man unjustly imprisoned and tied with the kind of chains that Herolt had himself seen.[25]

One Franciscan exemplarist employed images of wind, forest, river crossings, and disease as metaphors for spiritual danger. He told of a Norman lawyer (apparently of canon law) who, "like many others of his calling" did not follow the right path.[26] While crossing a bridge over the Seine at Rouen, he was lifted up into the air and transported as far as the church of Ste. Marie de Près. He was violently dropped down, dying of severe wounds and fractures. In a tale found in John Gobi's *Scala coeli*, a knight's doubts concerning taking up the cross were worked out as he dreamed of himself poised on a bridge perched above a high and deep canyon.[27] Bridges remained dangerous places, and many (not only children) were to trip and fall off, caught in a rushing river or mill wheel. Another tale told of a certain bailiff near Dublin who was traveling from town to town, when he was approached by a demon wielding a double-edged battle-axe.[28] After making the sign of the cross, he began to confess his sins. With each sin that he confessed, a mound of earth rose up around him, eventually forming a defensive tower against the Devil's siege. The bailiff confessed and undertook a life of penitential poverty. In another tale, a terrible pestilence was attributed to the hosts of quarreling demons who hovered over field and forest. Anyone who saw this would fall down in a stupor and might even die. Thomas of Okayn, Bishop of Clonfert (Ireland), held a great convocation and preached the Word of God, warning that only faith in the Lord, penance, and prayer would weaken the demons.[29]

A Dominican exemplarist, provided two highly graphic tales in which the lake and forest served as the tools of the preacher's message of retributive justice and penance.[30] In one case, a certain friar had failed to recite the commemorative mass for two recently deceased brethren. That night, in a dream, he came to a lake filled with many men mired up to their knees. He was ushered into a boat which filled him with fear, for it was both rudderless and lacking oarsmen. Those mired in the lake were forced to push the boat with their bare hands. On one side of the lake he spied a beautiful and noble city; on the other, the object of his journey, a great palace. The next night, in the frightful palace, he encountered the two dead brethren suffering for their sins. When he awoke, he received permission from the Dominican chapter to have more private masses said for the dead friars. The third night, he saw them being led to the beautiful city.

In another tale, the same exemplarist told of a cleric who had passed through the forest in which his princely patron had often hunted. Enveloped in a dense cloud, he was separated from his companions and was taken by horse to a great palace in which his patron was seated on a flaming chair wearing a fiery crown, suffering at the hands of his own victims. He cried out from his infernal throne, "I am he whom you seek and this is my throne and the crown weighs more than the whole world."[31] The deer that prodded him with their horns were the same deer he had once skinned and dehorned in the same forest. The two black hunting dogs who lacerated his flesh had belonged to two men whom he had hanged because they refused to allow their dogs to run for him in the forest. And the youth who thrust him from his throne, grabbing his crown and stabbing him in the heart, was the same man whom he had once killed with his own hands in the forest. The forest now served as the site of his own retributive punishment and the cleric's means of reaching the next world.

In literary sources, the journey across sea, forest, or other perilous regions often served as a touchstone to assist the hero to uncover his personality and as a means of forming character.[32] The forest-desert motif was a common setting for chivalric tales in courtly literature, often as a site of trial and adventure, which experienced a marked revival in the fourteenth century. Merchants crossing the abyss may be rewarded with shipwreck, piracy, and banditry, or by great profits, while souls who cross over may reach either heaven or hell. A standard biblical source for the perils of the sea was the episode of the "vigils of the night," when Jesus was seen walking on Lake Galilee. Richard of St. Victor likened the tempestuous sea to the inconstancy of the world and described the winds as the temptations of the Devil. In his *Convivio* Dante likened the merchant who reaches his home port safely after many setbacks to the noble soul who achieves eternal life after the sufferings of the world.

If the doctrine of *contemptus mundi* had nourished contempt for the beauty of the cosmos, the hagiographers who reported the lives of those saints whose activity focused on remote regions continued to praise the monastic site as a kind of innocent paradise blessed with an abundance of water, trees, and vines, prior to the attendant evils of urbanization.[33] The forest remained a site of desertlike solitude [*eremum*], a kind of frontier haven for hermits, runaway serfs, murderers, soldiers of fortune, defeated armies, demons, fairies, and dwarfs. An old chapel such as the one dedicated to Catherine of Fierbois, which witnessed a revival after 1375, was situated in such a densely forested region.[34] The desert and remote forested regions remained a central image as a result of biblical and postbiblical precedents as the site of refuge by such sainted figures as Elijah, Moses, and St. Anthony. Angelo of Clareno's *Apologia* (ca. 1317), for example, provided a long list of such personages who fled into the wilderness in order to avoid persecution by evil forces.[35] Angelo thus justified the flight of the persecuted Celestinians in the face of attacks by their Franciscan foes, aided by the Inquisition. This monastic theme was secularized as a consequence of the revival of such classical sources as Vergil's *Bucolics*, in which the fields and forests became the sites of pastoral, nonurban pleasures. Both Boccaccio and Petrarch expressed a preference for the countryside.[36]

The Perils of the Deep

The uncharted, uncontrollable world which lay on the periphery of civilization often demanded supernatural intervention in order to fend off disaster. As Michel Mollat has pointed out, ex-voto offerings were particularly widespread among persons subject to natural dangers, such as seamen.[37] The sea was depicted as the realm of Satanic and infernal powers such as the Beast of the Apocalypse, which failed to respond to rational means of appeasement, but could be controlled only with divine assistance. Peopled by pirates and subject to unexpected tempests, the sea demanded the countermagic of saints who could fend off the dangers of the deep which threatened coastal dwellers, sailors, merchants, fishermen, and other seafarers. Such was the role played by an earlier saint, Lawrence of Dublin, for example, whose miracles focused on the dangers of the stormy seas separating Ireland from England.[38] The inconstancy and violence of the sea could readily destroy the livelihood of seamen and their extended families.[39] The catastrophic loss of Duke John of Arundel's fleet on its journey to France in 1380, in which over twenty-five ships along with their crews and baggage were lost, was regarded by the monastic chronicler of St. Albans, Thomas of Walsingham, as the just consequence of the rape and spoliation which his armies had wreaked on those in their path. This national catastrophe found its parallel in the many local shipwrecks and personal tragedies which threatened the lives of those whose livelihood depended on the sea.[40]

Some of the saints, as patrons of a particular order, region, or profession, were credited with saving their clients from the perils of the sea journey, although they were not otherwise identified as aids against shipwreck. Many thus acquired a reputation as patrons of villagers, fishermen, merchants, and others whose livelihood was dependent on calm seas, clement weather, and freedom from attack by pirates, rival armies, and pagan or Saracen marauders. Even passengers who had arrived safely, considering the perils of sea travel, might fear that their baggage had been lost on the way.[41] Mary of Cervellone was therefore invoked by a group of Mercedarians in the course of a voyage from North Africa to Barcelona in 1289 to assist in the redemption of Christian captives; and Raymond of Penyaforte aided voyagers between Barcelona and Majorca.[42] Nicholas of Tolentino rescued persons nearly drowned in the Fiume Chienti, at sea near San Clemente on a journey to Civitanova; and came to the aid of those attacked by pirates near the port of Recanati.[43] Gerard Cagnoli assisted sailors and merchants who plied their trade in the western Mediterranean between Sicily and Pisa, both sites of his relics. Bartolomeo Albizi said of his power, "In the water and air obedience was shown to him when frequently persons about to go to sea commended themselves to the saint; some would procure for themselves a bit of his tunic, some [would acquire a bit] of his hair, or something else of his against the dangers of the sea. Afterward, entering the sea, they made the sign of the cross with Gerard's relics over the water and wind, and returned safely from every terror [found in] sea or wind."[44] In the same way, Yves of Tréguier protected fishermen and merchants off the rocky coast of Brittany, which was so treacherous that proximity to the shore could be a formula for danger; one miracle reports the loss of thirty-nine persons in a storm-tossed boat a mere stone's throw from land in August 1308 near Saint-Pol de Léon; six were rescued by a fishing vessel. A survivor suggested that one reason for the catastrophe was that the boat had been overburdened with passengers and cargo.[45]

Both Peter of Luxemburg and Urban V protected travelers who

were subject to Saracen corsairs along the littoral from Barcelona to Naples; Thomas Cantilupe of Hereford aided those involved in trade in the Irish Sea, English Channel, and Atlantic coast (especially the sea lane linking Bristol and Gascony); Louis of Toulouse assisted merchants and fishermen in the western Mediterranean,[46] while Bridget of Sweden was active among the voyagers in the Baltic[47] and Mediterranean,[48] and among lake-fishers of the north, who were subject to the perils of suddenly melting ice and pagan marauders.[49] Catherine of Fierbois protected ferrymen, pilgrims, merchants, and travelers plying such internal waterways as the Loire and Vienne;[50] and Amalberga of Ghent is even portrayed assisting fishermen who caught a turbot so large it could not fit into their net, endangering their boat.[51] The danger of drowning likewise affected persons at sea for recreational purposes, like a wealthy family of Motrone, whose small boat overturned in the channel off Pisa.[52]

The precision found in many of these stories may provide a glimpse at the role of the sea, lake, and river as means of transportation, the kinds of cargo and their value, the sites of danger, and the types of vessels (and occasionally the ship's name) which plied Europe's trade routes in the fourteenth century.[53] The report of a ship endangered on the route between Pisa and Avignon, for example, lists the names of ten of the fourteen men on board, allowing a reconstruction of the crew, passengers, and their origins.[54] The kinds of vessels employed (e.g., *pamfil, barca, sagetia, galea, linho, banqueta*) and the treacherous points along the littoral may also be identified.[55] Yves of Tréguier's protocol also suggests that most of the accidents occurred close to shore in the dangerous bays that dot the rocky Breton coastline. Alain de Landehoez, for example, reported that he was in a small boat along with three other persons a stone's throw from shore in mid-July 1314, when the vessel hit a rock. The boat split in two and the victim floated about gripping a small plank from morning til sunset, when he was discovered; both he and a second passenger survived, he believed, only because of a vow to St. Yves.[56]

In the north, the perils of shipwreck were compounded by fear of falling into enemy territory. For example, at vespers (about 5:00 p.m.) during the vigils of Easter, possibly in 1374, three soldiers (*milites*) had been fishing in the Baltic Sea off Reval.[57] They were suddenly driven by heavy winds (called a *Cabris*) into pagan territory and were captured by twelve pagans, who despoiled them of all their goods, except for a tunic. As one of the Christians invoked Bridget of Sweden's aid, an infidel responded, "Isn't she the one who would snatch you alive from our hands?" The nonbelievers decided to do away with their prey, and took them out to sea in order to throw them overboard, tying their hands behind their backs with stones to serve as ballast to insure that they would sink. The first captive was thrown overboard, but managed to survive. The pagans then decided to club them to death; again, with no success, owing to Bridget's miraculous intervention. They therefore exclaimed, "Look, the one they invoked is helping them. [Beware] lest she take vengeance on us, because she is so powerful, she deprives water of its strength and stays our hand. She may take vengeance on us." It is here suggested that even nonbelievers had seen the saint. The captives were set free and reached Christian territory with unusual speed.

Many sea disasters might have been avoidable, but the reduction of trade and the shortage of manpower which characterized the late middle ages may well have led to reduced maintenance of ships and the consequent likelihood of shipwreck. One succinct example illustrating the fear of shipwreck on the personal level comes from the 1388 protocol of Canon John of Rimini: "On 1 November 1388 Francesco Curto of the parish of S. Maria de Curto said that he had been in a boat on a sea island with a great fortune, when they lost the sail and could not reach land because a strong wind was blowing. He vowed to the blessed John and the wind immediately stopped."[58] Not only is the danger of shipwreck here noted, but also its economic consequences—namely the loss of a fortune.

Forest Dangers

The forest was another natural site of danger. Packs of wolves periodically invaded nearby villages and, as in the tale of Little Red Riding Hood, these beasts allegedly preferred the flesh of little children found playing away from the protection of home, sometimes even snatching children from their homes.[59] The "holy greyhound" St. Guinefort gained a reputation as the protector of small children, having defended his master's infant child against the dangers of a wolf who had stolen into the infant's bedroom. Covered with the dead wolf's blood, the dog Guinefort was slain by his master, who mistakenly believed that the child had been victimized by his faithful guard dog.[60] Margaret of Louvain was herself consumed by wolves, and her shrine also served as a site for the cure of ailing children. In a case near Pisa reported in 1347, the wolf preferred to abduct a mare, which was later found unharmed;[61] and at Massa Trabaria, a sheep taken by a wolf into the forest was to be found only half-dead several hours later, owing to a vow to Rayner of San Sepolcro.[62] The fear of marauding wolves is given voice in the following miracle:[63] "On the same day [27 August 1388] Diodolo de Belacro said that he had lost a mare, and could not find her, and had fallen into despair about it. When he had commended her to the blessed John [canon of Rimini], she immediately jumped up and joyfully leaped out, coming out to him from a dense forest and thus avoiding the mouth of wolves." In this case, several common fears of the period are noted: the presumed loss of income due to the mare's disappearance, the encroachment of the forest, and the depredation caused by marauding wolves.

In addition to beasts of prey, the forest was inhabited by bands of thieves and cutthroats, often unemployed or demobilized soldiers, not all as benign as Robin Hood, who was himself largely an invention of the late fourteenth century.[64] The merchants, peasants, and travelers who were victimized by these denizens of the forest played a central role in many of the miracle collections. The processes of Dorothy of Montau and Bridget of Sweden, who appealed to inhabitants of Europe's untamed frontier region, are especially rich in such reports. A well-documented case told of two women passing through the forest near the church of Vrigstad in the diocese of Lincöpen.[65] Apprehended by a thief (who had been at large for over six years), they were taken to a pond hidden deep in the forest, robbed, and threatened with drowning. After escaping, they encountered two local women who told them that for many years no one would venture into that forest since it was inhabited by wild beasts. The same protocol tells of a seven-year-old girl who had disappeared for ten days in the forest surrounding the village of Karby in Finland, inhabited by bears, wolves, snakes, and other wild beasts. She returned after following a sheep that had strayed from its flock.[66] Nevertheless, the forest could serve as a route of escape. A woman of Heiligenbeil captured by Lithuanians in 1401 had witnessed the death of her two children and husband. Having been worked to the bone, and hearing that she was to be burned, she escaped during Easter 1404 to a forest situated in the border region; at first, fearful of wolves, she hid in a cave without food for four days; and then subsisted on herbs and roots, until she crossed the Memel river into Christian territory.[67]

Domestic Dangers

If the world of nature was fraught with danger, the home and workplace were no less perilous. The number of work-related accidents that appear in miracle collections perhaps bears witness to the aging stock of tools and work implements and poorly constructed domestic dwellings that could collapse on their inhabitants.[68] It has been suggested that the stagnation of the medieval economy in the fourteenth century was caused not simply by natural disaster and depopulation, but also by low capital investment and a lack of technical ideas, which could have improved the deteriorating situation.[69] Unhealthy and unprotected working conditions, long working hours (perhaps aggravated by a shortage of laborers after the plague), and quarrels which might break out among workers could enhance the likelihood of injury, which could lead to prolonged unemployment, permanent injury, or even death.[70] Among the accidents reported were: the collapse of carts burdened with goods or produce, causing injury, loss of goods, and possible death;[71] riding accidents;[72] falls into a river from barges laden with goods;[73] falls from ladders,[74] stairs,[75] or open windows;[76] injuries from carrying heavy objects;[77] and injuries from threshing during harvest.[78] A particularly graphic case describes an injury incurred during the installation of a large bell at the Benedictine abbey of St. Victor at Marseilles.[79] As the bell was being lifted to the top of the clock tower, both the rope and pulley broke, and a heavy piece of the bell landed on the bell-maker after he had fallen. He was saved from certain death by making the sign of the cross and asking the aid of Urban V in the course of his fall. Since Urban V had served as abbot at St. Victor and had been responsible for its restoration and enrichment, it is not surprising that he was here invoked.[80]

Nor were animals spared. Those domesticated animals whose loss, injury, or disease could cause anxiety include pigs, asses, chickens, sheep, and cattle.[81] The loss of an ass, which served as the only beast of burden for many a poor family, could be catastrophic.[82] The spread of murrain among cattle and sheep was endemic.[83] A Breton servant, Adelicia de Parco, for example, reported that in 1315 many animals had died, so that her one surviving calf did not even have enough milk.[84] The horse in particular had become not merely an instrument of military conquest, but also a source of income, and its loss, theft, or injury could cause severe hardship.[85] A man of Strasbourg in the service of Pierre Scatisse, head of the accounts office (*magister camere computorum*) of the king of France, reported that the seven horses caught in a conflagration at the hospice in which he was lodged were valued at 100 gold pieces, a considerable sum. A ferryman and a merchant of Pisa both estimated their horses to be valued at forty florins; and a knight was willing to pledge one florin should his steed be cured.[86] At the same time, cases in which horses caused fatal injury, particularly to children (who recovered only after divine intervention), may have made their way into the law courts, suggesting that a rather anthropomorphic attitude toward the natural world remained a feature of both learned and popular culture.[87] Thus, John Gobi told how a knight and his faithful steed who perished while courageously fighting the Saracens went to heaven together.[88] Such episodes lend credence to Esther Cohen's argument that the human and animal were incorporated into one framework of justice.[89]

Another justifiable fear was the fear of fire (sometimes caused by arson), which destroyed crops,[90] consumed animals,[91] or burned down houses, threatening their inhabitants.[92] Fire might spread rapidly, since homes often doubled as warehouses for the storage of grain, wood, or other commodities, and were constructed with walls adjoining other dwellings.[93] Infant children were especially vulnerable.[94] Because of the close concentration of village homes, a change in wind direction could cause widespread damage, as occurred in the Breton village of Villa Guegin in about 1310, when such a conflagration raged for two days.[95] The entire village of Cugliano near Montepulciano was similarly threatened by an uncontrollable fire.[96]

The Plague

The best-documented scourge of nature was the plague, whose terrible depredations beggared all other catastrophes and encouraged the veneration of about fifty saints. Such acts of God were seen as the just consequences of *ira Dei* over the sinfulness of humanity. As one chronicler reported, "Since people knew of no remedy for the event, many thought it was a miracle and God's vengeance."[97] Moribund cults which focused on distress and rescue were reactivated, like the cult of Gauderic of Agricola, which was revived after eight thousand persons had supposedly perished in the region of Roussillon and Perpignan in 1384.[98] Sebastian, for example, was presumably promoted because of the similarity between the arrow marks of his martyrdom and those which appeared on the bodies of plague victims.[99] He was implored to intercede "in order to mitigate God's wrath."[100] As Gilles le Muisit recounted:

> It had been reported that the relics of St. Sebastian were to be found in a tomb at the monastery of Saint-Pierre d'Hasnon. At the time when the plague raged, a large number of people gathered and came there: nobles, knights, women, members of the clergy, canons, religious of every order, and persons of both sexes, displaying a great and wonderful piety. But when the death toll ceased following All Saints' Day, the pilgrimage and devotion also ceased. Likewise at Saint-Médard de Soissons, where it was said that the body of the martyr St. Sebastian rested, when the pestilence raged throughout France, persons from every region, sex and status gathered there. When the torment ceased, the pilgrimage and devotion also ceased.[101]

The lingering fear engendered by plague—even after its peak had crested—was voiced by a pilgrim who appeared on Tuesday, 8 April 1399, at the shrine of Catherine of Fierbois:[102] "Durant Vigier of Cozes in Saintonge appeared that day and said that a very great plague [*mortalité*] had then gripped his country. When he saw that so many people had died, he vowed his entire income to Madame St. Catherine; [and] that he would bring everyone of his house who had survived the plague to the chapel. He reported that no one of his house died in said plague."

The need for publicly unifying ceremonies and cults was especially acute in this period, since God's anger was credited with bringing the pestilence, war, and other ills suffered by humanity in retribution for its public and private sinfulness.[103] Since the church regarded the plague as a result of God's justifiable wrath at human sinfulness, appeasement of the divinity demanded acts of group penance, collective appeals to God, and public exorcism ceremonies in which all quarters of the city could be purified. Because of the collective nature of the threat of plague, many services were held to placate God's wrath.[104] In 1349, Pope Clement VI composed a mass designed to drive away the plague, "Missa pro vitanda mortalitate," and granted indulgences of up to 260 days. During the course of the lighted processions aimed at protecting a stricken city, waxen candles the length of the ramparts might be constructed, capable of burning for years, and symbolizing the envelopment of the city in God's merciful grace. A graphic description of the measures taken to ward off the plague at Cyprus in 1361 is found in the life of Peter Thomas by Philippe de Mezières.[105] Hearing of the rapid spread of disease in Rhodes, Turkey, and Syria, Peter approached King Peter of Cyprus in order to organize mass penitential acts to free the island of the impending "scourge of God" (*flagellum Dei*). At Famagusta thirty to forty persons had perished per day, but the sermons, masses, procession, and fasting at Famagusta and Nicosia under Peter's direction eventually halted the disaster.

The plague typically appeared in cycles of six to thirteen years; the most severe years were 1347–9, 1360–3, 1374, and 1383–4; and the miracle collections provide valuable corroborating evidence of its distribution and severity.[106] The provost and canon of the see of Majorca reported that the severe plague that raged on the island in 1375 had been followed by a food shortage and famine, so that he doubted whether he or any of his *familia*, numbering eight persons, would survive.[107] A man of Weissenstein visiting Inchenhofen in 1405 said that thousands had already perished from the plague in his region.[108] Dorothy of Montau took part in pilgrimages to Aachen and Einsiedeln in late August 1384 after all of her children had died, presumably during the previous year.[109] The miracles of Remigius in France in 1349 are devoted exclusively to plague victims; and those of Giovanni di Callio deal with a small town near Urbino stricken in 1373–4.[110] Catherine of Siena acquired much of her reputation in this way during the outbreak of 1373–4.[111] Within two or three years of seeing the first signs, a patient generally died; and one Matteo di Cenni di Fazio, for example, the rector of the hospital of Santa Maria della Misericordià, who had himself cared for victims, detected such signs on his body. Although physicians predicted his imminent death, Catherine had urged him to get out of bed and to continue his charitable work. He was soon cured and the saint was credited with turning evil into good.

The canonization record of Urban V is particularly rich in material concerning the effects of the plague in southern France in the 1370s.[112] The higher mortality rates among the young are borne out in these reports. All of the interlocutors, reporting miraculous cures despite the virulence of the epidemic and its high death toll, recount the swelling, fever, and weakness, and the telltale sores that appeared near the victim's groin; while those with means turned first to physicians for aid, others recognized the signs of approaching death, and despaired for their families or themselves, ordering the administration of last rites and preparations for the anticipated funeral and burial. Jean Oliver, a judge of Aix, however, whose training presumably acquainted him with the contemporary view of the disease as a result of human sinfulness, blamed the impending death of his sole surviving child (the others had already been felled by the plague) on his own sins. After two physicians (one perhaps Jewish) had delivered the grim prognosis that his son would not last the night, he promised that should he live, the child would be given over to the service of God. He said, "Oh Jesus Christ, blessed Son of God, *do not abandon me* [Job 10.2] because of my great sins by punishing me with the loss of my children and with the fact that this one child may scarcely survive. And you, blessed Virgin, Mother of God, beseech your only begotten Son to grant me this grace; and if he should live, I will commit him to the service of God." Since his son remained in pain as sunset approached, Jean added, "Oh most blessed Pope Urban, since I believe you are a saint in the eyes of God, I beseech your sanctity, that you should intercede before God so that my loving son should not die of this disease. If he should live owing to the intervention of your holy prayers, I will commit him to join the congregation of your sons, the monks of St. Victor of Marseilles, and as quickly as I can, I will present my son to your tomb with his offering."[113]

Recent historians may view technological and medical backwardness, overpopulation, or a poorly constructed and maintained infrastructure as the root causes of many of the aforementioned accidents and the disproportionate damage wrought by fire, shipwreck, plague, or storm. The general anxiety and fear characteristic of the fourteenth century was viewed by contemporaries, however, as the result of natural disasters. And such catastrophes were regarded as the just consequences of *ira Dei* over the sinfulness of humanity. Within the context of the medieval worldview, if God had brought such natural disasters on a sinful humanity, his propitiation by means of a vow and its fulfillment could bring about its reversal, particularly if the victim was blameless. This view of the immanent presence of both God and his Satanic opponent in nature was shared not simply by the popular classes, but also by their saintly and noble patrons. When the Gascons were devastating Ansouis in Provence in 1358, and a great storm darkened the area, it was feared that the enemy would scale the walls under cover of darkness. Dauphine of Languedoc therefore uttered a prayer for the exorcism of the Devil, and the tempest ceased.[114]

SEVEN

The Ravages of War

The perils of nature were compounded by the scourge of war. In time of war the *fama* or reputation of the saint and the power which accrued to those possessing his or her sacred relics were responsible for the enthusiasm with which recognition of a cult was sought. The fortuitous discovery (*inventio*) of long-lost relics, the scramble to acquire relics belonging to one's political and military foes (which sometimes went as far as theft), and the festivities surrounding the cult could symbolize state power and express unity in time of conflict. The humanist chancellor of Padua and hagiographer Sicco Polenton was forthright in his view of relics as a source of patriotic pride: "Prelates, religious, priests, clergy and lay, filled with devotion came to the monastery of Santa Maria de Porciglia of the white monks of Padua, along with other persons from distant regions, driven by the *fama* of the glorious miracles which an Omnipotent God deigned to perform in praise of His name and in the city of Padua" through Anthony of Padua.[1]

The following prayer for aid directed at John Gueruli by citizens of Verucchio captures the relationship of client and patron which continued to characterize much popular piety: "O fortunate land [*patria*] of Rimini, in which the sweet smell and body of [the blessed John] are to be found, whereby our God in these days operates and performs in our people such miracles."[2] For the presence of sacred relics allegedly aroused the senses of sight, sound, or smell. The joy displayed by the discovery of the relics of Garland of Caltagirone in late June 1327 was symbolized by the miraculous sound of ringing bells and the lighting of the lamps in early summer; such light was also reported in 1343 by the abbot around the tomb of Martin, a hermit-tailor buried at San Benigno in Genoa.[3] When Dauphine of Languedoc's body was removed for burial sweet music allegedly filled the air, which some at first falsely believed was produced by actors and musicians.[4] The relics of Thomas Aquinas at San Severino left a sweet "odor of sanctity" lingering on those with whom they had been in contact.[5]

If the patron saint had served as a balm against personal distress, his or her public role was no less recognized. The honor accorded local relics was often renewed with greater vigor in wartime. In 1338, the people of Passau found themselves besieged by their own bishop. One of the local residents, who had been especially devoted to Godehard of Hildesheim, recommended that they seek the aid of this locally born saint who had aided residents of the diocese in the past. He suggested that the saint could assist them to avert the disaster which God's anger (*ira Dei*) might bring upon them. The city's elders agreed, and, following a vow to Godehard, the duke of Bavaria intervened and brought about peace between the bishop and his people.[6] The oft-noted dedication of the Sienese army to the Virgin prior to the decisive battle of Monteperti in 1260 represents only one more dramatic example of the kind of faith in the saint's protection (illustrated in public art and legend) which had become commonplace. The people of Modena likewise continued to attribute the safety of their city to the merits of John the Baptist. Following an attack on the city in 1324, for example, Henry of Flanders, count of Lodi, had a vision at one o'clock in the afternoon in the forest of a bearded old man telling him that owing to the protection of John the Baptist, Modena had not been destroyed. Likewise, Galeazzo Visconti had been urged by the Milanese to destroy Modena stone by stone. He twice had a vision of the saint warning him that as long as he nourished such an aim, although populated by sinners, the city would withstand his siege. He must first promise to rebuild the town should he desire victory.[7] John the Baptist also extended his protection to the city of Genoa, which was protected from the army of King Charles VI of Sicily in 1386, as was the city of Mondovì.[8] In addition to patrons such as John the Baptist and Godehard, newer figures emerged to protect their compatriots in time of war. Even a hermit saint such as Giovanna of Signa, who had largely ministered to the lame and diseased, was recognized as "defender of the city" in 1396 for her service in wartime.[9] The Augustinian hermit Nicholas of Tolentino also protected locals involved in warfare between Ghibelline

San Severino and Guelph Tolentino in about 1311, and persons imprisoned by the *podestà* of Perugia in 1324.[10]

The miraculous reestablishment of peace and harmony to a troubled village, monastery, clan, or city was a common hagiographical
theme and was regarded as a God-given event. In 1338, for example,
shortly after the beginning of the Hundred Years' War, Philip VI of
France asked the bishop of Nîmes to celebrate masses, have sermons
delivered, and have processions conducted for the peace and defense
of the realm, thus bestowing a quasi-official status on the preacher.
Battles were likewise preceded and concluded with religious rites,
such as confession and communion, while the clergy prayed for the
safety of the troops. In 1412, for example, relics were displayed at
Paris to insure the victory of Charles VI against the Duke of Berry.[11]
One of the hoped-for results of the miracles of Bernardino of Siena
was an end to the continuing war between Guelphs and Ghibellines
in Aquileia.[12]

Politically, a commune such as Florence or Venice, which had acquired lands both far and near, heralded its imperial pretensions by
looting its newly won territories of key relics; and the conquered
lands were expected to adopt the cults of the victor as a sign of their
subservience. While the civic festivals of Venice are perhaps both
the best documented and most widely known, this phenomenon was
not limited to the towns and villages of the south. Legislation regulated the celebration of feast days, and prohibited certain forms of
labor, luxurious garments, gaming, and blasphemy during festivities.
The confirmation of confraternities (associated with neighborhoods,
professions, convents and churches), the protection of relics, the
cult's expenditures, and the conduct and responsibilities of its guard-
ians were regulated by both synodal and municipal statute.[13] The inflation of public ceremonies beyond the regular liturgical calendar
generated during the plague period demanded increased expenditures
on candles, banners, wax, wine, and the other paraphernalia of the
procession and cult.[14]

Assistance in Wartime

The utilitarian value of pilgrimage as a guarantor against the depredations of war was attested by Honoré Bonet:

> I declare that all pilgrims and Romers whatsoever, in whatever country they may be, are under the safeguard of the Holy Father of Rome, and can travel in time of war and of truce . . . And pilgrims have other privileges, for victuals must not be sold to them at a higher price than that of the country, and they have to pay no tolls, and require no safe-conducts, for he who is lord and father of all Christians, namely the pope, has given them safe-conduct. Such safe-conduct is extended to prelates, chaplains, deacons, *conversi*, hermits, pilgrims, to oxherds, and all husbandmen and ploughmen with their oxen, when they are carrying on their business.[15]

Patron saints of the martial aristocracy (who may have suffered relatively greater losses during this period) such as Maurice, George, and Michael, received wide currency in time of war.[16] Relics of a military nature, such as the sword of St. Maurice, were venerated; and many new cults—not otherwise directly identified with the martial class—protected their votaries against the enemy. Thomas of Hereford protected Englishmen harried by the Welsh and French;[17] Dauphine of Languedoc aided Provence and Aquitaine against the invading Spaniards under Henry of Trastamare in 1361; and the cult of Dominic of Silos was revived to assist Spaniards battling the Moors in southern Spain.[18] Urban V served as patron to partisans of the Guelph and French causes in Italy and France in the years just prior to the Great Schism, rescuing soldiers in distress, and extending his patronage to an entire region.[19] Merchants, pilgrims, seamen, fishermen, papal emissaries, and soldiers plying the dangerous, stormy coastal waters off southern France and Italy reported being saved following an appeal to the recently dead pope;[20] as had victims of the plague that ravaged Avignon, Marseilles, and adjacent areas in the years 1374–6.[21]

Assistance in time of war might merely take the form of prescient knowledge of a coming victory. Dorothy of Montau had allegedly warned of coming dangers, and foretold the victory of the Teutonic Knights against the Lithuanians, and it was believed that peace between the duke of Lithuania, the king of Poland, and the lords of Prussia was due to her prayers.[22] In 1314 or 1342, the Franciscan Gerard Cagnoli foretold the approaching peace with Pisa. In 1338, when Robert of Anjou laid siege to Termini in Sicily, he reportedly said, "Fear nothing, because in a few days, lacking water, the army will return home." Shortly afterward, the army retreated because of a shortage of water.[23] Likewise, when Guglielmo Raimondo Moncada, who had been appointed first lord of Augusta in 1336 by King Frederick II of Sicily, had been deprived of his castle, he was told by Gerard that within seven months his property would be restored.[24]

Such patronage continued to extend to those battling on Europe's non-Christian frontier: Bridget of Sweden assisted those facing nonbelievers in Scandinavia;[25] Dorothy of Montau assisted the Germans against their Lithuanian adversaries; merchants, pilgrims, soldiers, and Christian seamen battling Moslem corsairs in the Mediterranean were aided by Mary of Cervellone and Andrew Gallerani, among others.[26] The miracles of Wenceslas highlight the continued use of the miracle as a means of converting the nonbeliever. An imprisoned pagan allegedly said, "If the God of St. Wenceslas and the God of the Christians frees me from this wretched state because of his piety, and restores me to my former condition, I will believe in Christ and accept the baptism of salvation and will give my son to that martyr in eternal servitude." His chains thereupon loosened, and although tightened by the guards, they opened again and he was let free.[27] Even when the nonbelievers were friendly, Christians fearing death in foreign climes beseeched the aid of their patron. A young pilgrim visiting the shrine of Leonard of Inchenhofen in 1360 reported that while at Szepes in Hungary among nonbelievers, his leg had been injured. He was frightened by the sight of the dead being burned in a dung heap; his pagan host, nevertheless, promised to bury him in a field marked by a cross should he die. A vow to Leonard saved him from death.[28]

The Vagaries and Inequity of War

The collective violence produced by such conflicts as the Hundred Years' War and the Italian communal struggles had led to a deterioration in the practice of feudal warfare.[29] The medieval "art of war" had recognized a considerable number of noncombatants, including pilgrims, hermits, oxherds, ploughmen, husbandmen, peasants, merchants, and persons possessing a safe-conduct. The abduction of draft animals, laborers, and ploughs had been prohibited, along with the burning of fields and vineyards, while a truce itself functioned as a general safe-conduct.[30] Bona fide safe-conducts were of two types: "de grace," protecting its bearer against all acts of war and prosecution or arrest; and "de guerre," a sealed document paid for by the recipient, and whose status and value depended on the power of the issuing agency.

Furthermore, a contractual relationship existed between captive and captor whereby the prisoner was not to be killed or tortured, and although placed under lock and key, could not be threatened with death. Injuries inflicted on a prisoner by an outside party were regarded as trespass against his captors; and since he was transformed into a noncombatant, he automatically possessed a safe-conduct. Both Paris of Pozzi and Angelo of Perugia argued that the relationship between captor and captive was akin to that of the lord to his vassal.[31] Like the vassal, the prisoner must be loyal to his master; he must not dispute his captor's right to a ransom, while anathemas might be invoked against him should he fail to fulfill his obligations. A life-threatening, fearful, or unhealthy situation was also regarded as sufficient grounds to release a prisoner from his bond.[32] As Paris of Pozzi said, "The victor ought not to treat [his captive] badly or torture him for the sake of ransom."[33]

The prisoner was regarded as a noncombatant whose lands were technically immune from war. The taking of ransom had become one of the mainstays of war and its assumed profitability a cause for the continuation of armed conflict. Ransom arrangements were sometimes fixed by charter and traditionally could not exceed the prisoner's resources, generally equal to about one year's full revenue from the captive's estate; although in practice no fixed rule existed.[34] Christine de Pisan warned against excessively cruel ransom demands, "that the man be not undone thereby, and his wife and children destroyed and brought to poverty." She praised the Italian custom whereby if a man of arms is taken prisoner, he loses only his house and harness and need not forfeit his entire livelihood in order to ransom himself; she regarded the imprisonment and constraint of a man for a ransom he could not pay as tyrannical, and considered all who did so as damned.[35] The right to ransom was heritable, which often further prolonged the agony of the unfortunate prisoner. Excessive ransom demands, coupled with long imprisonment in unsafe and unsanitary conditions, was widespread. A French knight, serving as a captain on the church's side in 1376, for example, was imprisoned with his men for six and a half months at Acona, and guarded by twenty-four men; the captain himself was watched day and night by a special guard; the ransom demanded of Gregory XI for their release was 20,000 florins.[36] He managed to escape with a companion and found enough money in the treasury of the *castro* to free his men. A nobleman of Lautrec escaped in both 1372 (after thirteen weeks in prison) and 1376 (after fourteen weeks) from the Armagnacs.[37]

Despite traditional gentlemanly rules of conduct, the fourteenth century had witnessed a considerable debasement in the morality of war. The miracle collections suggest that formerly protected populations, such as pilgrims, were no longer spared. The citizen soldier and the knightly warrior had been replaced by the soldier of fortune whose aims were pecuniary. Pay rates differed enormously and large numbers of men, no longer controlled by a centralized military system, demanded payment. Problems of supply and victualing enhanced the pillage and general insecurity.[38] Among the other prohibitive costs of war were armaments, uniforms, fortifications, and ransoms—all made doubly difficult because of the general decline of economic activity. Freebooters, routiers, and arsonists roamed the countryside, extorting what were regarded as unjust demands from noncombatants. A pilgrim to Compostella, whose group was despoiled by the Armagnacs, appealed to Urban V for aid.[39] A man who had opposed the willingness of his fellow villagers to surrender to Galeazzo Visconti of Milan had his tongue slit and his eyes torn out, and was imprisoned for forty-three days in harsh conditions until regaining his speech.[40] A merchant traveling from Avignon was threatened with hanging when captured by a band of armed infantrymen;[41] one prisoner was mercilessly beaten by his captor.[42]

Although torture was considered an unacceptable means of extorting payment, Paris of Pozzi noted that mercenaries even tortured peasants.[43] Reprisals, such as the infamous sack of Limoges in 1370, became commonplace. Jean Froissart was particularly graphic about the infamies of war suffered by men, women, and children at Limoges, although the Duke of Lancaster had been expected to treat defeated knights chivalrously.[44] Honoré Bonet further warned against the excesses of those wars which were untempered by the former rules of chivalry:

> In these days all wars are directed against the poor laboring people and against their goods and chattel. I do not call that war, but it seems to me to be pillage and robbery. Further, that way of warfare does not follow the ordinances of chivalry of the ancient custom of noble warriors who upheld justice, the widow, the orphan and the poor. And nowadays it is the opposite that they do everywhere, and the man who does not know how to set places on fire, to rob churches and usurp their rights, and to imprison their priests, is not fit to carry on war.[45]

It should not be assumed, however, that the nobility behaved better than their upstart mercenary competitors. A man was held captive at Forchheim (ca. 1386) by a nobleman who, it was said, "held his own nobility in contempt."[46] The Hungarian army in 1312 allegedly destroyed a beekeeper's apiary and took the honey, leaving the owner with enough for one hive. After a vow to Cunegunda, he increased his holdings to fifty hives.[47]

The Provencal freebooter Bertrand de Born (ca. 1140—ca. 1215) himself had once written: "And it will be a happy time, for the usurers will be robbed of their property, and pack animals will no longer be able to journey in peace on the roads, nor will the townsmen and the merchants on the road from France travel in safety. He who takes willingly will become wealthy."[48] As a contemporary proverb attributed to Talbott went, "Si Dieu descendoit sur la terre, il se feroit pillard."[49] The merchant Falduccio di Lombardo wrote to Francesco Datini on 25 June 1389 of the impassable roads in southern France, "Provence seems to be a great cave of brigands because of the wars which rage here; everything is wild."[50] Nevertheless, this ruinous condition was not uniform. Robert Boutruche has noted that while the plains of north and northwestern France, the Agenais, and

Quercy were in ruins, the Béarnais and Alsace were spared.[51] The French cities apparently suffered less than the countryside during the Hundred Years' War, and such periods as 1340–73 and 1379–1405 were marked by a temporary hiatus in the orgy of destruction. Seignorial land was perhaps more affected than smaller holdings; and viticulture, market-gardening, and stock-breeding suffered perhaps more than grain crops.[52]

The victor was not necessarily spared. Barbara Hanawalt suggests, for example, that the highest rates of homicide in the Northamptonshire rolls which she examined coincide with the years 1346–9 and 1360–9, when the English armies had returned home following the great victories of Crécy and Calais in 1346–7 and the Treaty of Brittany in 1360.[53] Indeed, the view that the wars of the fourteenth century led to a kind of "golden age of brigandage" in which unemployed mercenaries and soldiers or displaced peasantry threatened wayfarers, finds ample evidence in the miracle collections. Nonetheless, Eric Hobsbawm's argument that the dislocation of the peasantry by the forces of market capitalism was a prime cause of banditry and peasant protest against the oppressor (which was favorably viewed by the community as just revenge) is not clearly confirmed, since the identity and social background of the thieves and brigands noted in miracle stories is not always clear.[54]

Many of the miracles in which a prisoner was freed from captivity suggest that in some way the contractual obligation had been broken by the captor and that divine intercession could therefore justifiably annul the anathema. The captor had overreached the bounds of equity by mistreating his prisoner, and divine intercession was required to secure his freedom. Many captors seem to have employed torture, although such protected groups as underage children, pregnant women, the aged, knights, barons, aristocrats, kings, professors, and the clergy were presumably exempt from such treatment.[55] Divine intervention could remedy such iniquity. In addition to the usual data required in the report of a miracle, such tales of miraculous escape often contain many of the following graphic details: the rank and identity of both captor and captive; the sites of capture and imprisonment; the date and time of capture and the length of time held; the dimensions of the prison; the number and height of the windows, if any; the number of guards; the kind and number of manacles; the injuries incurred prior to capture, during imprisonment and in the course of escape; the size of the ransom demand; the prayer uttered to secure release; the manner of escape (e.g., by means of rope, or stones); the means, if any, employed (such as dogs) by captors in pursuit of their escaped prisoner; and the distance traveled before reaching safety.[56]

A Cult Revived in France: Martial of Limoges

The roles of the saint and his or her cult as both a dispenser of justice and a rallying point for the establishment of social unity in a war-torn society may be illustrated in the fortunes of two older cults, those devoted to Leonard of Inchenhofen and Martial of Limoges, and the new cult of Charles of Blois. Newer cults dedicated to recently deceased figures enjoyed the fresh memory of their patron's charisma, and the support of a coterie of followers, family, and friends interested in forwarding their candidate. The cults of Leonard and Martial, on the other hand, were revived with great success in the fourteenth century, even surpassing their more recent competitors in social and geographical distribution. Both cults illustrate how the contemporary need for succor and affirmation in the face of the "terrors of history" and the social and military violence so evident during the period, could transform and revitalize long-established (although partially moribund) traditions. No clear class preference can be discerned in either cult: women and children, urban and rural folk, noble and serf make their appearance at their shrines, although the characteristic vicissitudes of the time are reflected in both.

Martial of Limoges began his cultic career as an example of the episcopal patron saint so common in the early middle ages. The purely legendary *Vita prolixior* of Martial's life by pseudo-Aurelian (late tenth—early eleventh century) suggests that he was of Jewish birth, but was baptized after hearing Christ preaching.[57] He was allegedly present at several of Jesus' miracles, including the raising of Lazarus, the Last Supper, and the Ascension. Following Peter to Antioch and then to Rome, Martial was then sent with two companions to evangelize Gaul. Although imprisoned, he founded a cathedral at Limoges, performed miracles and converted the region, continuing his evangelical activity at Bordeaux, Aquitaine, and Poitou.[58] Gregory of Tours, on the other hand, described Martial as one of the apostles to Gaul in the third century, and as the first bishop of Limoges. Although his apostleship was officially reiterated at the councils of Poitiers (1023), Paris (1024), Limoges (1028), and Bourges (1031), and he found an able propagandist in Adhemar of Chabannes and was supported by a string of bishops, Martial's status as one of the seventy-two direct disciples of Christ was not universally recognized.

Despite Martial's rather uncertain history, Limoges became a great center for the display of his relics, similar to Aix and Trèves.[59] The first such display (*ostensio*, although the term *votum* or *durante monstra* might also appear) had traditionally occurred in November 994, following Martial's intercession during an outbreak of St. Anthony's fire (i.e., erisypelas) in the regions of Aquitaine, Touraine, and Burgundy, which had exacted a heavy toll. Since many had approached the saint's shrine with the aim of securing a cure, the abbot of St. Martial at Limoges suggested three days of fasting by the entire population, followed by a procession of Martial's relics and those of other saints in the presence of the great prelates of Aquitaine. The procession followed a circuit around the city walls, and continued to Mount Montjauvy, culminating with the alleged cure of some seven thousand persons in the course of forty days. Adhemar of Chabannes noted in a sermon that Aquitaine had been devastated by sedition, fire, heavy rain, flood, and famine; as a consequence, local churches had called upon the faithful to pray and, in the course of the translation of Martial's relics from Solignac, miracles occurred. The greatest miracle was the disappearance of the plague.[60] Such translation ceremonies reportedly occurred in 1019, 1029, and 1094–5, when the saint's head may have been severed from his body; a special devotion was displayed toward the head as the site of the Holy Spirit's action during the saint's own lifetime. A special translation ceremony, accompanied by miracles, occurred in 1130; in 1183 aid was sought during a siege by Henry II; and miracles were reported at the *ostensiones* of 1300, 1317, and 1388. Other displays occurred in 1168, 1206, 1211, 1213–4, 1244, and 1283, in the presence of such dignitaries as

Louis VIII, Louis IX, and Philip III. When the notorious Black Prince took part in 1364, twelve persons suffocated in the throng.

In the fourteenth century the protective character of Martial's relics at Limoges received great impetus. Indulgences were granted to the site by such Limousin popes as Clement VI (1343) and Gregory XI (1376). Ceremonial displays occurred in 1306, 1308, 1364, and 1399; and the cult was actively supported by the Avignonese papacy and the municipal authorities, which sought to encourage the establishment of confraternities aimed at assisting the abbey of St. Martial, such as the Confrérie de Saint Martial du Sepulchre, and the Grande Confrérie de Saint Martial. In the fifteenth century, the relics were displayed in 1404, with the aim of putting an end to heavy flooding; in 1414 following the disastrous treaty of Troyes; following a royal victory in 1458; and in 1481 in order to request the fertility of the earth. After 1512 at Limoges and 1519 at St. Junien the display of Martial's relics tended to occur in seven-year cycles.[61] Surviving records suggest that a large number of pilgrims came to Limoges on such occasions, and that many injuries, and even death, resulted.

Following a period of great destruction and suffering in the Limousin (Limoges was sacked in 1371 by the Black Prince), a truce was concluded between the kings of England and France in 1388 and Martial's relics were displayed from Friday, 8 May, through Sunday, 14 June. The truce was signed on 18 August between Charles VI and the Duke of Berry on one side, and Richard II and the Duke of Lancaster on the other, going into effect on 2 September in the Limousin.[62] According to contemporary custom, such a truce would affect not simply individuals, but the entire region. The dossier of Martial's miracles was probably written sometime after August 1388 and before the end of 1389 by an apostolic penitentiary, perhaps at the behest of Abbot Geraud Jouviand, and suggests the propagandistic aim of justifying the cult's universality.[63] The miracles were recorded in formulary fashion, containing the witness's name, his or her geographical origin, the object of the miracle, an invocation to St. Martial, the fulfillment of the miracle, and the execution of the petitioner's promise.

As the anonymous editor testified: "In those days there occurred a pious display of the head of the glorious apostle by the monks and abbots . . . The church of God and the Christian people achieved unity, and the sweetness of peace was strengthened due to the prayers and merits of the saint." In addition to the attribution of the truce to divine intercession, the author expressed the view that popular enthusiasm was nourished by hopes that the Great Schism would soon be healed. Similar hopes are voiced in the protocol of Peter of Luxemburg. During the translation of Peter's relics in 1390 a local priest argued that "the whole display is a fake invented in order to attract pilgrims, especially because of the Schism."[64] Pope Urban VI was a highly unpopular figure who would soon be forced to leave Rome and seek refuge in Perugia, Lucca, and Genoa. As his death appeared near, his rival Pope Clement VII would thus remain alone, hastening a possible reconciliation of the two warring camps within the church.

The editor of Martial's protocol suggested that the people attributed the anticipated peace to the saint's intercession, which facilitated the performance of seventy-three miracles between about 1378 and 1389. He stated that the shrine is especially noted for the chains belonging to prisoners freed through the saint's merits. Such victims of tyranny were not only saved from death, but also avoided the loss of their goods. In particular, in the years prior to the ostensio, Limoges had been besieged by the hated Gaufroid de Testanegra, who is compared to the biblical princes of Edom, Moab, and Canaan who had kept the Hebrews from entering the Promised Land; as a result, the city had suffered severe food shortages. Philippe de Mézières describes Testanegra as the epitome of those persons of lowly birth who were enriched by army service and became great tyrants, living off pillage and ransom.[65] The display of Martial's relics had enabled pilgrims and victuals to reach the beleaguered inhabitants. The editor suggested that there was such an abundance of grain and other foodstuffs that the prices dropped by half.

The kinds of miracles found in this collection all reflect the difficulties of war: the failure of adversaries (particularly the English and their Breton allies) to honor safe-conducts, especially those of pilgrims;[66] the difficulty of mobilizing funds to redeem captives; the spread of dicing and other games of chance by roving freebooters; the confiscation or destruction of goods and chattel; the insecurities of travel, especially in the forest, which was populated with cutthroats, thieves, murderers, and wild animals; fears of unreliable or counterfeit currency;[67] the abduction of poor, defenseless captives, including children; the deliberate razing of villages and fields by enemy forces, leaving noncombatants dead or homeless; and the depredations caused by private warfare between henchmen and allies of the English and French crowns. The most vivid examples of miraculous intervention dealt with the salvation of captured soldiers and others, including formerly protected noncombatants, who were unable to pay exorbitant ransoms and were threatened with death. The general mayhem caused by the war did not spare persons of higher station, such as Martial Biza, guardian of the royal seal in the *baillis* of Limoges; Étienne d'Auvergne, royal notary at the chateau of Limoges; and a nephew of the abbot of St. Augustin de Limoges.

Nearly all of the miracles in this collection concern the difficulties of false imprisonment, hostage-taking, ransom, destruction of property, and loss of life which had accompanied the hostilities. Two examples will suffice to illustrate the kinds of victims aided by Martial's relics and the structure of the miracles contained in the collection. The first deals with a wine merchant whose goods were taken and whose life was endangered by English marauders, contrary to the traditional laws of war:

> Pierre Poyaudi of Masseret [Corrèze], after he had purchased four measures [*salme*] of good wine at Thiviers in the diocese of Périgeux, went to Limoges with his pack-animals. When he encountered the English, with his legs tied under the stomach of a horse, and with his hands behind his back, he was led in chains to the enemies' prison. In despair, seeing that he would lose all his wealth and that he himself was threatened with death, he cried out with a great wail to the blessed disciple of God, Martial, to take pity on him; should he free him from such inhumane treatment by his enemies, he would visit the most holy head of His disciple to give thanks to God with an offering [*imago*] of wax. Scarcely had he made his promise, when the French [*Gallici*], who could be seen from afar, attacked, and the English retreated. The captive was im-

mediately freed by them; recovering his wine and animals, he journeyed to Limoges with the offering he had promised, giving thanks
to God and his beloved disciple Martial.[68]

The postulant here conveys the despair, fear for both property and
life, and sense of injustice which bedeviled residents whose daily lives
were severely disrupted in the many combat zones of the Hundred
Years' War.

The second brief example may perhaps refer to the devastation
wrought by soldiers in the army of Charles VI, who took part in a
1387 expedition to Spain.[69] Under the former rules governing warfare the priest who was the victim (and who was perhaps under papal
orders) should have been immune from the reckless behavior of the
routiers:

> A certain priest of Poitiers on his way from Avignon, between the
> city of Valence and Vienne, was attacked by a band [societas] of
> armed men coming from Spain, who robbed him of a horse worth
> forty gold francs, and all of his money. The poor [pauper] priest,
> when he reached Vienne, hearing of the miracles performed during
> the display [ostensio] of said blessed head, prayed and vowed to the
> apostle of God, Martial, [saying] that, should his request be ful-
> filled, he would come as a pilgrim with a wax offering in order to
> honor that most holy head. When the vow had been made, the
> next morning the thieves came to the city and asked for the priest.
> Finding him, they restored both his horse and money.

In both of these cases, although much graphic detail is provided, the
occurrence of a miracle is barely proven, and many of the circumstances remain unreported. The merchant's tale reports that at the
time of his vow, the French were seen approaching, and thus he
might have been freed in due course. The restoration of the priest's
horse and money may have been the result of some order from a superior, unrecorded in this report.

Several of Martial's miracles were performed on Englishmen, as if
to suggest that the blessings of the saint encompassed the region, and
could thus even extend to the enemy. The following miracle clearly
voices the alleged extension of Martial's power to both friend and foe:

There was an English squire from the fortress of Beynat [(*sic*) now destroyed, situated near Monceaux and Argentat] in the diocese of Limoges. When he went out with many of his retainers to plunder the region, they had to cross a dangerous spot in the Dordogne river. The aforesaid [squire] fell down when the belt or reins with which his horse was bound broke and, losing control, his mount fell into the raging water. As the squire sank, he remembered that he had heard at another time of the display [*ostensio*] of said blessed head [of Martial]. He vowed, as he could, to God and the blessed Martial, that should the saint by his prayers free him from his danger, he would attend the display of [the saint's head] with a certain weight of wax for him and his horse, and that he would never take up arms against any Christian. When the vow had been made, it immediately seemed to him that a man led him out from under the water, and that his horse followed him. Both of them got out of the water unscathed. They were embraced by the observers, who believed that he had drowned, as they were to report afterward. He then went as a pilgrim on bended knee the distance of a stone's throw to venerate said very holy head; and, fulfilling his vow, tearfully reported that he would never have escaped without the miraculous assistance of the saint.[70]

The editor here demonstrates his desire to prove the universality of Martial's power; hence the cult's recognition by the aforementioned English squire, whose commander was Olimbarbe, who had assisted the pro-English seigneur of Turenne against Limoges in the Hundred Years' War.[71] The rather precise report of the reasons he and his steed fell into the Dordogne, coupled with his companions' assumption that he had drowned, is intended to prove that under normal circumstances, without an invocation to the saint, the squire and his horse would not have survived. This suggests that the editor was aware of the demand of theologians and canonists that the verifiable miracle must occur contrary to the normal processes of nature.

The miracles of Martial covered a radius of about sixty miles from Limoges, and often occurred in fortresses held by the English in which French soldiers were held captive, such as Châlusset, Beynac, Le Chastang, Courbefy, and Chanac. Many of those who were aided by Martial uttered a formulary prayer to the saint. Three adherents of the lord of Donzenac who were imprisoned at Chanac (Corrèze) by the viscount of Turenne, cried out: "Oh most pious consoler of captives, whose pious intercession frees captives from the fires of Hell and loosens the tyrant's yoke, we beseech you to aid us in our tribulation."[72] Such direct quotation of the prayer of the suing believer is often found in this collection.[73] The prayer generally includes an invocation to the saint in liturgical style, the request itself, and a promise to go on pilgrimage or provide an offering.

A Cult Revived in the Empire: Leonard of Inchenhofen

A second cult which received great impetus in the fourteenth century was devoted to Leonard of Inchenhofen. It attracted suppliants from a wide geographical distance, focusing on Bavaria, Hungary, Austria, and adjacent regions. The circumstances of carnage and spoliation which encouraged this revived cult find voice in the words of Conrad, a priest of Salzburg, whose 1360 testimony was recorded by the Cistercian chaplain Eberhard of Fürstenfeld:

> I was once in such misery and poverty because war reigned between the princes of the county, and I was despoiled of my possessions. Considering my wretched condition, and finding that I could be aided by no human solace, I sought refuge in that outstanding confessor of God, St. Leonard. I visited the boundaries [limina] of his shrine on the day of the beheading of John the Baptist [29 August] in 1358. As a consequence of the intervention of his holy merits, I was restored to my earlier status and was enriched by wealth and honor. I therefore arranged to have this double-winged dish made with the greatest care in order to honor him. I gathered together the relics of all the saints [who appear on the plate] into one. And because at the time I was an unworthy chaplain of Aufhofen [near Branau] near the river In, I thought of making this plate in order to honor a certain altar, since I was very fond of such relics. That same night St. Leonard appeared to me in the garb of a monk admonishing and saying to me, "Bring this plate [embossed] with the saint's relics to me without delay at Inchenhofen."[74]

Many of the features observed in the cult of Martial of Limoges may be found in the devotion to Leonard of Inchenhofen: an early history shrouded in mystery; a flowering in the eleventh century, reported by Adhemar of Chabannes; and special concern for prisoners. Like Martial, the cult of St. Leonard had been centered at Limoges, and enjoyed great popularity beginning with the Crusades. By 1960, five hundred and eighty-three sites of the cult had been identified in thirteen European countries. Leonard's activity was especially related to the freeing of prisoners and other assistance in time of war, along with protection from brigands. The characteristic emblematic medal displayed by pilgrims to Leonard's shrine at St. Léonard de Noblat consisted of a fortified tower, fetters, a kneeling suppliant and the saint himself—a semiotic illustration of the necessary elements in a typical rescue miracle.[75] Similar illustrations of Leonard freeing prisoners appear in contemporary illuminated manuscripts. The utterly fabricated legend described Leonard as a scion of the Frankish nobility born during the reign of the Emperor Anastasius (491–518).[76] A disciple of St. Remigius, archbishop of Rheims, he refused the offer of a bishopric from his friend Clovis, and preferred to retire to the monastery of St. Maximin at Micy and to assist Remigius in providing solace to prisoners. As a result of helping to relieve the labor pains suffered by the Frankish king's wife, he was allowed to construct an oratory in honor of the Virgin at Nobiliacum, where a religious community bearing his name—St. Léonard de Noblat— became the center of a small town. His cult, however, can be reliably dated only from the eleventh century, and was soon to become widespread in Bavaria, Austria, Swabia, and Siponto.

In the early twelfth century, Leonard was credited with assisting soldiers during the Crusades, leading to the dissemination of his cult throughout Europe. If devotion to Leonard at Noblat somewhat diminished during the Hundred Years' War as a result of the English occupation, which hindered the movement of pilgrims to his shrine, this was more than compensated by the rise of his cult in Bavaria. In the words of the great Dominican historian and inquisitor Bernard Gui, who described the miracles of Leonard as too many to count, "At the present time, in both east and west, he is well-known among confessors; he wears down iron gates, breaks bolts into pieces, shatters chains, opens prisons, reveals the dens of thieves, and restores to their families those who have been imprisoned."[77] The monastic chronicler Renier of Liège wrote that in 1212 Leonard had freed fifteen captives during a storm. In the early fifteenth century such works as *Le livre du miracle de Bacqueville, La Vie de Monsieur Saint Leonard*, and *Le livre du champ d'or* by Jehan Petit, spread word of Leonard's benevolence to noble prisoners of war to a wider audience. The autobiography of Jean Regnier, who was held captive in Beauvais in January 1432, contained a long digression on St. Leonard, and included a promise to make a pilgrimage to Corbigny should he be freed from prison.[78]

The most widely known tale involving Leonard occupies an undefined space between miracle and romance. It was reported that in the late fourteenth century two thousand French gentlemen led by the count of Nevers had replied to King Sigismund of Hungary's call for aid against the Turkish Sultan Bayezid. In the course of the Turkish victory of Nicopolis in 1396, three noblemen were taken prisoner by the Turks: Charles Martel, seigneur of Bacqueville in Normandy; Alfonse de Dampierre, seigneur of Biville in Normandy; and Étienne de Lisle, seigneur of Beaune in the Gâtinais. Brought before the sultan to deny their faith, they were tortured, harangued, and condemned to death. A slave to whose care they had been entrusted, in the course of a religious debate, baited them to plead for aid from one of their saints. Having spent the better part of the night praying for Leonard's help, they fell asleep, and the next morning found themselves transported to their native land. The sire of Bacqueville found himself in the forest of his own estate, where some woodsmen informed him that his "widow" was about to wed the rich sire of Brachy. He arrived at the chateau as the wedding cortege was about to commence, whereupon a servant, not recognizing him because of his white beard and the ravages of captivity, reported that a pilgrim was seeking alms from the mistress of the castle. Martel rejected the mere offer of money, and insisted on speaking directly to her before the wedding. Although the lady said that her husband was assumed dead, since he had not been heard from for a year, the mysterious guest reported that he had in fact seen the sire of Bacqueville. When he produced their wedding band, the nuptial banquet turned into a homecoming feast and a chapel was built at the chateau in Leonard's honor.

Such rescue tales served to spread Leonard's renown near and far, and suggest how a saint's cult could become the inspiration for courtly romance. Perhaps the leading site by the fourteenth century was, however, the village of Inchenhofen in Upper Bavaria, about thirty miles southeast of Augsburg, where a series of local clerics devotedly recorded the miracles attributed to their patron. Many of the private and public ills of the time find expression in the detailed catalog of Leonard's benefactions at Inchenhofen for about two hundred years beginning in 1258: civil disorder, plague, social conflict, false imprisonment, theft, family conflict, and sexual exploitation. In the early twelfth century, Leonard's cult at Noblat and Limoges had been largely patronized by the Benedictine and Cistercian orders. By the fourteenth century the nobility had taken up his cause, and after about 1400 the peasantry had become enthusiastic believers, turning Inchenhofen into one of Europe's leading pilgrimage sites. Pilgrims arrived from such faraway places as Italy, Hungary, Poland, and even Ethiopia, although most came from an area extending about three hundred miles from the shrine. Like the shrine of Catherine of Fierbois, the cultic center at Inchenhofen functioned without the physical presence of Leonard's relics, an increasingly common phenomenon in the late middle ages.

Leonard's career at Inchenhofen was attributed to the 1258 miraculous revelation of the theft of three chickens found in the saddle pack of a soldier passing by the shrine with his two companions. Sometime thereafter, the saint took revenge on a hungry groom in the Swiss army who had forcibly taken a loaf of bread from a poor woman of Kühbach while she and her fellow villagers were on pilgrimage. In return for freeing the thieving groom from his misery, the army promised to spare and respect Leonard's shrine. On the day when the foundation stone of Leonard's chapel was laid (1310 or 1346), an attempted theft was revealed. A stonecutter suggested stealing a pfennig from Leonard's altar in order to buy some tantalizing belladonna being sold outside the church. Failing to heed his companion's warnings, he purchased the fruit; when he began to eat, his hands stuck to his mouth and were freed only when he beseeched Leonard's help. In 1346, a convicted homicide awaiting execution managed to escape from an impregnable fortress after his prayers to Leonard. Thus, the first several miracles attributed to St. Leonard of Inchenhofen all served as solace to the victims of violence, often military in origin.

A Contemporary Saint: Charles of Blois

The Hundred Years' War has often been regarded as the furnace in which French nationalism was forged. Those saints who achieved recognition as symbols of resistance to the English yoke played an important role as the agencies through which this new-found national unity was voiced. Some, such as Catherine of Fierbois and Martial of Limoges, had long been the objects of local venera-tion. Others, themselves the victims of foreign invasion, such as Charles of Blois, Duke of Brittany, and Mary of Maillé, achieved rec-ognition as symbols of resistance. Mary of Maillé's husband Robert (d. 1362) had supported the defeated King John of France in Picardy and was himself maimed and crippled during the period of the king's imprisonment in England (19 September 1356 to 24 October 1360).[79] As Mary's Franciscan biographer noted, their castle at Sillé was devastated and forty-six local nobles were killed. At this time, he noted, the hated English "invaded cities, towns, castles, villages, churches, monasteries, and led captives away to their fortresses." Lord Robert of Sillé was taken to the chateau of Guernelle and a ransom valued at three thousand florins was demanded for his release. Because of Mary's tardiness in providing payment, he was poorly treated, refused food, threatened with death, and forced to survive on his own urine. Through her prayers, he was visited by the Virgin and saved. Restored to his wife, they both continued to assist victims of war, supplying ransom money to those in need and adopting three war orphans. Although she herself was despoiled of her property, Mary prevailed on the king, who was at Tours, to free criminals and captives condemned to death.

During the Hundred Years' War the cults of Catherine of Fierbois, Martial of Limoges, and Charles IV of Brittany rallied local patrio-tism against the depredations of the English and their allies. An ex-ample of the growth of a new cult in the midst of hostilities is the cult surrounding Charles of Blois, Duke of Brittany. Like many of his countrymen, he was captured, ransomed, and killed in battle. After Charles was captured by the English, Pope Innocent VI sent a letter to Edward III in 1358 protesting the terms of his ransom.[80] Before the battle of Auvray in 1364, Charles had reportedly declared, "I am going to defend my people, and may it please God, that this conflict should only be between me and my adversary, so that others should not die because of it."[81] As Contamine has noted, such confrontation of rival chiefs in single combat paralleled the solemn and ritual confrontation of warring armies. A classic duel in 1370 between one soldier who praised the superior honor and loyalty of the Bretons against his Gascon rivals is described in all its ritual detail in Charles's process. Despite the Gascon's proven skill, the Breton, who invoked Charles, defeated his foe in the presence of over four hundred persons.[82]

Charles was portrayed as the antithesis of the freebooters and routiers who were then ravaging much of France; his court was allegedly free of the bribery and corruption which had become commonplace elsewhere, aiding the poor and contributing wood from his own forests to rebuild the churches destroyed during hostilities; harvests were allegedly abundant under his rule, and villages which had sided with his foes were spared.[83] Breton soldiers who escaped imprisonment and villagers whose homes were pillaged and looted claimed Charles's benevolent aid; and merchants traveling in forests infested with thieves were spared, believing that Charles's aid had restored their property and saved their lives.[84] This patronage even extended to those who had supported the English.[85]

The cult of the martyred Charles did not flourish without opposition. Fearing the agitation in favor of his dead rival, on 1 February 1368 Duke John IV of Brittany ordered some English Franciscans to whitewash a mural containing a portrait of the former duke alongside the arms of Brittany contained in a cycle of the life of St. Francis at the Franciscan church of Dinan.[86] On 2 February, Duke John arrived and was satisfied that the image had been removed, although the bishop of St. Malo questioned its destruction and wanted to consult the pope. But the appearance of bloodstains on the fresco during a mass held the next day (3 February) was to become an important episode in the agitation in favor of Charles's canonization. Witnesses reported that the crowd shouted, "Look at the bleeding image of the lord Charles; no one can doubt his sanctity," for blood was flowing from both his heart and neck. Two soldiers attached to Duke John however mocked the communicants, saying, "False hicks and country folk, you believe him to be a saint, but you are lying. Lying bumpkins, by saint George, he is no saint." One of them climbed up to touch the image, and the other grazed it with a small knife in two spots, saying, "Look at his face, if he's a saint he'll bleed now." One of the witnesses at Charles's canonization trial, the knight Godfrey Budes (who had experienced other miracles at Charles's hand), climbed a ladder to inspect the fresco. He found drops of a liquid which appeared to be blood, and said, "You can readily see that it is blood." The Englishmen, still unconvinced, said that he spoke evil and was acting against the present duke. The canonization inquiry was to hear much testimony to the effect that no one had colluded to smear blood on the fresco.

Such animosity toward Charles's cult forms a focal theme of his miracles. Another miracle concerned an Englishman who in 1373 had come to Tréguier to visit the shrine of the Breton Yves Helory.[87] On the road his companions said to him, "We are near the village of Guincamp; let's go to see the tomb of the lord Charles, the former duke of Brittany, who has performed many beautiful miracles." The Englishman reportedly replied, "You believe he's a saint. By saint George, he's no saint, nor do I believe he is . . . I beseech him to perform such a miracle on me, that I can't make a pilgrimage to the blessed Yves before I've been forced to visit the church where he [Charles] is buried." The man suddenly fell ill, made a vow to visit Charles's tomb, and was cured. The witness then reported seeing Charles's former detractor threatening to duel with anyone who doubted his sanctity. Doubts concerning Charles's sanctity were further voiced by one Bertrand de Beaumont, who served in the army of the count of Rohan in September 1371 during the siege of Becquerel, which was occupied by the English. Bertrand called Charles a "malus homo, pillator et depredator."[88] Although warned of the duke's uprightness and saintliness, he nevertheless cried out, "Let me die by that evil cannon if it is not as I say." Another witness heard him say, "Let's not talk about the lord Charles, because he is not really a saint, nor do I believe he's a saint as far I can see." A Breton soldier who had belonged to the duke's retinue said, "I ask the lord Charles, if he has power before God, to show you today and perform a miracle in your presence, and if you die by the evil cannon [it will prove] that you are a liar." To this Bertrand angrily replied "Amen." During the siege he was mortally wounded by cannon fire and died. Charles's detractors, as Englishmen, cast doubt on the Breton's powers; they did not deny the institution of sainthood per se, but often preferred to invoke St. George as a more effective patron of English interests.

A tale of such false faith told by Jean Burgarelli de Sompniac of Lautrec in the diocese of Castres and found in the process of Urban V, reads like a contemporary adventure novel.[89] In 1372 he was captured by the Armagnacs and held prisoner for thirteen weeks, unable to pay the ransom demanded. After vowing to approach the shrine of Urban V barefoot bearing two wax candles of four *librae*, he was freed from his irons within two or three days and escaped, but failed to fulfill his vow. In July 1376 he was again captured by the Armagnacs and brutally confined in chains for fourteen weeks. Fearing the possible loss of both his goods and his life, he turned to Urban, saying, "O blessed Urban, just as you once saved me during my first captivity, through your holy merits, please assist me in my captivity, and intercede before God. I have failed to complete my vow, but will do so as soon as I can, and in addition to the original vow I will offer an image of two *librae* if I can escape." Shortly thereafter, Jean discovered a small metal sickle which he fashioned into a key and after three days loosened the chains. Although still weighed down by a twenty-five-pound weight, he was shown by the saint how to elude his guards. The fortress was well fortified and lit by a full moon, but he managed to free himself, though he was injured in the attempt.

The special patronage which Charles displayed toward his fellow Bretons is the subject of one of the most detailed reports of a duel to be found in the miracle collections.[90] In 1370, A Gascon soldier had defamed Breton fighting men, saying that "the Gascons are better and more honorable men of arms, and more faithful" than the Bretons. His Breton adversary therefore challenged him to single combat; after both had ceremoniously "thrown down the gauntlet," a date was set for the duel (which was witnessed by over four hundred persons). The Breton invoked many saints, including Charles, vowing to avoid wine and visit his tomb should his rival be vanquished. In addition,

Charles's name was embroidered in large letters on his sleeve. Although the Gascon was a bigger and stronger man who had defeated three men of arms in duels, the Breton killed his rival.

A witness at Charles of Blois's canonization trial (1367) spoke of waxen images of men and women, tibias, hands, arms, heads, eyes, ships (at least one hundred), castles, and homes deposited at the duke's shrine at Guincamp by pilgrims from Gascony, Spain, Normandy, and other regions.[91] These offerings might even include altarpieces and other objets d'art, providing employment for artists, sculptors, ceramicists, and other artists and craftsmen.[92] Supplying such mementos and ex-voto offerings could become something of a cottage industry. One of the witnesses reported having been reduced to poverty by continuous warfare in Brittany, so that he could scarcely support his family.[93] He beseeched Charles to either provide him with some money or show him how he could earn enough for his needs. He then had several visions in which the dead duke instructed him to make mementos for those visiting the shrine. His first three were tin images of armed men. But he remained fearful that the current duke's animus to the cult would endanger his livelihood. Charles's cult had clearly become a rallying point for those who opposed the usurper who had replaced Charles as duke and supported the English invader against France; but it also extended to non-Bretons battling in his region.

The cults of Charles of Blois, Martial, and Leonard thus illustrate many of the themes of popular piety in the fourteenth century, in which the ruinous anxieties of a violent, unpredictable, and war-weary age found expression. The rescue miracle, wherein the endangered victim seeks divine intercession in order to escape the perils of war, nature, and injustice, had become an increasing element in the pantheon of miracles. The immediate cause of this appeal to the supernatural was often the life-threatening danger and attendant evil wrought by military conflict, which in a time of total war, had begun to affect all classes, ages, and professional groups. Regarding war as a judgment from God, the church had merely condemned its unjust fruits.[94] And the saints and their relics could serve as succor against the misery it engendered. Paradise was increasingly portrayed as a fortress similar to those found in the fourteenth century, the religious being portrayed as warriors, and the saints and angels as an army battling the forces of Satan.[95]

Divine intervention had become the only means of assuring the
restoration of the equity and justice which had been destroyed during
hostilities and of balancing the growing disregard of the earlier rules
of military conduct. While the interests of the local clergy in fostering these cults is apparent, the presence of noble and peasant, male
and female, urban and country folk, friend and foe as participants in
the cult is clearly designed to guarantee universal recognition of the
saint and his relics by the faithful. The cults of both Martial of Limoges and Charles of Blois suggest a growing sense of national identity in a France torn by war. The most common genres of rescue miracle in these collections deal with: (1) the revenge wrought on
Englishmen and their allies who doubt the sanctity of the local saint;
(2) the enemy's willingness to lay down his arms in return for assistance from the local patron, whose protection may extend to all distressed persons in his territory; or (3) heroic escape from the clutches
of the enemy despite nearly impossible odds. The foreign invader is
portrayed not simply as a political foe, but also as a violator of the
traditional, civilized rules of war.

EIGHT

Conclusion

A ugustine had defined the miracle as any difficult, unusual event which exceeds the faculties of nature and surpasses the expectations or ability of the observer to comprehend, so as to compel astonishment.[1] He had limited miracles to those phenomena whose "unnatural" character was merely a consequence of the observer's limited understanding of the laws of nature. God produces what appear to be miraculous transformations in the natural world as a means of revealing himself and may make use of such agents as angels and saints to do so.[2] Miracles are essentially an acceleration of the normal processes of nature whereby the seeds (*semina seminum*) inherent in nature are activated.[3] These phenomena occur in such an unusual way that they are termed miracles, and are intended to teach us a lesson. This Augustinian view was to lay the groundwork for the later medieval concern with eliminating through judicial or scientific means those alleged miracles which could be rationally understood, despite the gullibility and ignorance of the untrained observer.

Miracle and Nature

T he thirteenth-century scholastics attempted to adapt the Christian notion of miracle to their understanding of natural law.[4] In the *De potentia*, following Gregory the Great, Thomas Aquinas stressed that holy persons perform miracles through both prayer and the power of grace; both of these means are open to any person possessing faith, for such faith makes one worthy of performing a miracle.[5] On the one hand, God himself has defined nature; therefore he cannot act against it. Nevertheless, he may act outside the normal patterns or laws of nature as we know them. Such an unusual event provokes our admiration or amazement, and is thus termed a *miraculum*. But it may be astonishing to us simply because we do not know the cause, although this cause may be known to others. In that case, such phenomena may not be termed miracles.[6] The considerable detail found in the miracles we have examined stems partly from the scholastics' attempts to verify the "unnatural" character of the supernatural events reported by the believers.

Thomas introduced the distinction between those miracles that are above nature (*supra naturam*), against nature (*contra naturam*) and apart from nature (*praeter naturam*). The miracle above nature is one in which God endows matter with a form which nature is unable to attain, such as the Incarnation of the Word; or when nature, while it can turn matter into a certain form, nevertheless cannot do so with respect to particular matter. For example, nature may bring dead persons in general back to life, but not a specified dead person. A miracle is against nature when the disposition of the material in which it occurs contradicts what actually occurs, for example, a virgin gives birth. An event is apart from nature when God has produced an effect which nature can produce, but he does so in a way which nevertheless cannot be attained by nature, such as when Christ turned water into wine.

Albertus Magnus's (d. 1280) discussion of the nature of miracle largely attempted to limit those phenomena which are termed miraculous by stressing that transformations in nature may in any case be attributed to the latent causal elements or seeds from which all things are created.[7] As long as God's creatures are fulfilling their divinely ordained intention, nature is not contravened. An event may perhaps be termed against nature when an object acts against its own inherent, particular nature. When God, however, restores sight to the blind, movement to the lame, or life to the dead, he is merely reversing the deprivation of physical characteristics which are inherent in humankind. The Austrian polymath Engelbert of Admont (ca. 1287–8), whose views adhered closely to those of Albert, summarized the thaumaturgical miracles of Jesus as the natural result of a spiritual transformation wrought by contact with God.[8] Each illness is thereafter described as a physical manifestation of a psychic weakness; and the ability to cure such diseases is passed on to the Apostles (Matthew 12.5). In his discussion of God's mastery over the elements, Engelbert argued that the "transformations" wrought in nature have a rational explanation, and merely constitute the bringing to fruition, through divine intervention, of the seeds inherent in nature. Nevertheless, such changes can be brought about both by heavenly forces (God, the angels, saints, prophets) and infernal forces (the Devil, demons, Pharaoh's magicians). Truly divine miracles, however, redound to the benefit of the faith and confound its foes. According to these scholastic standards, occasions of divine assistance against the plague and inclement weather which bedeviled the later middle ages represent classic instances of the role of miracle in restoring the imbalance of nature.

Theological speculation thus aimed at deemphasizing the miracle as a focal witness to the truths of the faith and sought to draw the believer's attention away from the fascination with supernatural intervention in favor of the words and deeds of the saints, their simplicity, chastity, poverty, and charity.[9] But as the examples which have been discussed in the preceding chapters suggest, both the learned and the *illiterati* both regarded the miracle as a form of divine intervention (like the ordeal) in order to restore the God-ordained order and equity inherent in nature and society. Like other hagiographical sources, the contemporary miracle must be read on two levels. On the one hand, it sanctified certain stereotypical themes of Christian faith, often based on the prototypical miracles of the Old and New Testaments. On the other hand, the specific difficulties characteristic of the period, such as war, plague, high infant mortality, and disasters of nature, find their solution. The miracles presented in the previous chapters played the necessary corrective role of restoring the regular (and natural) mechanisms of justice by returning property to the dispossessed, saving the innocent from torture, imprisonment, and hanging. And just as the breakdown of the state demanded appeal to the divine, so the restoration of health and balance to the Christian family, its fertility, and its continued survival required the punishment of adulterers and those who dabble in witchcraft, the cure of those possessed by the Devil, and the protection of the tender infant from the dangers of accident and childhood disease.

Since many of the ills which befell the period were regarded as the consequence of divine anger against human vice, the vow (which is an organic part of the miracle) could assist in the propitiation of God. His vengeance was a response to human violence, which included: (1) suicide, (2) the violence of the state against its own citizens through false and brutal punishment of alleged malefactors, and (3) widespread brigandage, theft, and piracy. Likewise, the endemic military conflict of the fourteenth century had led to a sharp deterioration of the rules which governed medieval warfare. Formerly protected noncombatants were now subject to ransom, imprisonment, and loss of income and liberty, which could be redressed only through miracle. The image of the saint as a dispenser of justice is found in the miracle collection of Bertha of Cambrai, for example, a Frankish saint buried at St. Amand whose body was elevated in 1081 and translated in 1288.[10] Here, the just punishment of a local nobleman who had violated church privileges is reported. The son of a magnate who had legally contributed land to the monastery of Maroeuil suffered justifiable divine revenge when he forcibly tried to recover this land just prior to the translation ceremonies. This unfortunate donor may well have found himself in the position of many contemporary Flemish noblemen who faced the dwindling of their fortunes in the late thirteenth century, partly as a consequence of high indebtedness. Such noblemen had often sought to regain lands which had been given to the church.[11]

Unity and Dissent

As in earlier periods, the miracle continued to function as a means of defining the community of the covenant and heralding the impending rule of God.[12] Each cult delineated the boundaries of community and remained an integral part of the economy of the supernatural by bringing together victim, family, friends, neighbors, fellow countrymen, and believers in a community of the faithful. The cult and miracle served as sacred means of spiritually circumscribing the village, urban, and national community within a geographic space populated by a defined group of people and as a socially and religiously legitimate agency for the expression of familial, communal, or patriotic pride and cohesion.[13] As Peter Brown has noted, the early bishops had often "orchestrated" the cult of the saints in order to legitimize their positions, and miraculous healings were transformed from private to public events.[14] The patron saint was credited with miraculously putting an end to plague, bringing a good harvest, keeping the enemy at bay, and reinforcing the sometimes fragile unity of tribe, city, and state. Such phenomena were documented and publicized among members of the congregation as a means of both strengthening communal solidarity and fashioning the community of believers.[15]

These values continued to characterize the fourteenth-century miracle. All of the miracles reported in the earlier chapters had occurred in the presence of witnesses and suggest the continuing crystallization of a collective consciousness which, as Fontaine has argued, constituted the "spiritual psychology" of the middle ages.[16] The observers of such miraculous events remained eternally bound together as participants in a sacred community. Each of the miracles cited earlier, while focusing on a central recipient (*miraculé*), created a community of faith, whether at the village or regional level. The cults devoted to Leonard, Martial, and Charles of Blois, in particular, which assisted in the rescue of both noncombatants and distressed prisoners of war, may also be regarded as emblematic of the kind of protonationalism which characterized the later middle ages.

This role of the miracle as a social bond which cut across lines of class, sex, age, and status remained one of its central features. The fullest protocols invariably include a broad spectrum of urban and rural folk, male and female, young and old, lay and religious, knightly and untitled. As one of the ecclesiastics present at the preparation of the body of Urban V for burial, kissing the hands and feet of the dead pope, reportedly said, "This body possessed a most holy soul, and served as the dwelling-place of the Holy Spirit. The blessed soul which inhabited this body interceded for us."[17] Urban's canonization protocol further recorded that "persons of high, medium and low station" were devoted to the saint.[18] The mutual patron-client relationship inherent in the miracle was further illustrated during the course of a war between Galeazzo Visconti of Milan and the marquis of Montferrato, when Milanese (i.e., antipapal) forces attempted to capture Lugnoni in the diocese of Vercelli. Although all the residents were willing to surrender, one man was adamantly opposed. Severely injured, he was unable to speak for forty-three days. Hearing of the miracles of Urban V, he vowed to build a chapel in the late saint's honor should he regain the power of speech (which he did).

The desire to possess relics, to take part in the cultic procession, and to experience or witness a miracle were hallmarks of popular piety, particularly at a time when the wrath of God (*ira Dei*) had brought about such otherwise inexplicable calamities as plague, warfare, high mortality, and natural disaster. The reputation of the miracle-worker and his or her relics was the foundation of the saint's cult, and much of the energy of the believers was focused on expressing their patriotism and membership in the Christian polity through participation in local cults. As society became more complex, the liturgical calendar became more crowded in order to accommodate those new professions, political entities, religious orders, and dynasties which sought divine approval and social or political recognition and glorification. The tailors' guild of Genoa, for example, patronized the cult of the hermit Martin; and the insignia of the Malatesti adorned the tombs of Gregory and John of Verucchio.[19] After about 1200 there was a clear inflation of ritual and ceremony, which encompassed mystery plays and penitential processions, later transformed into the elaborate pageants of the High Renaissance. In addition to the regular liturgical calendar and rites related to changes in the life cycle (baptism, confirmation) each town and village celebrated at least one annual festival during which the triumphal cart, venerated statue, civic banner, and sacred relic were paraded through the streets, often accompanied by mystery plays, entertainment, preaching, and religious ritual. It has been persuasively argued that such festivals, like the feast of St. Mark at Venice, constituted the nucleus of civic consciousness. Considerable political symbolism was later introduced after the fifteenth century, whereby local patriotism was consecrated. Peyer has noted that in many of the former Byzantine cities of Italy, *dominium* had long correlated with the possession of the remains of the saint-protector, who guarded the citizens against attack.[20]

Most frequently, the hagiographer was satisfied with a summary listing of those who were thaumaturgically cured, like the list provided of those aided by the display of the sacred relics of Albinus at Cologne between 1327 and 1330: "the paralyzed, the lame, those with crooked legs, the bent, some crawling on the ground, others with humped or curved spines, the blind, the feverish, those suffering from a variety of other ailments, including those who had died or drowned; not only those suffering from human ills, but even horses and cattle experienced such cures."[21] Zita of Lucca's biographer reported that as a result of her miracles:

> The blind see, the deaf hear, the crippled and withered are brought back to life, the lame and twisted are straightened, the mute speak, the fevered are cured, the grief-stricken consoled, unclean spirits are purged from the body, the flow of blood is stanched, birth pangs are relieved, the sterile are made fertile, the heavy made lighter, the ulcerous cleansed, those bitten and held prisoner by beasts are freed, seamen are aided, the yoke of the imprisoned is reduced, those twisted out of shape did not feel the pain, in many it seemed as though heat in the fire and liquid in the water evaporated, persons hung and yoked are freed from the jaws of death, persons whose physicians had despaired because of their high fevers, were freed.[22]

John of San Gemignano suggested that Seraphina had "snatched the incarcerated out of prison, led those injured by drowning out of the water, navigated the shipwrecked to a safe port, and stanched the searing flames of fire."[23] John's list is a particularly apt summary of the kinds of rescue miracles examined in the present volume.

All believers could thus allegedly take an active part in the cult without regard to income, social class, age, or gender. Extant inventories of votive offerings also provide a reliable catalog of those who sought assistance. In 1307, the commissioners in the case of Thomas of Hereford provided an informative inventory of the kinds of votives that believers were continuing to deposit at the saint's shrine: children's shifts, walking sticks, carts, cloth, jewels (including brooches, rings, and pins), bells, iron chains, ships' anchors, lances, spears, swords, knives, coins, and candles, along with waxen and silver images in the form of ships, persons, animals, human limbs, and body parts.[24] As noted earlier, one of the witnesses at the canonization process of Charles of Blois had recounted the many waxen ex-voto images of men and women, tibias, hands, arms, heads, eyes, ships, castles, and homes brought by pilgrims to the duke's shrine at Guincamp in Brittany.[25] The offerings of patrons, penitents, pilgrims, and *miraculés* represent perhaps one of the most lasting contributions of the

religious cult to early Renaissance devotional art. In addition to giving visual expression to the local patriotic fervor which the cult engendered, such painted images themselves often became both the inspiration for religious meditation and the focus for the performance
of miracles.[26]

The possession of holy relics and the festivities surrounding their
veneration were regarded as a means whereby the transcendent, divinely sanctioned unity of the social polity was revitalized. But what
of those who failed to join in the general festivities, who mocked
and derided the efficacy of the relics, and thus threatened such long-
cherished unity? The miracle collections reveal continuing voices of
dissent from this theme of universal unity and the vengeance
wrought against those who doubted the power of God and his agents,
as a foil to illustrate such power and to verify the authenticity of dis-
puted relics.[27] Malcontents doubted the efficacy of a saint or his or
her relics on a number of grounds. Some had opposed a saint's political program, and thus questioned his or her ability to serve as a tool
of divine power; others regarded clerical greed as the basis of the establishment of a cult; while some cast doubt on the institution of
sainthood and relic-worship per se. Their expressions of skepticism
were met with divine retribution. One of the great miracles of the
period had been the discovery of the cross and the instruments of the
Passion engraved on the heart of Clare of Montefalco after her death
in August 1305, which aroused the entire city and brought visitors
from near and far.[28] Several days after the miraculous discovery, a certain Simon dei Gilii of Spoleto, along with family and friends, including the *podestà* and other local notables, was shown the saint's
heart. Unable to refrain from laughter at the sight of the relic, he
began to joke and mock it, comparing the heart to that of an animal.
He was immediately stricken with a very serious nosebleed that could
not be stanched. It ceased only after the priest placed the relic over
his face and made a vow to God and St. Clare. Much weakened by
the event, he became a devotee of Clare's monastery of Santa Croce,
its relic and saint. This tale is illustrative of the central role of the
miracle as a means of encouraging ideological conformity.

The continuing examination of family and social structure and
roles, dream life, and popular religion as revealed in such sources may

appear to suggest a patchwork of often contradictory beliefs and behaviors, which cast doubt on the stereotypical characterization of the middle ages as an "age of faith" or "age of chivalry."[29] Nevertheless, on the deepest level of faith in the transcendent, late medieval culture does appear to possess some semblance of unity, which finds expression in times of great fear and distress, when the innocent suppliant appeals for divine aid against the exigencies of a violent and unjust world. Even those persons punished for blasphemy expressed doubts about the relics or virtues of a particular saint, rather than the principle of immanent divine Providence itself. The invocation to a saint is based upon some prior acquaintance with the reputation of the relics as potential sources of divine intercession. Not only does this saint's grace extend to long-standing devotees, but it also encompasses the sacred space surrounding the site of the relics, and even protects foreigners, including hostile ones. The receipt of divine grace is contingent on a conditional pledge or vow, whose fulfillment entails a public expression of penance and announcement of one's devotion. The participant's narrative contains two elements central to the rescue miracle: (1) an attempt on the part of the participant to explain, however briefly, the natural cause of this dangerous predicament; and (2) a strong sense of injustice or inequity, which can be put right only through the mercy of divine intercession.

Notes

Notes to Chapter One

1. John A. Hardon, "The Concept of Miracle from St. Augustine to Modern Apologetics," *Theological Studies*, 15 (1954), 229–57; Bernhard Bron, *Das Wunder: Das theologische Wunderverständnis im Horizont des neuzeitlichen Natur-und Geschichtsbegriffs*, 2nd ed. (Göttingen, 1979); for a summary of earlier material, see Benedicta Ward, *Miracles and the Medieval Mind: Theory, Record, and Event 1000–1215* (Philadelphia, 1982).

2. Paul Rousset, "Le sens du merveilleux à l'époque féodale," *Le moyen âge*, 62 (1956), 25–37.

3. Documentary evidence concerning miracles is hereafter cited by the name of the cult, followed by references according to the bibliographical list of cults. E. g., Gandolph, 708.

4. For a survey of the period, see, e.g., George Holmes, *Europe: Hierarchy and Revolt, 1320–1450* (London, 1975); Robert Lerner, *The Age of Adversity: The Fourteenth Century* (Ithaca, 1968); Michel Mollat du Jourdain and André Vauchez, eds., *Un temps d'épreuves (1274–1449)* (Paris, 1990); Francis Rapp, *L'Eglise et la vie religieuse à la fin du moyen âge* (Paris, 1971); Johann Huizinga, *The Waning of the Middle Ages*, trans. E. Hopman (London, 1924); John Bossy, *Christianity in the West, 1400–1700* (Oxford, 1987); Daniel Waley, *Later Medieval Europe* (London, 1975); František Graus, *Pest-Geissler-Judenmorde: Das 14. Jahrhundert als Krisenzeit* (Göttingen, 1989); Jacques Le Goff et al., *L'homme médiéval* (Paris, 1989).

5. E. Adamson Hoebel, *The Law of Primitive Man: A Study in Comparative Legal Dynamics* (Cambridge, Mass., 1967), 263.

6. Beatrice B. Whiting, *Paiute Sorcery*, in *Viking Fund Publications in Anthropology*, 15 (New York, 1950).

7. E. E. Evans-Pritchard, "The Notion of Witchcraft Explains Unfortunate Events," in *Witchcraft, Oracles, and Magic among the Azande* (Oxford, 1937), 18–32.

8. Bernardino of Siena, ed. Delorme.

9. André Vauchez, *La sainteté en Occident aux derniers siècles du moyen âge d'après les procès de canonisation et les documents hagiographiques* (Rome, 1981), 547; Pierre-André Sigal, *L'homme et le miracle dans la France médiévale (XIe-XIIe siècles)* (Paris, 1985).

10. Urban V, 204–5, no. 119.

11. Michel Mollat, "Sentiments et pratiques religieuses des gens de mer en France du XIIIe au XVIe siècle," *Revue d'histoire de l'Eglise de France*, 70 (1985), 305–15.

12. Robert Muchembled, *Culture populaire et culture des élites* (Paris, 1978), provides an excellent account of the daily life and fears of the laboring classes; see also idem, *La violence au village (XVe—XVIIe siècle)* (Turnhout, 1989).

13. On the rehabilitation of the miracle as a historical source, see Sofia Boesch Gajano, "Il culto dei santi: Filologia, antropologia e storia," *Studi storici*, 23 (1982),

119–36. For such studies see Jean-Claude Schmitt, *Le saint Levrier: Guinefort, guérisseur d'enfants depuis le XIIIe siècle* (Paris, 1979); Joseph Claude Poulin, *L'idéal de sainteté dans l'Aquitaine carolingienne* (Quebec, 1975); Ronald Finucane, "Pilgrimage in Daily Life: Aspects of Medieval Communication Reflected in the Newly-Established Cult of Thomas Cantilupe, Its Dissemination and Effects upon Outlying Herefordshire Villagers," in *Wallfahrt und Alltage im Mittelalter und früher Neuzeit* (Vienna, 1992), 165–217; Pierre-André Sigal, "Maladie, pèlerinage et guérison au XIIe siècle: Les miracles de saint Gibrien à Reims," *Annales: Économies, sociétés, civilisations*, 24 (1969), 1522–39; Jacques Dalaran, "Jeanne de Signa, ermite toscane du XIVe siècle ou la sainteté ordinaire," *Mélanges de l'Ecole française de Rome: Moyen âge*, 98.1 (1986), 161–99; Vauchez, *La sainteté en Occident;* idem, *Les laïques au moyen âge: Pratiques et expériences religieuses* (Paris, 1987). On pre-Christian survival in medieval religion, see Nicole Belmont, "Superstition et religion populaire," in *La fonction symbolique: Essais d'anthropologie*, ed. Michel Izard and Pierre Smith (Paris, 1979), 53–70; see Emile Benveniste, *Le vocabulaire des institutions indo-européens*, 2 vols. (Paris, 1969), under such terms as *saint* for an indication of the continuing employment of certain elemental concepts in religion. An excellent introduction to hagiographical research is Réginald Grégoire, *Manuale di agiologia: Introduzione alla letteratura agiografica* (Fabriano, 1987). Ronald C. Finucane, *Miracles and Pilgrims: Popular Beliefs in Medieval England* (London, 1977), which deals with several English cults of the twelfth and thirteenth centuries, is perhaps the most thorough discussion of popular belief and practice.

14. Some possible sources are cited in Pierre Boglioni, "Pour l'étude de la religion populaire au moyen âge: Le problème des sources," in *Foi populaire, foi savante* (Paris, 1976), 93–148. Although there is no complete catalog of hagiographical *topoi*, the following have proven helpful: J.-P. Migne, *Index de miraculis*, in *MPL*, 219: 332–62; the indices in each volume of the Socii Bollandiani, eds., *Acta sanctorum . . .* , 68 vols. to date (Paris, 1863–1940) [hereafter cited as *AASS*, followed by day, month, and volume within the month]; Stith Thompson, *Motif-Index to Folk Literature*, 6 vols. (Bloomington, Ind., 1989); Frederic Tubach, *Index exemplorum* (Helsinki, 1969); Ebenezer Cobham Brewer, *A Dictionary of Miracles* (Philadelphia, 1897; reimpression, Detroit, 1966); Peter Toldo, "Leben und Wunder der Heiligen im Mittelalter," *Studien zur vergleichenden Litteraturgeschichte*, 1 (1901), 20–35; 2 (1902), 87–103, 304–53; 4 (1904), 49–100; 5 (1905), 337–53; 6 (1906), 289–333; 8 (1908), 18–74; 9 (1909), 451–60.

15. On canonization see Henricus de Segusio [Hostiensis], *Summa aurea*, ed. Nicholas Soranza (Lyons, 1537), 187^{vi} *Decretales Gregorii noni*, III, tit. 45, cc. 1 and 2, in *Corpus iuris canonici*, 2 vols., ed. Emil Friedberg and Lewis Richter (Leipzig, 1879); see also Geoffrey of Trano, *Summa*, ed. Leonhard a Lege (Venice, 1570), 158; Innocent IV, *Apparatus quinque librorum decretalium*, ed. P. Roselle (Venice, 1610), 546ff. For the rules governing the interrogation of witnesses, see *Decretales Gregorii noni*, II, tit. 20, c. 52, *De testibus et attestionum*. For a good study of contemporary canonization practices, see Margaret R. Toynbee, *S. Louis of Toulouse and the Process of Canonisation in the Fourteenth Century* (Manchester, 1929).

16. Allucio, 232–7; Lucian, 812–3.

17. Dauphine of Languedoc, 79.

18. For an early prototype, see Innocent IV's letter of 27 November 1252, to the papal commissioners, in Rose of Viterbo, ed. Abate, 226–7: "Testes legitimos, quos super vita, conversatione ac miraculis recolendae memoriae Rosae puellae Viterbiensis

debetis recipere, prius ab eis prestito juramento, diligenter examinare curetis; et de omnibus quae dixerint interrogetis eosdem: quomodo sciunt, quo tempore, quo mense, quo die et quibus mense, quo die et quibus praesentibus, quo loco, ad cuius invocationem, quibus verbis interpositis; et de nominibus illorum, circa quos miracula facta dicuntur; et quot diebus antea eos viderant infirmos; et quanto tempore visi sunt sani; et quo loco sunt oriundi; et interrogetis de omnibus circumstantiis diligenter; et circa singula capitula fiant, ut expedit, quaestiones praedictae; et sic series testimonii et verba testium fideliter redigantur in scriptis." See also the bull of Innocent IV initiating the inquiry into Clare of Assisi in Zefferino Lazzeri, "De processu canonizationis S. Clarae," *Archivum franciscanum historicum*, 5 (1912), 645: "quo tempore, quo mense, quo die, et quibus praesentibus, quo loco, ad cuius invocationem et quibus verbis interpositis, et de nominibus illorum circa quod miracula facta dicuntur." See also Celestine V, ed. Seppelt, LII, for questions.

19. Thomas of Hereford, ed. *AASS*, 585–6, which concentrates on thaumaturgical miracles: "276. The third article [of the inquiry] deals with the miracles of said lord Thomas; concerning which the witnesses were first to be asked, testifying why, how often, and how God had acted through him, or for his sake [*pro eo*], both in the course of his life and after his death. Second, if they testify about said miracles, they are to be asked the sources for their knowledge. Third, if said miracles occurred above [*supra*] or against [*contra*] nature. Fourth, what words were used by those who sought to have said miracles performed, and how they invoked God and said lord Thomas. Fifth, if in accomplishing said miracles, herbs, stones, and any other natural or medicinal materials were used; and if incantations or trickery [*superstitiones*] or forms of deceit [*fraudes*] were involved in the operation of said miracles. Sixth, if, after said miracles had been accomplished, due to these miracles faith or devotion had grown among those persons at whose invocation or petition said miracles had occurred; or among those persons for whom the miracle had occurred; or among others to whom it became known; and they had glorified God. 277. Seventh, who were the persons in whom said miracles had occurred, their age and social condition; where were they from and who were their parents. Eighth, whether before said miracles had occurred, the witnesses had been acquainted with those persons who had allegedly experienced said miracles; if so, then for how long had they seen them healthy. Ninth, for how long and of what ailment [*aegritudo*] were they miraculously cured; how long had they suffered before the miracle took place, and for how many days before [the miracle] had they seen them suffering from such an ailment and how they knew they were suffering from such an ailment. Tenth, whether after the miracle they were fully and completely cured and healthy; and whether continuously and without pause, and for how long they were healthy, and for how long after said miracle had the witness seen them healthy and free of their ailment. Eleventh, in what year, month, day, place and with which persons present, whether said miracles occurred immediately or later [i.e., ex post facto]. Twelfth, if they occurred after the fact, how long afterwards did they become known in the places in which they were said to have occurred. Thirteenth, whether there is and was public knowledge of said miracle; if so, then for how long and from what time in the places in which said miracles were said to have occurred and in other places."

20. A. Thomasetti, ed., *Bullarium diplomatum et privilegorum Romanum pontificum*, 24 vols. (Turin, 1857–72), 4: 229–34 [hereafter referred to as *BR*]. The earlier canonization bulls often listed proven miracles in a rather stenographic manner.

21. *BR*, 4: 236–41, 291–4, 497, 529–32, 616–24; the only exception is the case of

Thomas Aquinas, 382–8. For predominance of children, see Christian Krötzl, "Christian Parent-Child Relations in Medieval Scandinavia According to Scandinavian Miracle Collections," *Scandinavian Journal of History*, 14 (1989), 21–37.

22. Vladimir Propp, *Morphology of the Folktale*, trans. Laurence Scott, 2nd ed. (Austin, 1968), 53; cf. Réginald Grégoire, *Manuale di agiologia*, 305–20; cf. also William Heist, "Hagiography, Chiefly Celtic, and Recent Developments in Folklore," in *Hagiographie, cultures et sociétés, IVe—XIIe siècles*, ed. Sofia Boesch-Gajano (Paris, 1981), 121–41, for fairy tale and miracle.

23. See for example miracles of Franciscan John of Rimini, ed. Dalaran; Martial of Limoges, ed. Lemaitre; on the notary see P. Weimar, "Ars notariae," in *Lexikon des Mittelalters*, 5 vols. to date (Zurich, 1977–93), 1: 1045–7. An example of the early, extensive use of notaries in the collection and authentication of testimony is found in the protocol of Odo of Novara, 325, in which two notaries were used. For a good example of a summarized account of the history of one papal inquiry, see Elzéar of Sabran, ed. Cambell.

24. August Potthast, *Regesta pontificum romanorum*, 2 vols. (Berlin, 1874–5), 7469, 10329; Hildegard of Bingen, ed. Bruder; Maurice of Carnoët, ed. Plaine; Simon of Collazzone, ed. Faloci-Pulignani.

25. Arnaldo Frugoni, ed., "L'Autobiografia di Pietro Celestino," in idem, *Celestiniana* (Rome, 1954), 43.

26. Natalie Z. Davis, *Fiction in the Archives: Pardon Tales and Their Tellers in Sixteenth-Century France* (Stanford, 1987), argues convincingly in favor of the reliability of the reports of notaries.

27. Clare of Montefalco, ed. Menestò, 452–4; other witnesses included Agnes, the wife of the notary Thomas of Montefalco, and the notary Petruccio Thomassii, 299–300, 391–3; for miracles performed on notaries, see the case of Thomas Aquinas, in BR, 4:382–8 (cited by John XXII); and Gerard Cagnoli, ed. Rotolo, "La leggenda," 438; for a notary's wife, see Celestine V, ed. Seppelt, 242–3. One of the witnesses in the protocol of Nicholas of Tolentino, Antonio Thomasii de Parisinis, who was cured by the saint, is identified as both a notary and a merchant (Nicholas of Tolentino, ed. Occhioni, 318). For another notary whose son was cured, and who played a key role in the dissemination of the cult, i.e., Johannes of Sulmona, see the protocol of Celestine V, ed. Seppelt, 229–30.

28. John of Bologna, *Summa notariae*, ed. Ludwig Rockinger, *Briefsteller und Formelbücher*, 2 vols. (Munich, 1864), 2: 664–5, 673ff.

29. See, e.g., the processes of Clare of Montefalco, Thomas of Hereford, and Yves of Tréguier. On notaries, see Patrick H. Daly, "The Process of Canonization in the Thirteenth and Fourteenth Centuries," in *St. Thomas Cantilupe Bishop of Hereford: Essays in His Honour*, ed. Meryl Jancey (Hereford, 1982), 125–35; Toynbee, *S. Louis of Toulouse*, 187–8.

30. Bernard Gui reports how the account of the life and miracles of Pope Benedict XI was immediately prepared according to such procedures. See Benedict XI, 14: "probata, testificata et iuramentis confirmata fuerunt coram notario et testibus convocatis in ecclesia Sancti Dominici Fratrum Paedicatorum de Parisio, paulo post sepulturam. . . ." The reports were given to Gaufrid de Allusiis, inquisitor of Carcasonne, who passed them on to Bernard Gui. Some thought-provoking remarks concerning the reliability of eyewitnesses are found in Aviad Kleinberg, *Prophets in Their Own Country: Living Saints and the Making of Sainthood in the Later Middle Ages* (Chicago,

1992), 40–70, discussing the barely believable scatalogical experiences of Christina of Stommeln reported by Peter of Dacia.

31. Mary of Cervellone, 160.

32. Honorina, 135, no. 27.

33. Rayner, 391–402.

34. Simon of Todì, 819, no. 28. For another contemporary notarized life and miracles see Humility of Faenza.

35. Catherine of Fierbois, ed. Chauvin.

36. Gerard Cagnoli, ed. Rotolo, "Il trattato," and "La leggenda"; for a protocol by a priest, see the case of Atto of Pistoia, 199ff. For a miracle recorded by local canons and canonesses at Liège in 1317, see Gertrude of Nivelles, 548. The disadvantages of the absence of trained personnel may perhaps be detected in the life (1417) of Brynolph of Scara, which reports that "pauca de multis," that is, very few of the many miracles, are recorded (Brynolph, 167).

37. Urban V.

38. On this trial, see Jean Le Mappian, *Yves de Tréguier* (Paris, 1981).

39. Thomas Helye, 614; Yves of Tréguier, ed. Borderie, 164–5; Charles of Blois, ed. Plaine et al. 248; Gerard Cagnoli, "Il trattato," 134; Thomas of Hereford, *Miracula ex processu*, 687.

40. Thomas of Hereford, Exeter College ms. 158, fol. 50^r–60^v. I am indebted to Ronald Finucane for providing me with a copy of the manuscript source. For further expressions of doubt see the marginal remarks in the process of Celestine V: "dubitatus an sit miraculum secundum papam" (ed. Seppelt, 256–7).

41. Celestine V, ed. van Ortroy.

42. Ibid., 474: "post multos discussiones et collationes diversas conscriptae fuerint, nullatenus debent in dubium revocari."

43. Jacopo Gaietano Stefaneschi, *Ordo romanus*, cc. 111, 115, in *Museum italicum*, 2 vols., ed. Jean Mabillon and Michele Germain (Paris, 1724), 2: 412–3, 418–24. See also Pietro d'Amelio, bishop of Senigallia, *Ordo romanus*, in ibid., 535–8, on the canonization of Bridget of Sweden. See also Bernhard Schimmelpfennig, ed., *Die Zeremonienbücher der römischen Kurie im Mittelalter* (Tübingen, 1973), 167–74; see also John Baptist Vitimiliensis, *De canonizatione B. Bonaventurae*, in *Miscellanea digesta novo ordine*, 4 vols., ed. Stephan Baluze (Lucca, 1744), 1: 471–87; L.-H. Labande, "Le cérémonial romain de Jacques Cajétan," *Bibliothèque de l'École des Chartes*, 54 (1893), 43–74.

44. Charles of Blois, ed. Plaine et al., 378–84.

45. *Multor* may refer to his profession rather than his name.

46. The very full attention to the gear worn by a victim who had been forced to cross the Rhone River at the castle of Sahon in order to flee from pursuing Bretons in 1374 also appears in Urban V's case (149–50). The man had entered a small boat, called a *batal*, heavily armed: "armatus de jupone, de tunica ferrea, et jaque de velluto, et cum bacineto ligato et stachato, ut est moris, braceriis et gantelletis, ense et cultello cincto, in pondere predicatorum arnesiorum quas C. L. librorum."

47. Thomas of Hereford, ed. *AASS*, 559: "The second article concerns his reputation and public opinion about him [*de fama et communi voce et opinione*]. Concerning these matters, the witnesses are first to be asked whether it is publicly believed and it is the commonly held view and belief of the people that said lord Thomas may be a saint. Secondly, if they testify concerning the above, they are to be asked how they know this, and where such an opinion is held; and beginning when they knew or heard

it said that it is a publicly held opinion. Thirdly, if they say that they have heard such things, they are to be asked from whom they have heard this, from how many persons, how often and where they heard such things said; and whether the persons from whom they had heard it were persons of good or bad reputation; whether they were particular friends, members of the household [*parentela*] of lord Thomas, or holders of benefices in the church of Hereford. Fourthly, they are to be asked in their deposition what they say or believe public opinion to be, what they call public opinion or the common belief of the people. . . ."

48. Hostiensis, *In quinque libros decretalium commentaria* (Venice, 1581), X, 3.45.1 (fol. 172a [s.v. *Venerantur*]).

49. Louis of Toulouse, *Processus*, 93.

50. Helen Enselmini, 512, for preface addressed to Sicco's son Lazaro. On Sicco see Alfredo Dalmaso, "Note sull'attività letteraria dell'umanista Sicco Polenton," *Studi trentini di scienze storiche*, 34 (1955), 3–27, 236, 264; 35 (1956), 22–48; Vittorio Rossi, *Il quattrocento* (Milan, 1945), 76, 190.

51. Dorothy of Montau, *Vita prima*, 560ff.; Bridget of Sweden, ed. Collijn, 106, for a comparison of the miracles wrought in Judaea and Egypt with those in the Scandinavian region. For the themes of early hagiography and the need to publicize miracles see Eberhard Demm, "Die Rolle des Wunders in der Heiligskonzeption des Mittelalters," *Archiv für Kulturgeschichte*, 57 (1975), 300–44.

52. Leonard of Inchenhofen, 184–5; Venturino of Bergamo, 38.

53. Peter Parenti, 89; André Vauchez, *La sainteté en Occident aux derniers siècles du moyen âge d'après les procès de canonisation et les documents hagiographiques* (Rome, 1981), 85, 175, 480.

54. Clare Gambacorta, 511; for universal celebration of the Alleluia of 1233, citing Psalms 148.12, see Salimbene de Adam, *Cronica*, ed. O. Holder-Egger, in *Monumenta germaniae historica: Scriptores*, 32 (Hannover, 1913), 70. Pietro Cantinelli, *Chronicon (ca. 1228–1306)*, ed. F. Torraca, in *Rerum italicarum scriptores*, 2nd ed., 31 vols., ed. R. A. Muratori (Città di Castello, 1900–75), 28: pt. 2. One of the best such texts is found in the 1325 testimony of the notary Berardo Appillaterre in Nicholas of Tolentino, ed. Occhioni, 123–4: "Item dixit quod a tempore obitus [1325] dicti fratris Nicolay pluries et pluries et sepe sepius et diversis temporibus et diversis annis, mensibus et diebus vidit et presens fuit quando multi et multi de diversis terris, provinciis et locis venientes ad terram Tholentini ad locum Sancti Augustini, ut iacet sepultus dictus beatus Nicholaus, ad archam ipsius dicentes publice et palam aliqui quod non viderant lumen et aliqui quod non potuerant ambulare et aliqui dicentes se fuisse oppressos a demonibus seu invasatos et aliqui dicentes se captivos et carceratos et aliqui dicentes se fuisse surdos et mutos et aliqui et multi et multi fuisse diversis infirmitatibus gravatos et liberatos precibus et meritis dicti beati Nicolay; et predicta etiam sacramento firmantes vera esse et offerentes aliqui unam oblationem et aliqui aliam, secundo quod dicebant se vovisse."

55. Urban V, 426: "maximarum, mediocrum et parvorum personarum"; Simon of Todì, 816, speaks of "meliores" and "maiores" at Bologna; Anthony of Padua, 58.

56. Peter Thomas, 168–84; see also Dorothy of Montau, ed. Stachnik, 46, for a report that pagans and gentiles heard of Dorothy's sanctity.

57. Catherine of Siena, ed. Laurent, 95.

58. William of Bourges, ed. *Analecta Bollandiana*, 321. St. Martin is cited as a precedent.

59. Wenceslas, ed. *Analecta Bollandiana*, 129. This is a late-thirteenth-century life.

60. Venturino of Bergamo, 68.

61. Gerard Cagnoli, "La leggenda," 440.

62. Henry of Treviso, 363.

63. Bernardino of Siena, 399–441.

64. The translation of the relics of the Dominican Peter Martyr, who had been assassinated by heretics at Milan, was accompanied by many vengeful miracles performed on doubters. See Peter Martyr, *Vita et miracula*, 704–7.

65. A Danish chronicler reporting on the translation of the relics of Margaret of Roskilde bemoaned the failure to provide a written record of her miracles. See Margaret of Roskilde, 719.

66. Lucian et al., 812–3. The first *inventio*, accompanied by miracles, had occurred in 1050, when the chapel of St. Saturninus was built. On 17 February 1326 Bishop Berengario granted an indulgence to the site; *Bibliotheca sanctorum*, 12 vols. (Rome, 1960–70), 8: 266–8.

67. See, e.g., Paule and Roger Lerou, "Culte des saints populaires et espace sacre," *Annales de Bretagne et les pays de l'Ouest*, 90 (1983), 233–47; F. Lautman, "Le territoire des reliques," *Annales de Bretagne et des pays de l'Ouest*, 90 (1983), 221–32.

68. Gerard Cagnoli, "La leggenda," 436–40.

69. The elaborate description of the musical instruments foreshadows the pageants characteristic of the Renaissance court. See Emanuel Winternitz, "Instruments de musique étrangers chez Filipino Lippi, Piero di Cosimo et Lorenzo Costa," in *Les fêtes de la Renaissance*, ed. Jean Jacquot, 3 vols. (Paris, 1956–75), 1: 379–95.

70. Neri was active in the mid-fourteenth century, was associated with Taddeo Gaddi, and was probably responsible for a series of frescoes in the Camposanto in Gerard's honor. See *Allgemeines Lexikon der bildenden Kunstler* (Leipzig, 1916), XIII, 311–2; Enzo Carli, *Pittura pisana del trecento* (Milan, 1962), 46–53; Miklos Boskovits, "Un apertura per Francesco da Neri," *Antichità viva*, VI, no. 2 (1967), 3–11.

71. This was characteristic of many such feast days; see Victor Turner, "The Center Out There: Pilgrim's Goal," *History of Religions*, 12 (1972), 191–230.

72. Amalberga, 100–6.

73. Martial, ed. Arbellot, 429; Zita of Lucca; *Vita et miracula Angeli Gualdensis*, in G. B. Mittarelli, *Annales Camaldulenses*, V, 59, 269, 290; p. 329, on funeral; *BR*, 4: 390, for papal reference to funeral of Bridget of Sweden; Margaret of Città, ed. *Analecta Bollandiana*, 22–36. On Peter of Luxemburg's funeral on 5 July 1387 at Avignon, when all work stopped, see *AASS*, 2 July I, 516. The public enthusiasm surrounding the cult of Marcolinus of Forlì (d. 1397) is discussed in Kleinberg, *Prophets in Their Own Country*, 31–7.

74. Simon of Todì, 816–20.

75. Celestine V, ed. Herde, 289ff.; Contardo of Este, 447; Clare Gambacorta, 503–16; Gandolph of Binasco, 711.

76. Joachim of Siena, ed. Soulier, 13.

77. S. Lukes, "Political and Social Integration," *Sociology*, 9 (1975), 291.

78. Aaron J. Gourevitsch, *Les catégories de la culture médiévale*, trans. Hélène Courtin and Nina Godnieff (Paris, 1983), 302–4.

79. Gerard Cagnoli, "Il trattato," 177.

80. Michael Goodich, "Miracles and Disbelief in the Late Middle Ages," *Mediaevistik*, 1 (1988), 23–38.

81. Jordan of Quedlinburg, *Sermones Dan de sanctis* (Strasbourg, ca. 1476), *Sermo* 192; for an illustration of the heavenly court envisioned by a contemporary saint see Bridget of Sweden, *Liber celestis*, in Pierpont Morgan Library, New York, ms. 498, fol. 4^v. A man in the *Miracula* of Giovanna of Signa reportedly asked his wife to beseech Giovanna to plead "ad pedes Domini." See Giovanna of Signa, ed. *AASS*, 286.

82. A. G. Little, ed., *Liber exemplorum ad usum predicatorum* (Aberdeen, 1908), 32.

83. Hervé Martin, *Le métier de prédicateur à la fin du moyen âge* (Paris, 1988), 346.

84. Gerard Cagnoli, "La leggenda," 419. The woman reported this vision to her confessor. The family was to build a chapel in Gerard's honor in the Franciscan church at Palermo in 1535.

85. A similar description of "the court of heaven" is found in the vision of a Dominican Tertiary woman in Francis of Siena, ed. Morini and Soulier, 37.

Chapter Two

1. Johann Huizinga, *The Waning of the Middle Ages*, trans. E. Hopman (London, 1924), 2.

2. Marc Bloch, *Feudal Society*, trans. L. A. Manyon (Chicago, 1961). For the violent ramifications of the plague and its attendant ills in one village, see J. A. Raftis, "Changes in an English Village after the Black Plague," *Medieval Studies*, 29 (1967), 158–77.

3. See, e.g., František Graus, *Pest-Geissler-Judenmorde: Das 14. Jahrhundert als Krisenzeit* (Göttingen, 1989).

4. John Grundmann, ed., "Documenti umbri sulla carestia, 1328–1330," *Archivio storico italiano*, 128 (1970), 207–53, on the consequences of war between Guelphs and Ghibellines in Umbria, 1328–30.

5. Leonard of Inchenhofen, 186: "Nam cum ista pestilentia ipsum replesset orbem, magnam aput nos violentiam hominibus inferre solebat."

6. Ibid., 188: "Post haec in vigilia sancti Bernardi venerunt locuste et brucus, quorum non erat numerus, que ob suam multitudinem lucem diei obtenebrantes et terram mirabiliter devastantes, maxima frugibus nocumenta intulerunt. Circa eadem etiam tempora grandis gwerra [sic] et dissensio inter Bavaros et Australes, in qua monasteri et ceteri pauperes multum vexati sunt." See Sigmund von Riezler, *Geschichte Baierns*, 9 vols. (Gotha, 1878–1914), 3: 80ff.

7. Mireille Vincent-Cassy, "Quelques réflexions sur l'envie et la jalousie en France au XIVe siècle," in Michel Mollat, *Études sur l'histoire de la pauvreté*, 2 vols. (Paris, 1970), 2: 487–502; P. Vaccari, "Le crisi delle classi nobiliari nei paesi europei durante il xiv secolo," *Studi storici in onore Gioacchino Volpe*, 2 vols. (Bologna, 1958), 2: 1045–59.

8. Leonard of Inchenhofen, 192 (1404). See Erich Keyser and Heinz Stoob, eds., *Deutsches Städtebuch*, 5 vols. to date (Stuttgart, 1952–74), 2: 383–6.

9. For a summary of historians' views see James Buchanan Given, *Society and Homicide in Thirteenth Century England* (Stanford, 1977), 40. On demography, see Roger Mols, *Introduction à la démographie historique des villes d'Europe du XIVe au XVIIIe siècle*, 3 vols. (Louvain, 1954–6), 2: 312ff., 207–8; Josiah Russell, *Population in Europe, 500–1500* (London, 1969).

10. Elisabeth Crouzet-Pavan, "Violence, société et pouvoir à Venise (XIVe—XVe siècles): Forme et évolution de rituels urbains," *Mélanges de l'École française de Rome: Moyen âge*, 96 (1984), 903–36.

11. David Herlihy, "Some Psychological and Social Roots of Violence in the Tuscan Cities," in *Violence and Civil Disorder in Italian Cities, 1200–1500*, ed. Lauro Martines (Berkeley, 1972), 140.

12. J. R. Hale, "Violence in the Late Middle Ages: A Background," in Martines, *Violence and Civil Disorder*, 19–37.

13. Richard C. Trexler, "Correre la terra: Collective Insults in the Late Middle Ages," in *Mélanges de l'École française de Rome: Moyen âge*, 96 (1984), 845–902.

14. Victor Turner, "The Center Out There: Pilgrim's Goal," *History of Religions*, 12 (1972), 191–230.

15. John Bossy, *Disputes and Settlements: Law and Human Relations in the Middle Ages* (Cambridge, 1983).

16. Clare of Montefalco, 498.

17. Alfredus Julien, "Evolutio historica compromissi in arbitros in iure canonico," *Apollinaris commentarium juridico canonicum*, 10 (1937): 187–232.

18. *Codex Theod.* 1.1.tit.xxvii.lex 1, in *Corpus iuris civilis*, ed. Theodor Mommsen and Paul Krüger, 3 vols. (Berlin, 1908–14); cf. Edward James, "'Beati pacificis': Bishops and the Law in Sixth-Century Gaul," in Bossy, *Disputes and Settlements*, 21–46, on sixth-century Gaul. For the freeing of a large number of prisoners from the gallows in Germany in the twelfth century see Giles, 393–422.

19. Ebenezer Cobham Brewer, *A Dictionary of Miracles* (Philadelphia, 1897; re-impression, Detroit, 1966), 379–80; František Graus, "Die Gewalt bei den Anfängen des feudalismus und die 'Gefängenenbefreiungen' der merowingischen Hagiographie," *Jahrbuch für Wirtschaftsgeschichte*, 1 (1961), 61–156, on an earlier period. For an *exemplum* concerning Dominic's preaching to the imprisoned disseminated by Étienne de Bourbon, see *Anecdotes historiques, légendes et apologues*, ed. A. Lecoy de la Marche (Paris, 1877), c. 158.

20. Hugh of Lincoln, ed. Douie and Farmer, II, 127–30.

21. *Corpus iuris canonici*, ed. Emil Friedberg and Lewis Richter, 2 vols. (Leipzig, 1879), c.1.x.5.32; c.12.x.1.43; c.1.x.1.43.

22. Vincent of Beauvais, *Speculum maius*, 4 vols. (Douai, 1624), vol. 2, *Speculum doctrinale*, X. 2003; Hostiensis, *Summa aurea*, ed. N. Soranza (Lyons, 1537), I. *De arbitriis*, fol. 69ᵛff. on a bishop and a cleric as arbitrators; cf. also Julien, "Evolutio historica compromissi," 87–232, which includes the relevant biblical citations and references to canon law.

23. Cf. A. M. Enriques, "La vendetta nella vita e nella legislazione fiorentina," *Archivio storico italiano*, ser. 7, 19 (1933), 85–146.

24. Martin Becker, "Changing Patterns of Violence and Justice: Fourteenth and Fifteenth Century Florence," *Comparative Studies in Society and History*, 18 (1976), 284.

25. Yvonne Bongert, *Recherches sur les cours laïques du Xe au XIIIe siècles* (Paris, 1949); Beaumanoir [Philippe de Rémi, sire de], *Coutumes de Beauvaisis*, ed. A. Salmon, 2 vols. (Paris, 1970–4), c. 1263.

26. Gene Brucker, "The Ciompi Revolution," in *Florentine Studies*, ed. Nicolai Rubinstein (London, 1968), 352 n. 1; see also S. Chojnacki, "Crime and the Venetian State," in Martines, *Violence and Civil Disorder*, 184–228.

27. *Gesta abbatum sancti Albani*, ed. H. T. Riley, 3 vols., *Rerum brittanicarum scriptores (Rolls series)*, 28.4 (London, 1967–9), 2: 163–76; see also 1: 407, 410, 423–5; 2: 27–8, 13–16, 163–76. *Vetus registrum Sarisberiensis*, ed. W. H. Rich Jones, 2 vols.,

Rerum brittanicarum scriptores (Rolls series), 78 (London, 1883–4), contains several reports of episcopal arbitration concerning financial rights in local parish churches.

28. Edward Powell, "Arbitration and the Law in England in the Late Middle Ages," *Transactions of the Royal Historical Society*, ser. 5, 33 (1983), 49–67; Esther Cohen, "Violence Control in Late Medieval France: The Social Transformation of the Asseurement," *Tijdschrift voor Rechtsgeschiedenis*, 51 (1983), 111–22; A. Amanieu, "Arbitrage," in *Dictionnaire de droit canonique*, 7 vols. (Paris, 1935–65), 1: 862–99.

29. Hostiensis, *Summa aurea*, I. *De arbitriis*, fol. 69ᵛff.

30. Bernard Cousin, *Le miracle et le quotidien: Les ex voto provencaux images d'une société* (Aix-en-Provence, 1983), deals with more recent cases, but has some very useful observations.

31. Julien Ries, *Le chemins du sacré dans l'histoire* (Paris, 1985), 25.

32. Esther Cohen, *The Crossroads of Justice: Law and Culture in Late Medieval France* (Leiden, 1993), provides much illuminating material on the ritual character of judicial proceedings.

33. Gérart Jugnot, "Les pèlerinages expiatoires et judiciaires au moyen âge," in *La faute, la répression et le pardon*, in Actes du 107e Congrès national des sociétés savantes, Brest, 1982, *Section de philologie et d'histoire jusqu'à 1610* (Paris, 1984), I, 413–20.

34. See the many articles in ibid., such as Pascal Texier, "La rémission au XIVe siècle: Significations et fonctions," 193–205. M. Bourin and B. Chevalier, "Le comportement criminel dans les pays de la Loire moyenne d'après les lettres de rémission (vers 1380—vers 1450)," *Annales de Bretagne et des pays de l'Ouest*, 88 (1981), 245–63, dealing with the six departments of the central Loire region of today, note that most of the letters from the period 1380–1450 deal with physical violence. Marie-Thérèse Lorcin, "Les paysans et la justice dans la région Lyonnaise aux XIVe et XVe siècles," *Le moyen âge*, 84 (1968), 269–300, which treats the Lyons area in a comparable period, notes theft as the principal crime appearing in the letters. Material concerning the kinds of persons who appealed to each cult appears in Roger Vaultier, *Le folklore pendant la guerre de Cent Ans d'après les lettres de rémission du Trésor de Chartes* (Paris, 1965).

35. Catherine of Fierbois, 15.

36. Urban V, 126, no. 4.

37. Yves of Tréguier, ed. Borderie, 196–200, for several witnesses with slightly conflicting evidence.

38. Ibid., 200–1.

39. Leonard of Inchenhofen, 188.

40. Urban V, 140–1, no. 27 testimony in June 1376.

41. Dorothy of Montau, ed. Stachnik, 239, no. 100.

42. Wenceslas, 124, c. 7; Gerard Cagnoli, 181, no. 11.

43. Bridget of Sweden, ed. Collijn, 633.

44. Gerard Cagnoli, "La leggenda," 426–7.

45. Ambrose of Siena, 198–9.

46. Ibid., 198.

47. Bartholomew of Pisa defined *rixa* as "quando ex ira invicem percuciunt et ideo rixa videtur quoddam privatum bellum." See Georg Dahm, *Das Strafrecht Italiens im ausgehenden Mittelalter* (Berlin, 1931), 362. Raymund of Penyaforte, *Summa* (Verona, 1744), III, 34, *De penitentiis*, 4: "rixa, tumor mentis, contumelia, clamor, indignatio, blasphemia."

48. Urban V, 331–2, no. 331; 241, no. 171; Leonard of Inchenhofen, 194 (1408).

49. Bridget of Sweden, 349–51.

50. For her support see G. Mollat, *Les papes d'Avignon (1305–1378)*, 10th rev. ed. (Paris, 1964); Bernard Guillemain, *La cour pontificale d'Avignon (1309–1376): Étude d'une société* (Paris, 1962).

51. Gerard Cagnoli, "La leggenda," 442–5.

52. Urban V, 142–3. Abbot Pierre de Banhac of Montmajour, a close confidant of the pope, was made cardinal in 1363.

53. Agnes, 728.

54. Gerard Cagnoli, "Il trattato," 183–4; on a horse thief at Corbien in the Dauphiné see Philippa Castellani, 98.

55. Catherine of Fierbois, 16.

56. Urban V, 198–9, no. 113.

57. Mollat, *Les papes d'Avignon*, 121–2.

58. Urban V, 267–8, no. 208. In another case, an inhabitant of Avignon named Stephan Mayseu had exhausted all his wealth in litigation. Within three days of a vow to Urban V, he won the case. See ibid., 358–9, no. 370.

59. Ibid., 197, no. 111.

60. Ibid., 234–5, no. 160. In another case, the prior of Condolet in the diocese of Rodez litigated two and a half years with the bishop of Rodez concerning his benefice. Beseeching Urban, he secured his benefice (303–4, no. 258).

61. See Jean-Daniel Morerod, "Taxation déciminale et frontières politiques en France," in *Aux origines de l'état moderne: Le fonctionnement administratif de la papauté d'Avignon*, in *Actes de la table ronde organisée par l'École française de Rome (Avignon, 23–24 janvier 1988)* (Rome, 1990), 333–4, for statistics of revenues in comparison to other dioceses.

Chapter Three

1. The following is a summary of Elisabeth Crouzet-Pavan, "Violence, Société et Pouvoir à Venise (XIVe-XVIe siècles): Forme et évolution de rituels urbains," *Mélanges de l'École française de Rome: Moyen âge*, 96 (1984), 903–36; M. Bourin and E. Chevalier, "Le comportement criminel dans les pays de la Loire moyenne d'après les lettres de rémission (vers 1380—vers 1450)," *Annales de Bretagne et des pays de l'Ouest*, 88 (1981), 245–63; Marie-Thérèse Lorcin, "Les paysans et la justice dans la région Lyonnaise aux XIVe et XVe siècles," *Le moyen âge*, 84 (1968), 269–300; Yvonne Lanhers, "Crimes et criminels au XIVe siècle," *Revue historique*, 240 (1968), 325–38; Sara Blanshei, "Criminal Law and Politics in Medieval Bologna," *Criminal Justice History*, 2 (1981), 1–30; Henri Platelle, "Moeurs populaires dans la Seigneurie de Saint-Amand d'après les documents judiciaires de la fin du moyen âge," *Revue Mabillon*, 18 (1958), 20–39; David Nicholas, "Crime and Punishment in Fourteenth-Century Ghent," *Revue belge de philologie et d'histoire*, 48 (1970), 288–334, 1141–76; Robert Muchembled, *La violence au village (XVe—XVIIe siècle)* (Turnhout, 1989); A. M. Enriques, "La vendetta nella vita e nella legislazione fiorentina," *Archivio storico italiano*, ser. 7, 19 (1933), 85–146; Barbara A. Hanawalt, "Violent Death in Fourteenth and Early Fifteenth-Century England," *Comparative Studies in Society and History*, 18 (1974), 197–220; Barbara H. Westman, "The Violent Family and Crime in Fourteenth-

Century England," *Journal of British Studies*, 13 (1973), 1–18; Martin Becker, "Changing Patterns of Violence and Justice: Fourteenth and Fifteenth Century Florence," *Comparative Studies in Society and History*, 18 (1976), 281–96.

2. Roger Grand, "Justice criminelle, procédure et peine des villes de France aux XIIIe et XIVe siècles," *Bibliothèque de l'École des Chartes*, 102 (1941), 51–108.

3. James Buchanan Given, *Society and Homicide in Thirteenth Century England* (Stanford, 1977), 193.

4. J. R. Hale, "Violence in the Middle Ages: A Background," in *Violence and Civil Disorder in Italian Cities, 1200–1500*, ed. Lauro Martines (Berkeley, 1972), 19–37.

5. Osmund, 71–3, for a man injured at Quidhampton, two miles from Salisbury, while trying to make peace between neighbors playing with a ball and stick.

6. Jacques Heers, *Family Clans in the Middle Ages*, trans. B. Herbert (New York, 1988), 52ff.

7. Michael Clanchy, "Law and Love in the Middle Ages," in *Disputes and Settlements: Law and Human Relations in the Middle Ages* (Cambridge, 1983), 47–67.

8. Crouzet-Pavan, "Violence," for summary.

9. Yves-Marie Bercé, *Fête et révolte: Des mentalités populaires du XVIe au XVIIe siècle* (Paris, 1976). For sermons of Jean Gerson delivered in 1401 and 1402 against both blasphemy and the "fête des fous," see Jean Gerson, *Oeuvres complètes*, 7 vols. to date, ed. P. Glorieux (Paris, 1960–93), 7: 409–12.

10. Thomas of Chobham, *Summa confessorum*, ed. F. Broomfield (Louvain, 1968), art.7, d.vi, qu.IIIa, c. 1 (p. 493). For the case of a saint who was herself killed by brigands in 1225, see Marie-Joseph Ollivier, "La B. Marguérite de Louvain," *Revue thomiste*, 4 (1896), 592–618.

11. Peter of Luxemburg, 511, nos. 211, 221; Charles of Blois, ed. Plaine et al., 397–8; Gerard Cagnoli, "Il trattato," 185, no. 14; Charles of Blois, ed. Plaine et al., 326–7.

12. Catherine of Fierbois, 39–40, for cloth robbed from an inn; Leonard of Inchenhofen, 191, for the theft of equestrian garments and gloves; Charles of Blois, ed. Plaine et al., 323, for wool and thread.

13. Gerard Cagnoli, "Il trattato," 185, no. 13. The event occurred in December 1346 or 1347, and the man promised the sizeable sum of ten *solidi* to Gerard's shrine.

14. Leonard of Inchenhofen, 191, for a horse stolen at Rothenburg valued at fifty florins in 1399; Peter of Luxemburg, 511, no. 222; Nicholas of Tolentino, ed. Occhioni, 182–3, for cattle stolen at Ascoli; Philippa, 98, for a horse stolen at Sisteron.

15. John Langdon, "Horse Hauling: A Revolution in Vehicle Transport in Twelfth- and Thirteenth-Century England," *Past and Present*, 103 (1984), 37–66; idem, "The Economics of Horses and Oxen in Medieval England," *Agricultural History Review*, 30 (1982), 31–40. For a case of hanging for theft, see Charles of Blois, ed. Plaine et al., 292.

16. Nicholas of Tolentino, ed. Occhioni, 321–3, for testimony of a merchant and notary whose cattle and palomino horse appeared to be suffering from a mortal disease.

17. Anna Benvenuti Papi, *In castro poenitentiae: Santità e società femminile nell'Italia medioevale* (Rome, 1990), 282.

18. Gerard Cagnoli, "Il trattato," 187: "Qui flens quia non videbat unde posset amplius lucrari necessaria vitae, instanter."

19. Ibid., no. 3; 189–90, no. 13. Another man was distressed over the loss of an ass, with which he earned his keep. (Ibid., 188: "asellus cum quo vitae necessaria lucra-

batur.") For a poor woman whose livelihood depended on the sale of pigs, see William of Norwich, 152–3.

20. Nicholas of Tolentino, ed. Occhioni, 267–8.

21. Urban V, 197–8, no. 112.

22. Ibid., 199–200, no. 114.

23. Charles of Blois, ed. Plaine et al., 377, for a purse with three or four florins lost by the seneschal of Angers, Jean; see also Peter of Luxemburg, 511, no. 222.

24. Gerard Cagnoli, "La leggenda," 413–4, no. 56.

25. For a classic case at Borgo San Sepolcro involving Francis of Assisi see Livario Oliger, ed., "Miracula S. Francisci," in *Archivum franciscanum historicum*, 12 (1919), 379–80, no. 52. The following cases are taken from Bridget of Sweden, ed. Collijn, 126; Stanislas of Cracow, *Vita majora*, 431–2; Leonard of Inchenhofen 189, 196, 198; Nicholas of Tolentino, ed. Occhioni, 84–5; Thomas of Hereford, ed. AASS, 668.

26. The following cases are found in Urban V, 224–5, no. 147; Thomas of Hereford, ed. AASS, 677; Leonard of Inchenhofen, 196, 188; Peter of Luxemburg, 509–10, no. 207; Stanislas of Cracow, *Vita majora*, 431–2; Thomas of Costacciaro, 601; Peter Parenti, 96.

27. For a long, detailed description of such a band in which many witnesses confirm the attempt to drown the victims, see Margaret of Hungary, ed. Franknoì, 321–5. The event occurred shortly after Easter in 1276.

28. Nicholas of Tolentino, ed. Occhioni, 267–8.

29. The term "tyrannus" is applied to Tietz von Ting, who had imprisoned a man of Reichenberg near Würzburg during an uprising against the bishop of Eichstadt. See Leonard of Inchenhofen, 194–5 (1411).

30. Ibid., 188. The phrase used is "cui proprietario attinebat."

31. Ambrose of Siena, 198.

32. Nicholas of Tolentino, ed. Occhioni, 114–5. The witness identified the victim as the judge Berardo Giacomo of Montemilione; he said the story could be corroborated by another judge, Giacomino Ugolini of Tolentino, who had been their fellow lodger at Bologna.

33. Ibid., 420; Urban V, 308–10.

34. Lucchesio of Poggibonsi, ed. AASS, 614.

35. Leonard of Inchenhofen, 191.

36. These come from Leonard of Inchenhofen, 196; Bridget of Sweden, ed. Collijn, 134; Thomas of Hereford, ed. AASS, 668. A woman of Montefalco reports being abducted in October 1300, at harvest season, by a band of seven thieves called *raspaldini*. Clare of Montefalco, 512.

37. Gerard Cagnoli, "Il trattato," 137–8, no. 12.

38. Edward Peters, *Torture* (Oxford, 1985); L. Chevallier, "Torture," *Dictionnaire de droit canonique*, 7 vols. (Paris, 1935–65), 7: 1294–1313; John G. Bellamy, *Criminal Law and Society in Late Medieval and Tudor England* (New York, 1984), 66, suggests that such torture was even used to reveal the location of stolen goods.

39. Caroline W. Bynum, "Material Continuity, Personal Survival, and the Resurrection of the Body: A Scholastic Discussion in Its Medieval and Modern Contexts," *History of Religions*, 30.1 (1990), 83, points out that of the 153 saints' lives found in James of Voragine's *Legenda aurea*, at least 75 contain reports of bodily dismemberment. See James of Voragine, *Legenda aurea*, ed. Th. Graesse (Breslau, 1890); on executions see ibid., Elizabeth of Thuringia, 767–8; Nicholas of Bari, 25–6; James the

Greater, 427. For drownings see ibid., Nicholas of Bari, 29; Mary Magdalene, 415–6; on wolves see ibid., Blasius, 167–8. For some graphic cases of torture, see ibid., the Maccabees, 454–5; Blasius, 168; Agatha, 171–3; Lawrence, 488–501; Matthew, 185; Vitus, 350; the Holy Innocents, 62–6; Sebastian, 108–13; and George, 262. Among recent studies of James's work are Alain Boureau, *La Legende dorée: Le système narratif de Jacques de Voragine* (Paris, 1984); and Sherry Reames, *The legenda aurea: A Reexamination of Its Paradoxical History* (Madison, 1985).

40. Leonard of Inchenhofen, 195.

41. Nicholas of Tolentino, ed. Occhioni, 112–3. The judge was Adcursus Gualterii Bonacursis, a doctor of laws at Tolentino and appellate judge and *maior sindicus* at Florence in June 1323, who testified at Nicholas's process in 1325. For a case of detention on suspicion of poisoning a river at Annoniac, see Philippa Castellani, 104. The man was redeemed by his wife.

42. Nicholas of Tolentino, ed. Occhioni, 587ff.

43. Ibid.; Urban V, 259–60, no. 198; 355–6, no. 365; Gerard Cagnoli, "Il trattato," 140, no. 25; 183–4, no. 8; 408, no. 38; Zita of Lucca, 514–5; Wenceslas, "Le dossier," 125, no. 8; Nicholas of Tolentino, ed. AASS, 663–4; Charles of Blois, ed. Plaine et al., 419.

44. A farmer of Verderia in the diocese of Aix had been tried at Nîmes for murder following the death of a canon who had quarreled with the farmer's lord. He was held for eight months and so weakened that he preferred death. Urban V, 242–3, no. 173.

45. Gerard Cagnoli, "La leggenda," 408, no. 38; Urban V, 259–60, no. 198.

46. Nicholas of Tolentino, ed. AASS, 663.

47. Leonard of Inchenhofen, 186.

48. One saint, a soldier who was accused of homicide and exiled along with his brother, was the Mercedarian Andrew de Gallerani, 52–7. For other cases, see Leonard of Inchenhofen, 197 (a man of Istria who came from Trieste to the shrine in 1416, and killed someone during a gambling fight); 191 (Strasbourg in 1400); 194–5 (Verona in 1411); 186 (Alsace in 1346); 188 (a man of Thann in 1364, whose parents were asked to pay 5,000 pounds at Strasbourg to redeem their son); Urban V, 355–6, no. 365 (a man of Le Puech whose goods were confiscated); Charles of Blois, ed. Plaine et al., 326–7 (a Breton imprisoned at Guincamp), 337, 372, 388, 391, 398, 405, 426; Angelo of Gualdo, V, 334 (a man of Stagio Noce in San Severino imprisoned at Fabriano); V, 266 (1306). An order was founded at Florence in 1343, one of whose duties was to accompany those condemned to death. See Giuseppe Rondoni, "I 'Giustiziati' a Firenze (dal secolo XV al secolo XVIII)," *Archivio storico italiano*, 28, ser. 5 (1901), 209–56.

49. Gerard Cagnoli, "Il trattato," 183.

50. Dorothy of Montau, ed. Stachnik, 240, no. 101.

51. Charles of Blois, ed. Plaine et al., 312–3.

52. Clare of Montefalco, 378.

53. Ibid., 478. The man's sister, who made the pledge to Clare, does not indicate whether he was exonerated or escaped.

54. Baudouin de Gaiffier, "Un thème hagiographique: Le pendu miraculeusement sauvé," in *Études critiques d'hagiographie et d'iconologie* (Brussels, 1967), 194–226; idem, "Liberatus a suspendio," in ibid., 227–32. The presence of earlier cases in *exempla* collections guaranteed that the general public was well acquainted with this miracle genre. One of the miracles of the Virgin involved a certain thief named Ebbo who was

held up by the Virgin so he could not strangle, and the second time she placed her hands around his throat so the rope would not cut into him. See A. G. Little, ed., *Liber miraculorum ad usum praedicatorum* (Aberdeen, 1908), 24–5. For an illustration of a man hung for theft (*furtum*) see Jacobus's encyclopedia (1360–75) in British Museum, Royal 6E.VII. pt. 1, 171ᵛ.

55. Charles of Blois, ed. Plaine et al., 197–208, for a full account, with several witnesses. Albizi's description of preparations for an execution at San Miniato is found in Gerard Cagnoli, "Il trattato," 137, no. 12: "essent parata vestimenta nigra ad induendum et fasciae ad oculos velandum et asini ad equitandum, ac statim sententia deberet ferri furcarum." See Esther Cohen, *The Crossroads of Justice: Law and Culture in Late Medieval France* (Leiden, 1993), 181–201, for an illuminating discussion of executions.

56. Peter of Luxemburg, 530–1, no. 67.

57. Thomas of Hereford, ed. AASS, 675; Oxford, Exeter College ms. 158, 19ᵛ–20ʳ. For another three-time hanging attempt see Yves of Tréguier, ed. Borderie, 188–9.

58. Leonard of Inchenhofen, 188–9.

59. Ibid., 190; Thomas of Hereford, ed. AASS, 632–6; Catherine of Fierbois, 22; Urban V, 458–9; see also Agnes of Montepulciano, 809 (2 cases); Lucchesio of Poggibonsi, ed. Bertagna, 456; Dauphine of Languedoc, 88, no. 81; Catherine of Fierbois, 2. A rare case of a man revived *after* execution is found in the *Legenda maiora* of Hedwig of Silesia. The man had been arrested and readied for execution at the order of Hedwig's husband Duke Henry of Silesia. Despite her pleas for mercy, he was executed. She reportedly revived him after his death. See Hedwig of Silesia, *Vita maior*, 555–6.

60. Zita of Lucca, 514–5.

61. Dorothy of Montau, ed. Stachnik, 345–6, no. 128. For a case near Aix see Dauphine of Languedoc, 88. In a case recorded in Gerard Cagnoli, "Il trattato," 140, a man had been accused of homicide after several witnesses underwent torture and falsely accused him of the crime in 1347. Here again, after a vow to Gerard, the false witnesses changed their testimony and the man was spared. Bridget of Sweden, ed. AASS, 559–60, for a man in Sweden accused of homicide who was asked to pay a fine in lieu of execution.

62. Joachim Piccolomini of Siena, ed. Soulier, 17–8.

63. Robert Bartlett, *Trial by Fire and Water: The Medieval Judicial Ordeal* (Oxford, 1986); Peter Brown, "Society and the Supernatural," in *Society and the Supernatural in Late Antiquity* (London, 1982), 302–32; Paul Rousset, "La croyance en la justice immanente à l'époque féodale," *Le moyen âge*, 54 (1948), 225–48.

64. Thomas Aquinas, *Summa theologiae*, ed. T. C. O'Brien et al., 61 vols. (New York, 1981), 2.2.95.8.

65. Urban V, 241, no. 171.

66. Ibid., 319, no. 303.

67. Ibid., 458–9, no. 51.

68. Ibid., 242, no. 173.

Chapter Four

1. See, e.g., Richard Kieckhefer, *Unquiet Souls: Fourteenth Century Saints and Their Religious Milieu* (Chicago, 1984); Donald Weinstein and Rudolph Bell, *Saints and Society: The Two Worlds of Western Christendom, 1000–1700* (Chicago, 1982); Michael

Goodich, *Vita perfecta: The Ideal of Sainthood in the Thirteenth Century*, in *Monographien zur Geschichte des Mittelalters*, 25 (Stuttgart, 1982); M. Glasser, "Marriage in Medieval Hagiography," *Studies in Medieval and Renaissance History*, ser. 2, 4 (1981), 3–34; André Vauchez, *La sainteté en Occident aux derniers siècles du moyen âge d'après les procès de canonisation et les documents hagiographiques* (Rome, 1981).

2. See, e.g., Caroline W. Bynum, *Holy Feast and Holy Fast: The Religious Significance of Food and Medieval Women* (Berkeley, 1987); Chiara Frugoni, "La giovinezza di Francesco nelle fonte (testi e immagine)," *Studi medievali*, ser. 3, 25.1 (1984), 115–44; Shulamith Shahar, *Childhood in the Middle Ages* (London, 1990); David Herlihy, *Medieval Households* (Cambridge, Mass., 1985). A good example of family reconstruction using a miracle as the source is Silvestro Nessi, "Appendice storico documentaria," in Clare of Montefalco, 623–4.

3. Paul Ramsey, "Human Sexuality in the History of Redemption," *The Ethics of St. Augustine*, ed. William S. Babcock (Atlanta, 1991), 115–45. The major sources are Augustine's *De nuptiis et concupiscentia, De bono conjugali, De civitate Dei*, and *De gratia Christi et peccato originali*.

4. Giovanna di Signa, ed. Mencherini, 384.

5. For a child of Montefalco born with one testicle as big as an egg, see Clare of Montefalco, 508–9; for another case of an enlarged testicle, see Martial of Limoges, ed. Arbellot, 422.

6. Gerard Cagnoli, "La leggenda," 406, no. 27; 407, nos. 32, 33.

7. Dorothy of Montau, ed. *AASS*, 512; Hedwig of Silesia, ed. Semkowicz, 514; Dauphine of Languedoc, 40. The chaste agreement between Elzéar of Sabran and his wife Dauphine of Languedoc is found in Elzéar of Sabran, ed. Cambell, 551. A certain knight named Isnard supposedly followed their precedent.

8. Eva Cantarella, "Homicides of Honor: The Development of Italian Adultery Law over Two Millennia," in *The Family in Italy from Antiquity to the Present*, ed. David Kertzer and Richard Saller (New Haven, 1991), 229–44.

9. Julius Kirshner, "Introduction to Part Two," in ibid., 147–9.

10. E. A. Hoebel, *The Law of Primitive Man: A Study in Comparative Legal Dynamics* (Cambridge, Mass., 1967), 262–7. On the relations between the divine and the earthly, see Annemarie de Waal Malefijt, *An Introduction to Anthropology of Religion* (New York, 1970), 7–9.

11. R. M. Smith, "Kin and Neighbors in a Thirteenth Century Suffolk Community," *Journal of Family History* (1979), 219–56; Thomas Tentler, *Sin and Confession on the Eve of the Reformation* (Princeton, 1977).

12. Smith, "Kin and Neighbors"; J. A. Raftis, "Changes in an English Village after the Black Plague," *Mediaeval Studies*, 29 (1967), 158–77.

13. Maria Pia Di Bella, "Name, Blood and Miracles: The Claims to Renown in Traditional Sicily," in *Honor and Grace in Anthropology*, ed. J. G. Péristiany and Julian Pitt-Rivers (Cambridge, 1992), 151–65; J. K. Campbell, "Honour and the Devil," in *Honour and Shame: The Values of Mediterranean Society*, ed. J. G. Péristiany (Chicago, 1966), 139–70.

14. See *Novellae*, 13, in *Corpus iuris civilis*, ed. Theodore Mommsen and Paul Krueger, 3 vols. (Berlin, 1908–14); Thomas of Chobham, *Summa confessorum*, ed. T. Bloomfield (Louvain, 1968), 25, for such sins. A long sermon on *luxuria*, delivered in 1418, and detailing the vices against nature, appears in Johannes Herolt, *Sermones de tempore et sanctis cum Promptuario exemplorum* (Strasbourg, 1492), fols. 123^r–124^v.

15. Georg Dahm, *Das Strafrecht Italiens im ausgehenden Mittelalter* (Berlin, 1931), 411ff.

16. Ibid., 411.

17. Ibid.

18. Ibid., 40.

19. Peter of Luxemburg, 518–9.

20. Julio Caro-Baroja, "Honour and Shame: A Historical Account of Several Conflicts," in *Honour and Shame*, ed. Péristiany, 79–137, on the medieval period; Julian Pitt-Rivers, "Honour and Social Status" in ibid., 19–77. On infamy in canon law see Vincent Tatarczuk, *Infamy of Law: A Historical Synopsis and a Commentary*, Catholic University of America Canon Law Studies, no. 357 (Washington, D. C., 1954).

21. For statistics of genres of miracle in this period, see Vauchez, *La sainteté*, 547.

22. Yves of Tréguier, ed. Borderie, 370, witness 12, for testimony at his canonization proceeding. Witness 33 reports another case of the satisfactory conclusion of a long-standing suit between family members after Yves's intervention.

23. Ibid., 12, 18, 24–5, 56, 74–5, 86, 118, 313.

24. Gerard Cagnoli, "La leggenda," 398.

25. Christiane Klapisch-Zuber, "Kinship and Politics in Fourteenth-Century Florence," in *The Family in Italy*, ed. Kertzer and Saller, 208–28.

26. Thomas of Chobham, *Summa confessorum*, 344; for the penitential trend in contemporary sermons, see Hervé Martin, *Le métier de prédicateur à la fin du Moyen âge, 1350–1520* (Paris, 1988); Larissa Taylor, *Soldiers of Christ: Preaching in Late Medieval and Renaissance France* (Oxford, 1992).

27. Philip Benizi, 83; for reform of prostitutes see also Dauphine of Languedoc, 470.

28. Bridget of Sweden, ed. Collijn, 513.

29. Danielle Jacquart and Claude Thomasset, *Sexuality and Medicine in the Middle Ages*, trans. Matthew Adamson (Princeton, 1988), 91.

30. Ibid., 84, on loss of reason.

31. Bernward of Hildesheim, 1033.

32. Jacques Chiffoleau, "Dire l'indicible: Remarques sur la catégorie du *nefandum* du XIIe au XVe siècle," *Annales: Economies, civilisations, sociétés*, 45 (1990), 289–324, which notes the increasing use of infamy as a legal category, and the large number of celebrated cases in the early fourteenth century in which this accusation was used.

33. Gerard Cagnoli, "Il trattato," 183.

34. Dahm, *Das Strafrecht Italiens*, 416–7.

35. Thomas of Chobham, *Summa confessorum*, III.xia (p. 36).

36. Vincenzo Licitra, ed., "Il *Liber legum moralium* e il *De regimine vite et sanitatis* di Bellino Bissolo," *Studi medievali*, ser. 3, 6 (1965), 405–54. For a summary see Michael Goodich, *From Birth to Old Age: The Human Life Cycle in Medieval Thought, 1250–1350* (Lanham, Md., 1989), 105–31. On late marriage of males and continuing dependence on family in Tuscany, see Christiane Klapisch-Zuber, *Women, Family, and Ritual in Renaissance Florence*, trans. Lydia Cochrane (Chicago, 1985), 41, 110.

37. Gerard Cagnoli, "Il trattato," 153.

38. For the scholastic discussion of witchcraft, see Joseph Hansen, *Hexenprozess und die Entstehung der grossen Hexenverfolgung* (Aalen, 1964), 157ff.; for citation, Thomas Aquinas, *Commentarium in quatuor libros Sententiarum*, IV, dist. 34, art. 3; and

Summa theologiae, 1ae, 51, 3.6, in *Opera omnia*, 26 vols. (Parma, 1852–73); and *Quaestiones disputatae*, 5 vols. (Turin, 1953), *De veritate*, XXV.7.

39. Peter Lombard, *Sententiarum libri quattuor*, ed. PP. Collegii S. Bonaventurae, 2 vols. (Quaracchi, 1916), IV.34.1. Other commentaries worthy of note are Albertus Magnus, *Commentarii in IV sententiarum*, IV.34.10, in *Opera omnia*, ed. A. Borgnet, 38 vols. (Paris, 1890–8); William Durand the Younger, *In Petri Lombardi Sententias theologicas commentariorum libri IIII*, 2 vols. (Venice, 1571), IV.34.1,2; Joannes Duns Scotus, *Quaestiones in quartum librum sententiarum*, IV.34.4, in *Opera omnia*, 26 vols. (Paris, 1891–1902).

40. Adolph Franz, *Die kirchlichen Benediktionen im Mittelalter*, 2 vols. (Freiburg-im-Breisgau, 1909), 1: 178–86.

41. Bonaventura, *Commentaria in quatuor libros sententiarum*, IV.34.2, in *Opera omnia*, 10 vols., ed. PP. Collegii S. Bonaventurae (Quaracchi, 1968), vol. 4.

42. The following cases are found in Gerard Cagnoli, "Il trattato," 183; Leonard of Inchenhofen, 193, 201, 203. For an adulterer of Marseilles who left his wife and journeyed to La Rochelle because of another woman, see Louis of Toulouse, *Processus*, 304–5.

43. Urban V, 125–6.

44. Leonard of Inchenhofen, 190; on disorders in 1387 against the Jews at Dinkelsbühl, see Ferdinand Seibt and Winfred Eberhard, eds., *Europa 1400: Die Krise des Spätmittelalters* (Stuttgart, 1964), 51. For canon law on adultery, see Thomas of Chobham, *Summa confessorum*, 345.

45. Peter of Luxemburg, 509, no. 206. This was reported in 1390.

46. Richard C. Trexler, "Correre la terra: Collective Insults in the Late Middle Ages," *Mélanges de l'École française de Rome: Moyen âge*, 96 (1984), 845–902; for exposure to public ridicule through caricature, see Samuel Edgerton, Jr., *Pictures and Punishment: Art and Criminal Prosecution during the Florentine Renaissance* (Ithaca, 1985).

47. Gerard Cagnoli, "La leggenda," 420.

48. Idem, "Il trattato," 153–4.

49. Idem, "La leggenda," 426–7.

50. Charles of Blois, ed. Plaine et al., 372–6.

51. Ibid., 320.

52. Ibid., 325–6.

53. Yves of Tréguier, ed. Borderie, 383–4.

54. Lucchesio of Poggibonsi, ed. *AASS*, 612. One of the most graphic tales of such fraternal rivalry appears in the miracles of William of Norwich, 231–6. A nobleman of Lorraine, claiming that his brother had despoiled him of his wealth, had burned down a canonry, killing all the inhabitants (including the brother). Penance was imposed by the archbishop of Trèves and Pope Eugenius II (ca. 1145–53) requiring him to wander about in irons for a year and restore the holy site he had torched. At the Holy Sepulchre, after a vow to William, the chains miraculously loosened. In another case in the same collection (William of Norwich, 236–41) the man murdered his brother and his children with a pitchfork, claiming that the brother had usurped his land.

55. Ambrose of Siena, 238.

56. For a good biography, see Jeanne Ancelet-Hustache, *Sainte Elisabeth de Hongrie* (Paris, 1947).

57. The following case comes from Nicholas of Tolentino, ed. Occhioni, 464.

58. Gerard Cagnoli, "Il trattato," 182.

59. Charles of Blois, ed. Plaine et al., 363–4.

60. Thomas of Hereford, ed. *AASS*, 668.

61. Yves of Tréguier, ed. Borderie, 168–72.

62. Joachim of Siena, ed. Soulier, 13.

63. Engelbert of Admont, *De miraculis Christi*, in Admont ms. 398, fols. 31^r–32^r·

64. Gerard Cagnoli, "Il trattato," 144–53; see also Charles of Blois, ed. Plaine et al., 389–91, for a twelve-year-old *furiosus*; and 240–4, for a child described as "demens et furiosa."

65. Yves of Tréguier, ed. Borderie, 174–81.

66. Bridget of Sweden, ed. Collijn, 575.

67. In the records of Nicholas of Tolentino, ed. Occhioni, 195, a man who tried to strangle his wife is described as a *furiosus*; and a woman of Camboro (p. 303), possessed by two evil men who had been executed, hurled foul vituperation at all and sundry. On the difficulty of distinguishing magic from exorcism, and its relationship to sexuality, see Peter Dinzelbacher, "Heilige oder Hexen?" in *Untersuchungen zu sozialen, rechtlichen und theologischen Reaktionen auf religiöse Abweichung im westlichen und ostlichen Mittelalter*, ed. Dieter Simon (Frankfurt-am-Main, 1990), 41–60.

68. Nicholas of Tolentino, ed. Occhioni, 323–30, 136–7.

69. For citation, see Hansen, *Hexenprozess*, 188.

70. Yves of Tréguier, ed. Borderie, 357–62.

71. Charles of Blois, ed. Plaine et al., 313–8.

72. Richard Kieckhefer, *Magic in the Middle Ages* (Cambridge, 1990), 192–3; Edward Peters, *The Magician, the Witch, and the Law* (Philadelphia, 1978), 129–37; Julio Caro Baroja, *The World of the Witches*, trans. O. N. V. Glendenning (Chicago, 1971); Jeffrey B. Russell, "Witchcraft," in *Encyclopedia of Religion*, 16 vols., ed. Mircea Eliade (New York, 1987), 15: 415–23.

73. Clare of Montefalco, 500–1, on two persons restrained at Clare's tomb after beating their heads against the wall. One was exorcised after spitting out a black beetle. A common phraseology is "cum tanta rabie quod vix potuerat teneri ligata"; see Gerard Cagnoli, "La leggenda," 406, no. 30.

74. Jean-Claude Schmitt, "Le suicide au Moyen Age," *Annales: Économies, sociétés, civilisations*, 31 (1976), 3–28, for a general survey.

75. For a graphic illustration of Judas hanging from a tree, see the article on Judas Iscariot in the encyclopedia (ca. 1360–75) attributed to the Cistercian Jacobus, in British Museum, Royal 6E.VII, pt. 2, fol. 339^v. The standard version appears in James of Voragine, *Legenda aurea*, ed. Th. Graesse (Leipzig, 1850), 183–6. For English translation see James of Voragine, *The Golden Legend*, trans. William Granger Ryan, 2 vols. (Princeton, 1993), I, 166–71, under the legend of St. Matthew. The miraculous rescue of a suicidal pilgrim to Compostella who had been accused of murder is described in James of Vitry, *Historia orientalis*, ed. Francis Moschus (Douai, 1597), 427.

76. Thomas Aquinas, *Summa theologiae*, 2a, 2ae, 65.5, in *Opera omnia*. He cites Augustine's *De civitate Dei*, ed. B. Dombart and A. Kalb, 2 vols., in *Corpus cristianorum: Series latina*, vols. 47–8 (Turnhout, 1955), 1: 20, 22, 23, 26; Aristotle, *Ethica Nicomichea*, 3 vols., trans. Robert Grosseteste, ed. R. A. Gautier, in *Aristoteles latinus*, 26, pts. 1–3 (Leiden, 1972–3), 5: 11.1138a11, lect. 17; 3: 6.1115a26, lect. 14; 3: 7.1116a12, lect. 15.

77. Dahm, *Das Strafrecht Italiens*, 348.

78. Peter Martyr, *Miracula . . . post mortem*, 716.

79. Philip Benizi, 82–4.

80. Nicholas of Tolentino, ed. Occhioni, 278–84.

81. Albertus Magnus, *Summa theologiae*, II.vii, tract.7, q.27.3; q.27.1, in *Opera omnia*, vol. 32.

82. See the treatises on melancholy cited in S. Muntner, ed., "Al-ha-Melancholia, le Regel Yovel ha-Elef le-moto shel-Yizhak ben-Shlomo Yisrael," *Ha-Rofeh ha-Ivri*, 25 (1952), 85–95 [Hebrew]; Stanley W. Jackson, "Acedia the Sin and Its Relationship to Sorrow and Melancholia in Medieval Times," *Bulletin of the History of Medicine*, 55 (1981), 172–85.

83. Urban V, 232–3.

Chapter Five

1. See, e.g., Christian Krötzl, "Christian Parent-Child Relations in Medieval Scandinavia According to Scandinavian Miracle Collections," *Scandinavian Journal of History*, 14 (1989), 21–37. Michel Vovelle, *La mort de l'Occident de 1300 à nos jours* (Paris, 1983), 35, notes that in the *Legenda aurea* by James of Voragine, 54 percent of the miracles deal with children for recent saints, while for the preceding period, the figure is 34 percent.

2. A. Higounet-Nadal, "Les facteurs de croissance de la ville Périgueux," *Annales de démographie historique*, 1982, 19; T. H. Hollingsworth, *Historical Demography* (London, 1969), 375–88; John Hatcher, *Plague, Population, and the Economy 1348–1530* (London, 1977), 26–9.

3. Michael Goodich, "Il fanciullo come fulcro di miracoli e potere spirituale (XIII e XIV secolo)," in *Potere carismatici e informali*, ed. A. Paravicini-Bagliani and A. Vauchez (Palermo, 1992), 38–57; William Christian, *Apparitions in Late Medieval and Renaissance Spain* (Princeton, 1981), 216–9, on children as visionaries.

4. H. Zielinski, "Elisabeth von Thuringen und der Kinder: Zur Geschichte der Kindheit im Mittelalter," in *Elisabeth: Die deutsche Orden und Kirche*, ed. U. Arnold and H. Liebing (Marburg, 1983), 27–38; André Vauchez, "Charité et pauvreté chez Sainte Elisabeth de Thuringe d'après les actes du procès de canonisation," in *Études sur l'histoire de pauvreté*, ed. M. Mollat, 2 vols. (Paris, 1970), I, 163–70; N. Ohler, "Alltag im Marburger Raum," *Archiv für Kulturgeschichte*, 67 (1985), 1–40; and Sperandea of Cingoli, 905ff., for *Appendix de miraculis*.

5. Thomas of Hereford, ed. *AASS*, 596–8; on canonization see Patrick H. Daly, "The Process of Canonization in the Thirteenth and Fourteenth Centuries," and R. C. Finucane, "Cantilupe as Thaumaturge: Pilgrims and Their 'Miracles,'" in *St. Thomas Cantilupe Bishop of Hereford: Essays in His Honour*, ed. Meryl Jancey (Hereford, 1982), 125–35, 137–44.

6. Petrus Roger [Pope Clement VI], *Sermones*, "Exsulta et lauda habitatio Sion . . . " [Isaiah 12.6] in Bibliothèque Sainte-Geneviève ms. 240, fol. 541ʳ.

7. Thomas of Hereford, ed. *AASS*, 612.

8. Peter Martyr, *Miracula . . . post mortem*, 712–27.

9. William of Bourges, ed. *Analecta Bollandiana*, 349.

10. Gerard Cagnoli, "Il trattato," 153–6.

11. Nicholas of Tolentino, ed. Occhioni, 116–30.

12. The changing fortunes of children are dealt with in John Boswell, *The Kindness*

of Strangers: The Abandonment of Children in Western Europe from Late Antiquity to the Renaissance (New York, 1988); Goodich, "Il fanciullo," 28–47; Shulamith Shahar, Childhood in the Middle Ages (London, 1990); Christiane Klapisch-Zuber, Women, Family, and Ritual in Renaissance Florence, trans. Lydia Cochrane (Chicago, 1985), 103ff., argues convincingly for the disproportionate abandonment of infant girls in early Renaissance Tuscany.

13. Gerard Cagnoli, "La leggenda," 415–6, 437, 438, 441; "Il trattato," 155, 149; William of Bourges, ed. Analecta Bollandiana, 334–7; Martial of Limoges, ed. Lemaitre, 123, 127; Giovanna of Signa, ed. AASS, 286; Peter Martyr, Miracula post mortem, 716, 717; Charles of Blois, ed. Plaine et al., 206–7.

14. See the case of a woman of Flanders who had borne three dead sons and as a result was despised by her husband, in Peter Martyr, Miracula . . . post mortem, 716.

15. Gerard Cagnoli, "La leggenda," 415–6, no. 61.

16. See also ibid., 417, nos. 61–7; 438, nos. 137–9; idem, "Il trattato," 140, no. 23; 155, nos. 1–12; idem, "La leggenda," 407, nos. 36–7; 439, no. 138, for a woman bearing after a twenty-year barren marriage; 441, no. 144, on problems of childbirth; Giovanna of Signa, 286, no. 17.

17. Nicholas of Tolentino, ed. Occhioni, 125.

18. Gerard Cagnoli, "La leggenda," 439, no. 138.

19. Peter Martyr, Miracula . . . post mortem, 717–8; on a woman married three times before she conceived, see Charles of Blois, ed. Plaine et al., 206–7.

20. Urban V, 290–2.

21. Ibid., 474–5.

22. Gauderic of Agricola, 1116.

23. Urban V, 153–4, no. 43.

24. Gerard Cagnoli, "La leggenda," 415.

25. Idem, "Il trattato," 182.

26. William of Bourges, ed. Analecta Bollandiana, 334–7.

27. Jacques Gélis, "De la mort à la vie: Les sanctuaires à répit," Ethnologie française, 11 (1981), 211–24.

28. Martial of Limoges, ed. Lemaitre, 123; cf. Thomas of Hereford, ed. AASS, 642–3.

29. Martial of Limoges, ed. Lemaitre, 127.

30. Charles of Blois, ed. Plaine et al., 304–5.

31. Clare of Montefalco, 373–4.

32. R. C. Finucane, "Children at Risk in Northern and Southern Europe: Illness and Accidents in Medieval Canonization Records," Paper presented at seminar, Children, Parents, and the Community: Medieval and Early Modern Perspectives, 28–29 April 1993, Linköping University, Sweden.

33. The terms used include alveus, fluvium, puteum, fons, fossatum, fovea, greppus, fontalis puteum, lixivius, congrius, lacerna, lacus, vivarium, and stagnum. It is not always clear what kind of body of water is intended. The translators in the trial of Thomas of Hereford, ed. AASS, 609–10, used three terms for the same body of water, apparently a pond. See also Simon of Montfort, 74; Thomas of Hereford, ed. AASS, 644–5; Dorothy of Montau, ed. Stachnik, 229; Leonard of Inchenhofen, 196 (1417).

34. Gerard Cagnoli, "Il trattato," 182, no. 2; Simon of Montfort, 85; Nicholas of Tolentino, ed. Occhioni, 585; Charles of Blois, ed. Plaine et al., 218, 384, 390–2; Martial of Limoges, ed. Analecta Bollandiana, 432–3 (no. 48) at Folles; Leonard of Inchen-

hofen, 193, at Scöbach in 1409; Bridget of Sweden, ed. Collijn, 131–2; Cunegunda, 733.

35. Stanislas of Poland, 424–5; Leonard of Inchenhofen, 196, in 1415; 197, in 1422; Clare of Montefalco, 509–10; Nicholas of Tolentino, ed. Occhioni, 282–3, 332–3, 335, 381–2, in 1315; Martial of Limoges, ed. *Analecta Bollandiana*, 429–30, at Montréal in the Dordogne; 432–3, at Noblat; Gerard Cagnoli, "La leggenda," 406, no. 31; "Il trattato," 134, nos. 5, 9.

36. Gerard Cagnoli, "Il trattato," 134, no. 3; Margaret of Hungary, ed. Franknoì, 375–8; 380–3, in 1276; Charles of Blois, ed. Plaine et al., 222; William of Bourges, 334–7; Leonard of Inchenhofen, 196 (1417); Dorothy of Montau, ed. Stachnik, 396–70; Nicholas of Tolentino, ed. Occhioni, 261–4, 292–3, 295–6, 308–9; Peter of Luxemburg, 499–500; Simon of Montfort, 86; Yves of Tréguier, ed. Borderie, 139–40.

37. Gerard Cagnoli, "Il trattato," 134, no. 3; 140, no. 35; Cunegunda, 737; Zita of Lucca, 531, miracle in 1377; Louis of Toulouse, ed. *Analecta Bollandiana*, 353; William of Norwich, 189; Richard Rolle of Hampole, *Officium*, 812; Louis of Toulouse, *Processus*, 384; Yves of Tréguier, ed. Borderie, 283–4, 295–6; Leonard of Inchenhofen, 192 (1403); Nicholas of Tolentino, ed. Occhioni, 332; Peter Martyr, *Miracula . . . post mortem*, 717–8.

38. Nicholas of Tolentino, ed. Occchioni, 164–5; Martial of Limoges, ed. Arbellot, 433.

39. Thomas of Hereford, ed. AASS, 643, 644, 645 in 1288; Nicholas of Tolentino, ed. Occhioni, 243; Dorothy of Montau, ed. Stachnik, 249.

40. Zita of Lucca, 615.

41. Thomas of Hereford, ed. AASS, 609–12; Ronald C. Finucane, "Pilgrimage in Daily Life: Aspects of Medieval Communication Reflected in the Newly-Established Cult of Thomas Cantilupe (d. 1282), Its Dissemination and Effects upon Outlying Herefordshire Villagers," in *Wallfahrt und Alltag im Mittelalter und früher Neuzeit* (Vienna, 1992), 180ff., deals extensively with this; idem, "Medieval Peasant Children at Risk: Village Reactions to Childhood Accidents and Apparent Death in Rural England, ca. AD 1300," Paper delivered at Mid-America Medieval Association, Wichita State University, 3 March 1990. Finucane is working on a study of children in miracle stories.

42. See, e.g., Peter Martyr, *Miracula . . . post mortem*, 716, concerning a French girl who had fallen into the Yonne river: "cuius mortis quatuor erant indicia certitudinis: videlicet magnum temporis spatium, rigiditas corporis, frigiditas, et negritudo." Christian Krötzl, "Evidentissima signa mortis: Zu Tod und Todesfeststellung in mittelalterlichen Mirakelberichten," in *Symbole des Alltags: Alltag der Symbole*, ed. Gertrud Blaschitz et al. (Graz, 1992), 765–75, discusses the standards of death in miracle stories.

43. Yves of Tréguier, ed. Borderie, 135–6, 155–6, 233–4; Charles of Blois, ed. Plaine et al., 193.

44. Thomas of Hereford, ed. AASS, 619; Martial of Limoges, 419; Yves of Tréguier, ed. Borderie, 132.

45. Thomas of Hereford, ed. AASS, 613; Clare of Montefalco, 408.

46. Peter Martyr, 709–10; Hedwig of Silesia, *Vita maior*, 620–1.

47. Charles of Blois, ed. Plaine et al., 208.

48. Thomas of Hereford, ed. AASS, 608–11; Yves of Tréguier, ed. Borderie, 146–7.

49. Yves of Tréguier, ed. Borderie, 147.

50. Martial of Limoges, ed. Lemaitre, 111.

51. Clare of Montefalco, 408–9.

52. Lucchesio of Poggibonsi, ed. *AASS*, 612; Bridget of Sweden, ed. Collijn, 131–2; Hedwig of Silesia, *Vita maior*, 620–1; Richard Rolle, 814; Thomas of Hereford, ed. *AASS*, 617–8; Amalberga, 100 (1327 at Ghent); Leonard of Inchenhofen, 197 (1417); Clare of Montefalco, 262–3, 393–4; 488, for a child sitting on a donkey carrying wine and bread in 1315–6 near Montefalco. In 1398 a three-year-old boy at Roggenhausen(?) in Pomerania was struck by a shovel wielded by his mother to shovel dung (see Dorothy of Montau, ed. Stachnik, 366).

53. Clare of Montefalco, 408, 501–2; Thomas of Hereford, ed. *AASS*, 613, 642; Leonard of Inchenhofen, 197 (Innsbruck, 1417); Dorothy of Montau, ed. Stachnik, 26, 77.

54. Honorina, 135, on a child of Achères drowned in the Seine discovered by two passersby and revived in the presence of nine persons.

55. Finucane, "Children at Risk" (1993).

56. Charles of Blois, ed. Plaine et al., 267–8.

57. See, e.g., James Bruce Ross, "The Middle Class Child in Urban Italy: Fourteenth and Early Fifteenth Century," in *Childhood in History*, ed. Lloyd de Mause (New York, 1974), 182–222.

58. Leonard of Inchenhofen, 197, in 1423.

59. Dorothy of Montau, ed. Stachnik, 229.

60. Hedwig of Silesia, *Vita maior*, 622–3.

61. Thomas of Hereford, ed. *AASS*, 626. I wish to thank Ronald Finucane for providing valuable correctives to the version in the *Acta sanctorum*. This is based on *Vat. Lat.* ms. 4015, fols. 188ʳ–203ᵛ. A summary also appears in Exeter College ms. 158, fols. 38ᵛ–39ʳ.

62. Charles of Blois, ed. Plaine et al., 208.

63. Ibid., 242–3.

64. Thomas of Hereford, ed. *AASS*, 608–9; cf. Finucane, "Medieval Peasant Children," on coroners.

65. Thomas of Hereford, ed. *AASS*, 612.

66. John of Bridlington, *Collectanea*, 123.

67. Thomas of Hereford, ed. *AASS*, 617. I again wish to thank Ronald Finucane for his corrections, drawn from *Vat. Lat.* ms. 4015, fols. 157ᵛ–165ʳ.

68. Thomas of Hereford, ed. *AASS*, 609–12.

69. Ibid., 642; Clare of Montefalco, 262–3, 393–4, 488.

70. Yves of Tréguier, ed. Borderie, 132–8.

71. Michael Goodich, *From Birth to Old Age: The Life Cycle in Medieval European Thought, 1250–1350* (Lanham, Md., 1989), 89–92.

72. The following comes from Thomas of Hereford, ed. *AASS*, 617; Charles of Blois, ed. Plaine et al., 363–6; and Yves of Tréguier, ed. Borderie, 259–60; cf. Finucane, "Pilgrimage," 200ff. on issues of time and distance.

73. Thomas of Hereford, ed. *AASS*, 617, 645, 683.

74. On frequency of crime, see John G. Bellamy, *Criminal Law and Society in Late Medieval and Tudor England* (New York, 1984); Barbara Hanawalt, *Crime and Conflict in English Communities, 1300–1348* (Cambridge, 1979); James B. Given, *Society and Homicide in Thirteenth Century England* (Stanford, 1977); Yvonne Lanhers, "Crimes et criminels au XIV siècle," *Revue historique*, 240 (1968), 325–38; M. Bourin and B.

Chevalier, "Le comportement criminel dans les pays de la Loire moyenne d'après les lettres de rémission (vers 1380—vers 1450)," *Annales de Bretagne et des pays de l'Ouest*, 88 (1981), 245–63.

75. Thomas of Hereford, ed. *AASS*; Leonard of Inchenhofen, 186; 187 in 1363 (Schliersee in Bavaria).

76. Yves of Tréguier, ed. Borderie, 151–2.

77. Ibid., 140.

78. Thomas of Hereford, ed. *AASS*, 610; cf. Charles of Blois, ed. Plaine et al., 235–6.

79. Yves of Tréguier, ed. Borderie, 235–6.

80. Thomas of Hereford, ed. *AASS*, 618.

81. Ibid., 610, 612; Dorothy of Montau, ed. Stachnik, 77.

Chapter Six

1. Jean Durst, *Before Nature Dies*, trans. Constance D. Sherman (Boston, 1970), 36–8.

2. Vincent of Beauvais, *Speculum maius*, 4 vols. (Douai, 1624), vol. 4, *Speculum naturale*, lib. 23, c. 1 (citing gloss on Genesis 26, Creation).

3. John Passmore, *Man's Responsibility for Nature* (London, 1974); Ian G. Barbour, *Technology, Environment, and Human Values* (New York, 1980); Wilhelm Ganzenmüller, *Das Naturgefühl im Mittelalter*, Beiträge zur Geschichte des Mittelalters und Renaissance, vol. 18 (Leipzig, 1914); Keith Thomas, *Man and the Natural World* (Harmondsworth, 1983), 22ff.; Jacques Le Goff, *The Medieval Imagination*, trans. Arthur Goldhammer (Chicago, 1988), 47–59, on wilderness.

4. Gerard Cagnoli, "La leggenda," 423–4, tells of a woman of Pisa who in 1347 envisioned a tornado on two successive occasions, and was told by Gerard that the areas drenched in rain symbolized the believers, and the dry regions the unbelievers. In another miracle (Ibid., 432) a man was caught in a heavy downpour in the forest while gathering myrtle.

5. On heavy rain, see Louis of Toulouse, *Processus*, 293. For floods at Tours in 1415, see Mary of Maillé, 764; at Orvieto in 1216, see Peter Parenti, 98; at Cahors in the 1340s, Peter Thomas, 57; Gerio of Montesanto, 158–9.

6. Jacques Chiffoleau, *La comptabilité de l'au delà: Les hommes, la mort et la religion dans la région d'Avignon à la fin du moyen âge (vers 1320–1480)* (Rome, 1980), 100ff., 441ff., for lists of natural catastrophes ca. 1330–1490, including floods, cold, snow, earthquakes, drought, plague, famine, wars; Pierre Guillaume and Jean-Pierre Pousson, *Démographie historique* (Paris, 1970), 47–8, on demographic consequences; Louis Stouff, *Ravitaillement et alimentation en Provence aux XIVe et XVe siècles* (Paris, 1970) on famine and malnutrition.

7. Jean Delumeau, *La peur en Occident (XIVe—XVIIIe siècles): Une cité assiégée* (Paris, 1978), on fear of natural catastrophe in the later middle ages.

8. British Museum, Royal 6.E.VI. pt. 2, 271ᵛ, *Infernus*.

9. Gregorio Penco, "Il simbolismo animalesco nella letteratura monastica," *Studia monastica*, 6 (1964), 7–38.

10. Anna Benvenuti Papi, *In castro poenitentiae: Santità e società femminile nell'Italia medievale* (Rome, 1990), 281.

11. Dorothy of Montau, ed. Stachnik, 104–5, 120.

12. Gerard Cagnoli, "Il trattato," 142; Urban V, 444–5.

13. Philip Benizi, ed. Soulier, 60–83.

14. Guillaume and Pousson, *Démographie historique*, 48.

15. The classic account is Millard Meiss, *Painting in Florence and Siena after the Black Death* (Princeton, 1951).

16. Catherine of Siena, ed. Franceschini, 126.

17. Cited in Papi, *In castro poenitentiae*, 282. The miracles of Stanislas of Cracow, ed. Kadlubek, 431, contain the following remark: "Sic beatus Stanislaus pontifex et martir gloriosus in celo et in terra et in igne et in aqua omnibus se invocantibus in veritate est adiutor in opportunitatibus, in tribulatione." Regarding Nicholas's mastery over "bodies, soul, death and demons," see Johannes Herolt, *Sermones de tempore et sanctis cum Promptuario exemplorum* (Strasbourg, 1492), fol. 236ʳ.

18. Celestine V, ed. Frugoni.

19. Seraphina, 235–42.

20. Dorothy of Montau, ed. Stachnik, 65.

21. Queen Eleonora of Sicily's fear of lightning and thunder led her to make a candle etched with a relic of Gerard Cagnoli and the prayer "In principio erat Verbum" on the Feast of the Purification. When a great storm arose in Catania, she placed such a candle in her window, the thunder and lightning subsided, and the storm ceased. Gerard Cagnoli, "La leggenda," 426. For a horse hit by lightning, see Dorothy of Montau, ed. Stachnik, 43.

22. Herolt, *Sermones*, sermo 108, fols. 154ᵛ–155ʳ.

23. Ibid., sermo 18, fol. 255ʳ–256ᵛ.

24. Ibid., sermo 108, fol. 155ʳ.

25. Ibid., sermo 4, fol. 236ʳ.

26. A. G. Little, ed., *Liber exemplorum ad usum praedicatorum* (Aberdeen, 1908), 41–2 n. 67.

27. John Gobi, *Scala coeli* (Strasbourg, 1483), no. 401.

28. Little, *Liber exemplorum*, 51–2, no. 95.

29. Ibid., 85–6, no. 142. See also Gobi, *Scala coeli*, nos. 400, 641, 642, 643, largely dealing with water, and the Virgin.

30. Stephen Forte, ed., "A Cambridge Collection of Exempla in the Thirteenth Century," *Archivum fratrum praedicatorum*, 28 (1928), 139–40, no. 201.

31. Ibid., 145–6, no. 311.

32. Several relevant articles appear in the special issue *L'Eau au Moyen Age*, in *Sénéfiance* (Aix-en-Provence, 1985).

33. Gregorio Penco, "Il senso della natura nell'agiografia monastica occidentale," *Studia monastica*, 11 (1969), 327–34. For an illustration of the pastoral attitude toward nature and the need to live in harmony with the beasts, expressed by the hermit Giovanna of Signa, see the frescoes discussed in Daniel Russo, "Jeanne de Signa ou l'iconographie au féminin: Études sur les fresques de l'église paroissale de Signa (milieu du XVe siècle)," *Mélanges de l'École française de Rome: Moyen âge*, 98 (1986), 201–18.

34. Catherine of Fierbois, 1, for the site of the shrine. On the forest, largely in literature, see Marianne Stauffer, *Der Wald: Zur Darstellung und Deutung der Natur im Mittelalter* (Berlin, 1959).

35. Angelo Clareno, *Apologia pro sua vita*, ed. Victorinus Doucet, *Archivum franciscanum historicum*, 39 (1948), 63–200.

36. B. Bennassar et al., *L'Ouverture de monde: XIVe—XVIe siècles* (Paris, 1977), 276–7, for a chapter on the fourteenth and fifteenth centuries by Guy Fourquin.

37. Michel Mollat, "Les ex-voto maritimes," *Bulletin de la société archéologique du Finistère*, 100 (1973), 263–73.

38. Lawrence of Dublin, ed. Plummer, 121–86.

39. Michel Mollat, "Sentiments et pratiques religieuses des gens de mer en France du XIIIe au XVIe siècle," *Revue d'histoire de l'Église de France*, 70 (1984), 305–15.

40. Thomas of Walsingham, *Chronica anglicana sancti Albani*, 2 vols., ed. H. T. Riley, in *Rerum britannicarum scriptores (Rolls series)*, 28.1 (London, 1863–4), 1: 423–5.

41. For a Franciscan who feared that his baggage had been lost, see Gerard Cagnoli, "La leggenda," 421.

42. Mary of Cervellone, 160, for statements of victims reported at a general chapter at Ilerda; Raymond of Penyaforte, ed. Balmé and Paban, 296.

43. Nicholas of Tolentino, ed. Occhioni, 234, 259, 320.

44. Gerard Cagnoli, "La leggenda," 425.

45. Yves of Tréguier, ed. Borderie, 275–7.

46. Louis of Toulouse, *Processus*, 123, 228, 229–30, 231–3, 295, 318, 322, 329.

47. Bridget of Sweden, ed. Collijn, 110–11.

48. Ibid., 205, 261, 314, 344–5, 371, 435, 496.

49. Ibid., 114, 132, 184–5.

50. Catherine of Fierbois, 3, 4–5.

51. Amalberga, 100; for the miraculous appearance of fish in a pool which formerly had none, on the date of her canonization, see Hedwig, *Vita maior*, 630.

52. Gerard Cagnoli, "La leggenda," 428–9, for a highly detailed report.

53. Paul Amargier, "Gens de mer en Méditerranée dans les années 1375–1390," in *Navigation et gens de mer en Méditerranée de la Préhistoire à nos jours* (Paris, 1980), 68–83, discusses the trials of Urban V, in which 26 of the 380 depositions came from sea folk. Geneviève Bresc and Henri Bresc, "Les saints protecteurs de bateaux 1200–1460," *Ethnologie française*, 9 (1979), 161–78, on Christianization reflected in the names of vessels.

54. Urban V, 147, no. 34.

55. Ibid., 129, 130, 147, 150–1, 182–3, 186–7, 195–6, 229–30, 241–2, 245–6, 248–9, 250–1, 275–7, 280, 301, 325–6, 342–3, 353–4, 359, 435–6, 436–7, 444, 457–8, 472–3.

56. Yves of Tréguier, ed. Borderie, 228–9; see also 158–9, 161–4, 209–10, 213–4, 276–7.

57. Bridget of Sweden, ed. Collijn, 134–5.

58. John of Rimini, 670, no. 126.

59. William of Bourges, ed. *Analecta Bollandiana*, 271; Zita of Lucca, 531.

60. Jean-Claude Schmitt, *Le saint lévrier: Guinefort, guérisseur d'enfants depuis le XIIIe siècle* (Paris, 1979).

61. Gerard Cagnoli, "Il trattato," 189–90.

62. Rayner of Borgo San Sepolcro, 401. For an attack of wolves near Paris in 1421, see Alexandre Tuetey, ed., *Journal d'un bourgeois de Paris (1405–1449)* (Paris, 1975), 154.

63. John of Rimini, 652, no. 21.

64. For the view that the Robin Hood tales were an expression of peasant discon-

tent, see Maurice Keen, *The Outlaws of Medieval Legend*, rev. ed. (London, 1977), 145–73; cf. John G. Bellamy, *Robin Hood: An Historical Inquiry* (Bloomington, 1985).

65. Bridget of Sweden, ed. Collijn, 126–7; Stanislas of Cracow, ed. Kadlubek, 431–2.

66. Bridget of Sweden, ed. Collijn, 138–9.

67. Dorothy of Montau, ed. Stachnik, 240–1.

68. For a collapsing house, see Peter of Luxemburg, 514; Urban V, 445–6; Charles of Blois, ed. Plaine et al., 222, 260–1; Cunegunda, 733. For the collapse of a newly built chapel on the Franciscan guardian of Genoa, Joannes de Margaroctis, in August 1346, see Gerard Cagnoli, "La leggenda," 408; for falling bricks, Gerard Cagnoli, "Il trattato," 139.

69. John Langdon, "Horse Hauling: A Revolution in Vehicle Transport in Twelfth- and Thirteenth-Century England," *Past and Present*, 103 (1984), 37–66; idem, "The Economics of Horses and Oxen in Medieval England," *Agricultural History Review*, 30 (1982), 31–40; R. H. Britnell, "Agricultural Technology and the Margin of Cultivation in the Fourteenth Century," *Economic History Review*, 30 (1977), 53–66.

70. Jean-Pierre Leguay, "Accidents du travail et maladies professionelles au moyen âge," *L'information historique*, 43 (1981), 223–33, largely on the fifteenth century, suggests evidence for this little-explored subject. On the decline of progress in the later middle ages, see Jean Gimpel, *The Medieval Machine: The Industrial Revolution of the Middle Ages* (London, 1977).

71. Peter of Luxemburg, on an accident in June 1387 at Avignon, 500–1, 530; cf. Urban V, 221–2; Thomas of Hereford, ed. AASS, 665; Dorothy of Montau, ed. Stachnik, 222, 366–7, 369–70.

72. Yves of Tréguier, ed. Borderie, 203–5.

73. Peter of Luxemburg, 501, 502, 519, 521.

74. Ibid., 502, 506; John of Rimini, 649.

75. Urban V, 158; John of Bridlington, *Collectanea*, 122.

76. Gerard Cagnoli, "La leggenda," 412, 435; "Il trattato," 135, 136.

77. Urban V, 144–5; Richard Rolle, *Officium*, 82–3; cf. Francis of Assisi, *Tractatus de miraculis*, 295, 296, for accidents incurred while building Franciscan churches.

78. Urban V, 322, 330–1.

79. Ibid., 451–2.

80. G. Mollat, *Les papes d'Avignon (1305–1378)* (Paris, 1964), 119–20.

81. Margaret of Città, ed. *Analecta Bollandiana*, 36. In Gerard Cagnoli, "Il trattato," 189, a family brought ex-voto offerings of both calves and pigs in thanks for difficulties that had been overcome. For a psychological study, see Regina Abt-Baechi, *Der heilige und das Schwein* (Zurich, 1983).

82. Gerard Cagnoli, "La leggenda," 431; Louis of Toulouse, *Processus*, 493.

83. Urban V, 207–8; Thomas of Hereford, ed. AASS, 668, 680; Gerard Cagnoli, "La leggenda," 413; Amalberga, 106.

84. Yves of Tréguier, ed. Borderie, 274: "quod fuit et erat magna mortalitas animalium."

85. Stanislas of Cracow, ed. Kadlubek, 427–8; John of Rimini, 652, 659; Gerard Cagnoli, "La leggenda," 431; Urban V, 333, for an injured horse; 378, for a stolen horse; Yves of Tréguier, ed. Borderie, 213–4, 292–3, on a horse nearly drowned at sea; Leonard of Inchenhofen, 189, on horse thieves.

86. Gerard Cagnoli, "Il trattato," 187ff., for several cases of injuries and disease involving horses; Nicholas of Tolentino, ed. Occhioni, 240; Jerome, 658; Louis of Toulouse, *Processus*, 289, 292, 300.

87. Esther Cohen, *The Crossroads of Justice: Law and Culture in Late Medieval France* (Leiden, 1993), 100–33, on the trials of animals. For a horse accused of murdering a child, see Yves of Tréguier, ed. Borderie, 295.

88. Gobi, *Scala coeli*, no. 404.

89. Cohen, *Crossroads of Justice*, 132.

90. Urban V, 221–3.

91. Ibid., 168–9.

92. Philippa Castellani, 102; Peter of Luxemburg, 514; Thomas of Hereford, ed. *AASS*, 653, 668, 676, 691; idem, Exeter College ms. 158, fol. 20ᵛ; Charles of Blois, ed. Plaine et al., 323, 384–5, 398; John of Bridlington, ed. *AASS*, 142; Yves of Tréguier, ed. Borderie, 184–5; Dorothy of Montau, ed. Stachnik, 379–80, for fire at the castle of Christburg in Pomerania; Stanislas of Cracow, ed. Kadlubek, 430, for a fire set by pagans in Prussia during a Crusade; Hedwig, *Vita maior*, 606, for a fire near Gnesen in 1263.

93. Philippa Castellani, 102; Peter Martyr, *Miracula . . . post mortem*, 716, 726; Charles of Blois, ed. Plaine et al., 384–50, Gerard Cagnoli, "La leggenda," 429.

94. Charles of Blois, ed. Plaine et al., 323.

95. Yves of Tréguier, ed. Borderie, 162–3.

96. Agnes of Montepulciano, 808; cf. also Amalberga, 106; Seraphina, trans. Mansfield, 37, for village.

97. J. Viard and E. Deprez, eds., *Chronique de Jean le Bel*, 2 vols. (Paris, 1904), 1: 222.

98. Gauderic of Agricola, 1116. One of the most popular plague cults was devoted to the pilgrim Roch of Montpellier, who had himself fallen victim to the disease. All of the sources, however, appear to date from the fifteenth century. It was reported that the councils of Constance (1409) and Ferrara (1439) did not move despite the ravages of plague, owing to the saint's posthumous intervention. See the discussion in Augustin Fliche, "Le problème de Saint Roch," *Analecta Bollandiana*, 68 (1950), 343–61. For a saint (Wendelinus) popularized during an outbreak at Trier in 1320, see *AASS*, 21 October IX, 346.

99. Marie-Madeleine Antony-Schmitt, *Le culte de Saint-Sebastien en Alsace* (Strasbourg, 1977), 10, for this suggestion.

100. Sebastian, ed. Mills, 412; on the theme of the wrath of God, see J. C. Payen, "Les *Dies Irae* dans la prédication de la mort et des fins dernières au moyen âge (À propos de *Piramus*, v. 708)," *Romania*, 86 (1965), 48–76. Aignan of Chartres, 321–35, represents an excellent introduction to such hagiographical *topoi* as (1) the revival of a cult devoted to an alleged follower of Paul, (2) God's vengeance as a source of public misfortune, (3) universal acceptance of a cult, (4) the rescue of relics from a disastrous fire, and (5) the festivities surrounding translation ceremonies. The author notes that the anger of God was often wreaked on the city of Chartres, bringing in its wake sedition, pestilence, infertility, and the destruction of churches.

101. Gilles le Muisit, *Annales*, ed. H. Lemaitre (Paris, 1966), 258.

102. Catherine of Fierbois, 20, no. 48.

103. Sebastian, ed. Mills, 410–8; Baudouin de Gaiffier, "Les sources latines d'un miracle de Gautier de Coincy," *Analecta Bollandiana*, 71 (1953), 100–32, esp. 125,

128; Sebastian, ed. *AASS*, 939–41; *Bibliotheca sanctorum*, 12 vols. (Rome, 1970–80), 10: 775–90.

104. Jacques Chiffoleau, *La compatibilité de l'au delà: Les hommes, la mort et la religion dans la région d'Avignon à la fin du moyen âge (vers 1320–1480)* (Rome, 1980), 379, on plague saints. Pierre Rézeau, *Les prières aux saints en français à la fin du moyen âge*, 2 vols. (Geneva, 1982–3), contains the vernacular prayers addressed to saints such as Petronilla, Adrian, Anthony of Padua, and Sebastian, who were regarded as aids against the plague.

105. Peter Thomas, 97, on plague in Cyprus.

106. Jean-Noël Biraben, *Les hommes et la peste en France et dans les pays européens et méditerranéens*, 2 vols. (Paris, 1975–6); for a graphic eyewitness account of the processions and preventive measures undertaken when the plague hit Paris in 1418, along with war and other catastrophes, see Tuetey, *Journal d'un bourgeois*, 111–16.

107. Urban V, 153–4.

108. Leonard of Inchenhofen, 193, no. 9. The phrase reads "X milia et quingenti," but this may not be an accurate reading.

109. Dorothy of Montau, ed. Westpfahl, II. 43–4.

110. Remigius, 337–43; John of Rimini, 648–77.

111. Catherine of Siena, ed. Laurent, 321–2, 431.

112. Urban V, 130, no. 14; 143–4, no. 31; 153–4, no. 43; 187, no. 92; 189–90, nos. 100–1; 200–1, no. 115; 225, no. 148; 226, no. 149; 228–9, no. 153; 248, no. 181; 254–5, no. 190; 255–6, no. 192; 264, no. 204; 268–9, nos. 209–11; 281, no. 227; 293, no. 243; 302, no. 255; 323, no. 311; 359–60, no. 372; 453, no. 40.

113. Ibid., 290–2, no. 241.

114. Dauphine of Languedoc, 300.

Chapter Seven

1. Antonio Rigon, "Devotion et patriotisme communal dans la genèse et la diffusion d'un culte: Le Bienheureux Antoine de Padoue surnommé le Pellegrino († 1267)," *Faire Croire: Modalités de la diffusion et de la réception des messages religieux du XIIe au XVe siècle* (Rome, 1981), 259–78.

2. John Gueruli, 425–53. A eulogy to Bologna dated 1177–8 states: "Iocundare, praeclara urbs Bononia, ac plurimum suavi modulatione vocum et angelicis tripudiis oportet te exaltare, quoniam multorum sanctorum patrociniis es decorata faciliter. O quam beata es, Bononensium civitas, et quam a confinibus civitatibus venerenda." Cited in Enrico Cattaneo, *Città e religione nell'età dei communi* (Milan, 1979), 61.

3. Garland, 541–51; Martin of Genoa, 804. See Patrick Geary, *Furta Sacra: Theft of Relics in the Central Middle Ages* (Princeton, 1978), on relic theft and "discovery" in the eleventh and twelfth centuries. Two more recent cases of relic theft include George of Cappadocia, ed. *AASS*, 133; and Paul Novus, ed. *AASS*, 639, whose body was taken from Constantinople to the monastery of St. George the Greater at Venice in 1222. For a history see Kenneth M. Setton, "St. George's Head," *Speculum*, 48 (1973), 1–12. The relics of St. Trypho were purloined from Boka Katorska, perhaps in the ninth century; evidence of a cult dates from 1006, but only in 1287 was papal approval given. See *AASS*, 10 November IV, 323–4.

4. Dauphine of Languedoc, 63–4.

5. Thomas Aquinas, ed. Prümmer, 57–160, for William of Tocco's *Vita S. Thomae*

Aquinatis (142–3 on episode); Bernard Gui, *Vita S. Thomae Aquinatis*, 160–263 (227–8 for episode); *Processus canonizationis S. Thomae Aquinatis Napoli*, 265–407 (324–6, 359–60 for episode); papal bull, 519–30 (for episode, 525–6); and G. Mollat, ed., *Lettres communes de Jean XXII*, 16 vols. (Paris, 1946), no. 1356.

6. Godehard, 651–2, for miracles of the thirteenth—fifteenth centuries.

7. John the Baptist, *Historia mediolana*, 655ff.

8. Idem, *De cineribus*, 676.

9. Anna Benvenuti Papi, *In castro poenitentiae: Santità e società femminile nell'Italia medievale* (Rome, 1990), 267–9.

10. Nicholas of Tolentino, ed. Occhioni, 175, 540.

11. Alexandre Tuetey, ed., *Journal d'un bourgeois de Paris (1405–1449)* (Paris, 1975), 62–4.

12. Bernardino of Siena, 399–441.

13. Jacques Heers, *Fêtes, jeux et joûtes dans les sociétés d'Occident à la fin du moyen âge* (Montreal, 1971); Richard Trexler, ed., *Synodal Law: Florence and Fiesole, 1306–1518*, in *Studi e testi*, 268 (Rome, 1975), 114–22; Ludovico Zdekauer, ed., *Breve ordinamenta populi Pistorii* (Milan, 1891), I.83, II.28, 224; Noël Coulet, "Jalons pour une histoire religieuse d'Aix au Bas-Moyen Age (1150–1450)," *Provence historique*, 22 (1972), 203–60. R. Derville, "La vie religieuse au XIVe siècle d'après les comptes de la cathédrale de Cambrai," *Revue d'histoire de l'Eglise de France*, 74 (1988), 213–33, reports the considerable expenditure involved in liturgical processions during the plague period. Vauchez's comment in *Faire croire*, 11, argues that in the later middle ages the people practiced religion by means of signs and gestures more than through liturgical language. The dismemberment of saints' bodies in order to supply relics for clients had continued apace, despite papal disapproval. See Caroline W. Bynum, "Material Continuity, Personal Survival, and the Resurrection of the Body: A Scholastic Discussion in Its Medieval and Modern Contexts," *History of Religions*, 30.1 (1990), 79.

14. Derville, "La vie religieuse."

15. Honoré Bonet, *The Tree of Battles*, ed. and trans. G. W. Coopland (Liverpool, 1949), 187–8.

16. Philippe Contamine, *La guerre au moyen âge* (Paris, 1980); Dante Balboni and Maria Chiara Celletti, "Giorgio," in *Bibliotheca sanctorum*, 12 vols. (Rome, 1970–80), 6: 511–31, on the flourishing of the cult in the fourteenth century.

17. Thomas of Hereford, ed. *AASS*, 683, 684, 685; Thomas of Hereford, in Oxford, Exeter College ms. 158, fols. 6ʳ, 29ᵛ, 30v.

18. Dauphine of Languedoc, 85–6; Dominic of Silos, 128–229, contains a large number of well-documented escapes from military imprisonment experienced by Spaniards fighting in the area of Granada before 1331.

19. Urban V, 124–5, 146–7, 149–50, 205–6, 238, 272–3, 284–6, 295, 309–10, 315, 332, 357–8, 432–3.

20. Urban V, 129, 136, 147, 149–50, 150–2, 159–60, 182–3, 186–7, 195–6, 202–3, 212–3, 226–7, 229–31, 241–2, 245–6, 248–9, 275–7, 280, 283, 301, 342–3, 352–4, 359, 435–7, 444, 457–8, 466, 472–3, 475. For a brief study of coastal life reflected in Urban's process, see Paul Amargier, "Gens de mer en Méditerranée dans les années 1375–1390," in *Navigation et gens de mer en Méditerranée de la Préhistoire à nos jours* (Paris, 1980), 68–83.

21. Urban V, 130–1, 143–4, 155–6, 187–92, 200–1, 207–8, 221, 225–6, 228–9, 232, 248, 254–6, 264–9, 281–2, 287, 290–3, 302, 311, 325, 359–60, 453, 467, 473–5.

22. Dorothy of Montau, ed. Stachnik, 63–6, 68–9, 145.

23. Gerard Cagnoli, "La leggenda," 422.

24. Ibid., 422–3.

25. Bridget of Sweden, ed. Collijn, 134–5, on three *milites* captured by pagans near Reval.

26. Andrew Gallerani, 56; Mary of Cervellone, 180.

27. Wenceslas, "Le dossier," 123 (c. 3).

28. Leonard of Inchenhofen, 186–7.

29. M. H. Keen, *The Laws of War in the Middle Ages* (London, 1965); Contamine, *La guerre*; Christopher T. Allmand, *Society at War: The Experience of England and France during the Hundred Years' War* (Liverpool, 1976).

30. Keen, *Laws of War*, 199.

31. Paris of Pozzi, *De re militari*, in Francesco Ziletti, ed., *Tractatus universi iuris*, 22 vols. (Rome, 1584–6), 16: 421ᵛ; see Keen, *Laws of War*, 152–7.

32. Bonet, *Tree of Battles*, pt. 4, c. 55; Keen, *Laws of War*, 179.

33. Paris of Pozzi, *De re militari*, 421ᵛ.

34. Contamine, *La guerre*, 195ff.; Bonet, *Tree of Battles*, 153.

35. Christine de Pisan, *The Book of Fayttes of Armes and of Chivalrye*, trans. William Caxton, ed. A. T. P. Byles, *Early English Texts Society: Original Series*, 189 (Oxford, 1932), 223–4 (cc. 17). The ransom sums are sometimes noted, e.g., a man of Grosseto imprisoned at S. Flora was asked to pay 150 florins (Agnes of Montepulciano, 809).

36. Urban V, 146–7.

37. Ibid., 284–6.

38. Philippe Contamine, *La France au XIVe et XVe siècles: Hommes, mentalités, guerre et paix* (London, 1981), contains many essays on the period. See no. 4 ("La Guerre de Cent Ans en France: Une approche économique").

39. Urban V, 135–6. For the case of a man of Ghent hung by his feet to pay ransom to Armagnacs near Paris, see Gerulph, 205.

40. Urban V, 432–3.

41. Peter of Luxemburg, 520–1.

42. Ibid., 509.

43. Paris of Pozzi, *De re militari*, 421ᵛ.

44. Jean Froissart, *Chroniques*, ed. J. M. B. C. Kervyn de Lettenhove, *Oeuvres de Froissart*, 26 vols. (Brussels, 1867–77), 8: 43.

45. Bonet, *Tree of Battles*, 189.

46. Leonard of Inchenhofen, 189.

47. Cunegunda, 741–2.

48. Cited in Daniel Waley, *Later Medieval Europe* (London, 1964), 124.

49. E. de Fréville, "Des grandes compagnies au quatorzième siècle," *Bibliothèque de l'École de Chartes*, 5 (1843–4), 246.

50. "Cette Provence parait être et est une caverne de brigands à cause des guerres qui ont sevi ici; toute chose y est sauvage." (*Annales Avignonnaises de 1382 à 1410: Extraites des Archives des Datini*, ed. R. Brun, *Mémoires de l'Institut historique de Provence*, 12 [1935], 105–42.)

51. Contamine, *La guerre*; Robert Boutruche, *La crise d'une société* (Paris, 1963).

52. E. Menkes, "Aspects de la guerre en Provence à la fin du XIV siècle," in *Economies et sociétés au moyen âge: Mélanges offerts à Edouard Perroy* (Paris, 1973), 465–76, on Trets in Provence.

53. Barbara Hanawalt, "Violent Death in Fourteenth and Early Fifteenth Century England," *Comparative Studies in Society and History*, 18 (1976), 197–220.

54. Eric Hobsbawm, "The Peasant and Brigand: Social Banditry Reconsidered," *Comparative Studies in Society and History*, 14 (1972), 494–505.

55. Edward Peters, *Torture* (Oxford, 1985), 49.

56. The most detailed reports are found in the protocol of Charles of Blois, ed. Plaine et al.

57. Jean-René Gaborit, "Marziale di Limoges," *Bibliotheca sanctorum*, 8, 1310–13; L. Duchesne, "Saint Martial de Limoges," *Annales du midi*, 4 (1892), 289–330.

58. Martial of Limoges, ed. *AASS*; see Adhemar of Chabannes, *Historiae libri tres*, III. 56, in *MPL*, 141: 69; and his *Epistola de apostolatu S. Martialis* in *MPL*, 141: 87–111; F. Wormald, "The English Saints in the Litany of Arundel ms. 60," *Analecta Bollandiana*, 64 (1946), 84–6, on the transformation of Martial into an apostle in the eleventh century.

59. For a history of the display of relics (*ostensiones*), see Louis Perouas, "Ostensiones et culte ds saints en Limousin: Un approche ethno-historique," *Ethnologie française*, 13 (1983), 323–36; Françoise Lautman, "Les ostensiones de Limousin," *Ethnologie française*, 13 (1983), 309–22; L. Duchesne, "Saint Martial de Limoges," *Annales du midi*, 4 (1892), 289–330; Françoise Lautman, "Le territoire des reliques," *Annales de Bretagne et des pays de l'Ouest*, 90 (1983), 221–32; Antoine Perrier, "Une manifestation populaire: Les ostensiones septennales," *Bulletin de la société archéologique et historique du Limousin*, 101 (1974), 119–56.

60. Marie-Madeleine Gautier, ed., "Sermon d'Adémar de Chabannes pour la translation du saint Martial le 10 Octobre," *Bulletin de la société archéologique et historique du Limousin*, 88 (1961), 72–83, for Adhemar's sermon.

61. Lautman, "Ostensiones."

62. Martial of Limoges, ed. Lemaitre, for details of truce; Keen, *Laws of War*, 205–6; Nicholas Upton, *De officio militari libri quattuor*, II, c. 13, ed. Edward Bysshe (London, 1654), 90.

63. Martial of Limoges, ed. Lemaitre; ed. Arbellot for text.

64. Peter of Luxemburg, 512, c. 227.

65. Philippe de Mézières, *Le songe du Vieil Pelerin*, ed. G. W. Coopland (London, 1969), 1: 530; cf. E. de Fréville, "Les grandes companies au quatorzième siècle," *Bibliothèque de l'École de Chartes*, 5 (1843–4), 232–53.

66. Martial of Limoges, ed. Lemaitre, nos. 1, 4, 25, 48, 55, 77.

67. Ibid., nos. 13, 14, 19, 35.

68. Ibid., 119–20, no. 36.

69. Ibid., 120, no. 38; Contamine, *La guerre*, 583–4.

70. Martial of Limoges, ed. Lemaitre, 106.

71. Ibid. For another case of a man of Spoleto, who, after being captured by papal forces, vowed never to fight again if freed, see Urban V, 315.

72. Martial of Limoges, ed. Arbellot, 442–3, no. 71.

73. Martial of Limoges, ed. Lemaitre, nos. 3, 16, 39, 46, 49, 59, 63, 72.

74. Leonard of Inchenhofen, 187. This plate, presented to Eberhard and prior Johannes, was described as containing illustrations of the following: the wood of the Holy Cross; the stone on which Jesus sat when he fasted in the desert; the oil of St. Catherine of Mt. Sinai; and portraits of Pope Gregory, Bishop Rupert (?), Virgil of Salzburg, Queen Cunegunda, Thomas of Canterbury, Mary Magdalene, King Oswald,

Pantaleon, Ursula, Margaret, Otolica(?), James, Lawrence, Andrew, Peter, Stephen, and Vitus.

75. Ernst Bernleithner, ed., *Kirchenhistorischer Atlas von Österreich* (Vienna, 1967), map no. 12 indicates that sites devoted to Leonard were the most popular. See Kurt Köster, *Pilgerzeichen und Pilgermuscheln vom mittelalterlichen Santiagostrassen* (Neuminster, 1983); and P. Loisseau et al., *Saint-Léonard-de-Noblat: Un culte, une ville, un canton* (n.p., 1988) on emblems related to Leonard. Gustav Bossert, "Der S. Leonhardskult in Württemberg," *Zeitschrift für württemburgische Landesgeschichte*, 3 (1939), 73–101, on German sites. For Leonard's cult in the crusader period, see A. Poncelet, "Boémond et S. Léonard," *Analecta Bollandiana*, 31 (1912), 24–44.

76. Benedetto Cigniti, "Leonardo di Nobiliacum," *Bibliotheca sanctorum*, 7: 1198–1208; A. Zimmermann, "Leonhard," *Lexikon für Theologie und Kirche*, 10 vols. (Freiburg-im-Breisgau, 1930–38), 6: 508–9; Ph. Rouillard, "Léonard (Saint) de Noblat," *Catholicisme: Hier, aujourd'hui, demain*, ed. G. Jacquemart, 10 vols. (Paris, 1948–85), 7: 362–3; F. Arbellot, *Vie de Saint Leonard* (Paris, 1863). A. Poncelet, *Commentarius praevius*, in AASS, in 6 November III, 143–55, is perhaps the best summary.

77. As cited in A. Poncelet, *De S. Leonardo confessore*, in AASS, 6 November III, 143, note 4.

78. Pierre Rézeau, *Le prières aux saints en français à la fin du moyen âge*, 2 vols. (Geneva, 1982–3), 2: 101.

79. André Vauchez, "Influences franciscaines et réseaux aristocratiques dans la val de Loire: Autour de la bienheureuse Jeanne-Marie de Maillé (1331–1414)," *Revue d'histoire de l'Eglise de France*, 70 (1984), 95–105.

80. Keen, *Laws of War*, 158; Heinrich Denifle, *La desolation des églises, monastères et hôpitaux en France pendant la guerre de cent ans*, 2 vols. (Paris, 1897–9), 2: 393, for the letter; terms of ransom in Thomas Rymer, *Foedera, conventiones, litera et cujuscunque generis acta publica*, 11 vols. (Hague, 1739–45), 3: pt. 1, 126–8 (10 August 1358).

81. Charles of Blois, ed. Plaine et al., 93: "Ego ibo defendere populum meum, placeret modo Deo quod contencio esset solum inter me et adversarium meum, absque eo quod alii propter hoc morerentur." For liturgical references to Louis IX as defender of France, see Robert Folz, "La sainteté de Louis IX d'après les textes liturgiques de sa fête," *Revue d'histoire de l'Eglise de France*, 57 (1971), 33.

82. Charles of Blois, ed. Plaine et al., 247–8.

83. Ibid., 161, 165, 173, 346.

84. Ibid., 215–8, on a woman who hid wine from pillagers in a riverbed; 241, on seven merchants carrying knives, silk, cloth, belts, etc., spared by routiers near Redon; 258, on a man who hid a purse filled with five gold pieces; see also 109, 282–3, 289, 294–5, 307–8, 319, 334–5.

85. Ibid., 215–8, 261–3, 305–6, 345, 361–2.

86. Ibid., 283–5, 293–7.

87. Ibid., 296–7.

88. Ibid., 303.

89. Urban V, 284–6.

90. Charles of Blois, ed. Plaine et al., 247–8; Robert Bartlett, *Trial by Fire and Water: The Medieval Judicial Ordeal* (Oxford, 1986), 103–26, on later medieval efforts to ban trial by battle.

91. Charles of Blois, ed. Plaine et al., 83–4, 398.

92. Gerard Cagnoli, "La leggenda," 417, e.g., reports that after being cured of a fever in July 1346, a wealthy citizen of Lucca offered two *pictores* to Gerard Cagnoli: "Propter quod, ut votum impleret fideliter, misit ad expensas suas Pisas duos pictores, qui, forma accepta de figura Sancti Gerardi et de ipsius informati miraculis, reversi Lucam, ipsum in ecclesiam Fratrum Minorum pinxerunt solemniter, ipsam imaginem sexdecim miraculis de patratis per eum mirabiliter accingentes." Owing to the cure of a Catalan merchant of Majorca who was visiting Pisa, *imagines* of wax also multiplied at the Franciscan convent on the island (Gerard, 420). For an image painted at Pistoia, see 424. The report of the translation of the relics of Peter Martyr in 1340 notes the artwork done by Pisani (Peter Martyr, *Vita et miracula*, 690). On the illustration of Peter's martyrdom by the friars at Gubbio despite the views of a blasphemer, see Peter Martyr, *Miracula . . . post mortem*, 713.

93. Charles of Blois, ed. Plaine et al., 395–8.

94. Philippe de Villette, abbot of Saint-Denis, said, "And just as men terrify flies without difficulty, so God resolves wars according to His will." See C. J. Liebman, ed., "Un sermon de Philippe de Villette, abbé de Saint-Denis pour la levée de l'Oriflamme (1414)," *Romania*, 68 (1944–5), 463–5. Philippe de Mézières said, "Victories come from Heaven." Giovanni da Legnano, in his *Tractatus de bello, de represaliis et de duello*, ed. T. E. Holland (Washington, D. C., 1917), 1ff. argued that while the celestial, spiritual war is the source of all war, specific wars occur when "the sensitive human appetite" resists reason. See Philippe Contamine, *La France au XIVe et XVe siècles: Hommes, mentalités, guerre et paix* (London, 1981), for a reprint of "L'idée de guerre à la fin du moyen âge."

95. Pierre Riché, "Les représentations du palais dans les textes littéraires du haut moyen âge," *Francia*, 4 (1976), 161–71, discusses the precedents in the early middle ages.

Chapter Eight

1. Augustine, *De utilitate credendi* 16.34, in MPL, 42: 40; see also *Contra Ioannem*, tract. 8, noted in John A. Hardon, "The Concept of Miracle from St. Augustine to Modern Apologetics," *Theological Studies*, 15 (1954), 231. *Contra Faustum* 26.3, in MPL, 42: 481.

2. Augustine, *De trinitate*, ed. W. J. Fountain, in *Corpus cristianorum: Series latina*, 50 (Turnhout, 1968), III.4–10; V.11–12.

3. Augustine, *De genesi ad litteram*, 6.13.24, in MPL, 34: 349; see also Augustine, *De verbis Domini*, 44, in MPL, 38: 253–42.

4. On the influence of Aristotle and the philosophy of nature in the schools, see Aimé Forest et al., *Le mouvement doctrinal du XIe au XVe siècle* (Paris, 1956), 205ff.; M. Grabmann, *Guglielmo di Moerbeke O. P. il traduttore delle opere di Aristotele* (Rome, 1946); Fernand van Steenberghen, *Aristotle in the West*, trans. L. Johnson (Louvain, 1955). See idem, "La philosophie de la nature au XIIIe siècle," in *La filosofia della natura nel medioevo: Atti del terzo congresso internazionale di filosofia medioevale* (Milan, 1966), 114–32, on the rise of Aristotelianism and natural law.

5. Thomas Aquinas, *Quaestiones disputatae: De potentia Dei*, 5 vols. (Turin, 1931), q. 6, art. 9; see also Gregory the Great, *Dialogi* 2.30, ed. Adalbert de Vogüe, 3 vols. (Paris, 1978–80). William McCready, *Signs of Sanctity in the Thought of Gregory the Great* (Toronto, 1989), provides an excellent introduction to the concept of miracle

in the early middle ages. Much of the scholastic argument is taken whole out of patristic sources.

6. Aquinas, *De potentia*, q. 6, art. 2. This is based on Aristotle, *Metaphysics*, rev. ed., ed. W. D. Ross, 2 vols. (Oxford, 1958), 1: 2.982b16.

7. Albertus Magnus, *Summa theologiae*, II. tract. 8, q. 31, in *Opera omnia*, ed. A. Borgnet, 38 vols. (Paris, 1890–8), vol. 32. Bernhard Bron, *Das Wunder: Das theologische Wunderverständnis im Horizont des neuzeitlichen Natur-und Geschichtsbegriffs*, 2nd ed. (Göttingen, 1979).

8. Engelbert of Admont, *De miraculis Christi*, Admont ms. 398. On Engelbert, see Rudolph List, *Stift Admont 1074–1974: Festschrift zur Neunhundertjahrfeier* (Admont, 1974), 131–45. The chief authority on the work of Engelbert is George Fowler, *Intellectual Interests of Engelbert of Admont* (New York, 1947), 63.

9. Caroline W. Bynum, *Docere verbo et exemplo: An Aspect of Twelfth Century Spirituality* (Missoula, Mont., 1979).

10. Bertilia of Cambrai, 157–8.

11. E. Warlop, *The Flemish Nobility before 1300*, 4 vols., 2 vols. to date (Courtrai, 1975–6), 1: 276–8, 314, 327.

12. Howard Clarke Kee, *Miracle in the Early Christian World: A Study in Sociohistorical Method* (New Haven, 1983), 156.

13. Numa-Denis Fustel de Coulanges, *The Ancient City*, trans. Willard Small, 3rd ed. (Boston, 1877), on the patron-god of antiquity. Peter Brown, *The Cult of Saints: Its Rise and Function in Latin Christianity* (Chicago, 1981), 40; Nicole Hermann-Mascard, *Les reliques des saints* (Paris, 1975), on relics.

14. Brown, *Cult*, 7ff.

15. An important source is Robert Grant, *Miracle and Natural Law in Graeco-Roman and Early Christian Thought* (Amsterdam, 1952), on nature and miracle in Hellenistic and early Christian periods; cf. H. Delhaye, "Les premiers 'libelli miraculorum,'" *Analecta Bollandiana*, 19 (1910), 427–34; Brown, *Cult*, 28.

16. Sulpicius Severus, *Vie de Saint Martin*, ed. Jacques Fontaine, 3 vols. (Paris, 1967–9), 1: 188–90.

17. Urban V, 427, no. 168.

18. Ibid., 429, no. 178.

19. Martin of Genoa, 804; John Gueruli; Gregory of Verucchio, 441.

20. Yves-Marie Bercé, *Fête et revolte: Des mentalités populaires du XIVe au XVIIIe siècle* (Paris, 1976), deals with the often violent carnivals associated with Christian feasts in the early modern period, which is far less documented for the fourteenth century; cf. Robert Muchembled, *La violence au village (XVe—XVIIe siècle)* (Turnhout, 1989); Edward Muir, *Civic Ritual in Renaissance Venice* (Princeton, 1981); Richard C. Trexler, *Public Life in Renaissance Florence* (New York, 1980); Enrico Cattaneo, *Città e religione nell'età dei communi* (Milan, 1979).

21. Albinus, 181–2.

22. Zita of Lucca, 513; for a similar list see Maio, ed. Vauchez, 371, on life (ca. 1330–5).

23. Seraphina, 235–42.

24. Thomas of Hereford, ed. *AASS*, 594–5; E. M. Gunk, *St. Thomas of Hereford* (Newport, Isle of Wight, 1978), 13; Arthur Thomas Bannister, *The Cathedral Church of Hereford* (London, 1924), 167–8; Ronald C. Finucane, *Miracles and Pilgrims: Popular Beliefs in Medieval England* (London, 1977), 98, 180.

25. Charles of Blois, ed. Plaine et al., 83–4, 398.

26. A study of the central role of the saint's cult in Renaissance art is found in Helene Wieruszowski, "Art and the Commune in the Time of Dante," *Speculum*, 19 (1944), 14–33; see also Rona Geffen, *Spirituality in Conflict: Saint Francis and Giotto's Bardi Chapel* (University Park, Pa., 1988); Daniel Arasse, "Entre dévotion et culture: Fonctions de l'image religieuse au XVe siècle," in *Faire croire: Collection de l'Ecole française de Rome*, 51 (Rome, 1981), 131–46; Jean-Philippe Antoine, "*Ad perpetuam memoriam*: Les nouvelles functions de l'image peinte en Italie: 1250–1400," *Mélanges de l'Ecole française de Rome*, 100 (1988), 541–615.

27. Paolo Golinelli, "Il santo gabbato: Forme di incredulità nel mondo cittadino italiano," in *Città e culto dei santi nel medioevo italiano* (Bologna, 1991), 63–90; Michael Goodich, "Miracles and Disbelief in the Late Middle Ages," *Mediaevistik*, 1 (1988), 23–38.

28. Clare of Montefalco, 459–61, 484–5, for several eyewitness accounts of the event.

29. J. M. Bak, "Medieval Symbology of the State: Percy E. Shramm's Contribution," *Viator*, 4 (1973), 33–63, for example, suggests a complex understanding of symbols of state, based on Germanic custom, scholastic political theory, ecclesiastic interpretation, biblical and Byzantine precedent, all of which changed in accordance with developing needs. In another example, Caroline W. Bynum, "The Body of Christ in the Later Middle Ages: A Reply to Leo Sternberg," *Renaissance Quarterly*, 39 (1986), 399–439, has suggested that what appears sexual to our contemporary eyes may not have been so in the middle ages. Her view is challenged in Richard Rambuss, "Epistemology of the Prayer Closet," Paper presented at Medieval Studies Conference, Kalamazoo, 1993, who argues that portrayals of the Passion of Christ do indeed possess a sexual dimension.

Cults Cited

Agnes. Thomas à Kempis, *Miracula post ser. 8 ad Novit*, in AASS, 21 January II, 726–8.

Agnes of Montepulciano. Raymund of Capua, *Vita S. Agnetis de Montepolitano*, in AASS, 20 April II, 792–812.

Aignan of Chartres. R. D. A. Clerval, ed., "Translationes S. Aniani Carnotensis episcopi annis 1136 et 1264," *Analecta Bollandiana*, 7 (1888), 321–35.

Albert of Trapani. "Vita S. Alberti confessoris ordinis Carmelitarum," *Analecta Bollandiana*, 17 (1898), 317–36.

———. *Acta et miracula Alberti*, in AASS, 7 August II, 226–35.

Albinus. Leonard Ennen, ed., *Quellen zur Geschichte der Stadt Köln* (Darmstadt, 1961), 4: 181–2.

Allucio of Campugliano. *Vita et translatio S. Allucii confessoris*, in AASS, 23 October IX, 232–9.

Amalberga of Ghent. *Miracula S. Amalbergae virginis*, in AASS, 10 July III, 100–7.

Ambrose of Massa. *Processus canonizationis . . .* , in AASS, 10 November IV, 566–608.

Ambrose of Siena. Gisbert et al., *Vita et miracula Ambrosii*, in AASS, 20 March III, 179–250.

Amicus. *Vita prima S. Amici*, in AASS, 3 November II.1, 92–5.

Andrew Gallerani. *Vita B. Andreae de Galleranis*, in AASS, 19 March III, 49–58.

Angelo of Gualdo. *Vita et miracula Angeli Gualdensis*, in Giovanni Benedetto Mittarelli, *Annales Camaldulenses ordinis Sancti Benedicti*, 9 vols. (Venice, 1755–73), 5: 59, 269, 290, 329.

Anthony of Padua. Léon de Kerval, ed., *Sancti Antonii de Padua vitae duae* (Paris, 1904).

Anthony of Padua (the Pilgrim). Sicco Polenton, "Vita beati Antonii Peregrini," *Analecta Bollandiana*, 13 (1894), 417–25.

This list contains only sources cited, and is not intended as a comprehensive list of all the primary sources relevant to the cults.

———. Thealdo de Soligio, "Miracula Beati Antonii Peregrini," *Analecta Bollandiana*, 14 (1895), 108–14.

Atto of Pistoia. *AASS*, 22 May V, 199–204.

Baudin. *Sermo de siccitate anno 1331 . . .* , in *AASS*, 7 November III, 393–4.

Benedict XI. Bernard Gui, "De vita prima et miraculis B. Benedicti papae XI," *Analecta Bollandiana*, 19 (1900), 14–36.

Bernardino of Siena. F. Delorme, ed., "Ex libro miraculorum SS. Bernardini Senensis et Ioannis a Capistrano," *Archivum franciscanum historicum*, 11 (1918), 399–441.

Bernward of Hildesheim. *Historia canonizationis et translationis S. Bernwardi episcopi*, in *AASS*, 25 October XI, 1033.

Bertilia of Cambrai. *Translatio Bertiliae*, in *AASS*, 3 January I, 157–8.

Bona of Poggibonsi. *Translatio Bonae*, in *AASS*, 29 May VII, 142–60.

Bridget of Sweden. Isak Collijn, ed., *Acta et processus canonizationis beate Birgitte* (Uppsala, 1924–31).

———. *De miraculis S. Birgittae*, in *AASS*, 8 October IV, 534–60.

Brynolph of Scara. Claudius Annerstedt, ed., *Vita S. Brynolphi episc. Scarensis . . .* , in *Scriptores rerum suecicarum medii aevi*, 3 vols. (Uppsala, 1818–76), 3: 141–83.

Catherine of Fierbois. Yves Chauvin, ed., *Livre des miracles de Sainte-Catherine-de-Fierbois* (Poitiers, 1976).

Catherine of Siena. M. H. Laurent, ed., *Il processo castellano*, in *Fontes vitae S. Catharinae Senensis historici*, IX (Siena, 1942).

———. Thomas of Siena, *Sanctae Catharinae Senensis Legenda minor*, ed. E. Franceschini, *Fontes vitae S. Catharinae Senensis*, X (Milan, 1942).

Celestine V. F. X. Seppelt, ed., *Die Akten des Kanonisationsprozess in dem Codex zu Sulmona*, in *Monumenta Coelestiniana: Quellen zur Geschichte des Papstes Coelestin V* (Paderborn, 1921), 211–334.

———. F. van Ortroy, ed., "Procès-verbal du dernier consistoire secret préparatoire à la canonisation," *Analecta Bollandiana*, 16 (1897), 475–87.

———. Peter Herde, ed., *Legenda de translatione sancti corporis eius . . .* , in Peter Herde, *Coelestin V (1294)* (Stuttgart, 1981), 289ff.

———. *Autobiografia*, ed. Arnaldo Frugoni, *Celestiniana* (Rome, 1954), 56–67.

———. Pierre d'Ailly, *Vita Coelestini V*, in Seppelt, 149–81.

———. Maffeo Vegio, *Vita Coelestini V*, in Seppelt, 183–208.

Charles of Blois. François Plaine et al., eds., *Monuments du procès de canonisation du B. Charles de Blois duc de Bretagne 1320–1364* (Saint—Brieuc, 1921).

———. A. Vauchez, ed., "Canonisation et politique au XIVe siècle: Documents inédits des Archives du Vatican de Charles de Blois, duc de Bretagne (†1364)," in *Miscellanea in onore di Monsignor Martino Giusti Prefetto dell'Archivio Segreto Vaticano*, 2 vols. (Rome, 1978), 2: 381–404.

Clare of Assisi. Zefferino Lazzeri, ed., "Il processo di S. Chiara d'Assisi," *Archivum franciscanum historicum*, 13 (1920), 403–50.

———. Thomas of Celano, *Vita Clarae*, in AASS, 12 August II, 754–68.

Clare Gambacorta. *Vita Clarae*, in AASS, 17 April II, 503–16.

Clare of Montefalco. Enrico Menestò, ed., *Il processo di canonizzazione di Chiara da Montefalco* (Perugia, 1984).

Claudius. P. F. Chiffolète, *Miraculorum Liber II*, in AASS, 6 June I, 647–60.

Contardo of Este. *Historia Contardi*, in AASS, 16 April II, 444–8.

Cunegunda. *Vita B. Cunegundis*, ed. Wojciech Ketrzyński, in *Monumenta poloniae historica*, IV, 682–774.

Dauphine of Languedoc. Jacques Cambell, ed., *Enquête pour le procès de canonisation de Dauphine de Puimichel comtesse d'Ariano* (+ 26.XI.1360) (Turin, 1978).

Dominic of Guzman. *Processus*, in Jacques Quétif and Jacques Echard, eds., *Scriptores ordinis praedicatorum*, 2 vols. (Louvain, 1961), 1: 44–58.

———. V. J. Koudelka, "Procès de canonisation de S. Dominique," *Archivum fratrum praedicatorum*, 42 (1972), 47–67.

———. A. Walz, ed., *Processus canonizationis S. Dominici*, in *Monumenta ordinis praedicatorum historica*, 16 (Rome, 1935).

———. Jordan of Saxony, *Libellus*, in AASS, 4 August I, 541–57.

Dominic of Silos. Sebastian de Vergara, ed., *Vida y milagros del taumaturgo español, Moysés segundo, redentor de cautivos, abogado de los felices partos, santo Domingo Manso, abad benedictino, reparador de el real monasterio de Silos* (Madrid, 1736).

Dorothy of Montau. Hans Westpfahl, ed., *Vita Dorotheae Montoviensis magistri Johannis Marienwerder* (Cologne, 1964).

———. John of Marienwerder, *Vita prima B. Dorotheae*, in AASS, 30 October XIII, 493–9.

———. Idem(?), *Vita*, in ibid., 499–560.

———. Richard Stachnik, ed., *Die Akten des Kanonisationsprozesses Dorotheas von Montau von 1394 bis 1521*, in *Forschungen und Quellen zur Kirchen-und Kulturgeschichte Ostdeutschlands*, 15 (Cologne, 1978).

Elizabeth of Portugal. *Vita et miracula*, in AASS, 4 July I, 173–97.

Elizabeth of Thuringia. Caesarius of Heisterbach, *Sermo de translatione beate Elyzabethe*, in A. Huyskens, ed., *Die Schriften des Cäsarius von Heisterbach über heilige Elisabeth von Thüringen*, in *Publikationen des Gesellschaft für Geschichtskunde*, 43.3 (1937), 281–90.

————. Theodore of Apolda, *Vita beatae Elisabethae*, in J. Basnage and H. Canisius, eds., *Monumentorum ecclesiasticarum et historicum sive Henrici Canisii Lectiones antiquae* (Antwerp, 1725), 4: 116–52.

Elzéar of Sabran. Jacques Cambell, ed., "Le sommaire de l'enquête pour la canonisation de S. Elzéar de Sabran, TOF († 1323)," *Miscellanea francescana*, 73 (1973), 438–73.

————. Francis of Meyronnes, *Libellus de vita*, in AASS, 27 September VII, 539–55.

Emetherius and Celedonius. *Translatio sanctorum . . . Emetherii et Celedonii*, in Enrique Florez et al., eds., *España sagrada*, 51 vols. (Madrid, 1747–1879), 31: 436–8.

Engelbert of Cologne. Caesarius of Heisterbach, *Vita, passio et miracula S. Engelberti*, in AASS, 7 November III, 623–84.

————. Fritz Zschaeck, ed., *Leben, Leiden und Wunder des heiligen Engelbert von Ceasarius von Heisterbach*, in *Publikationen der Gesellschaft für rheinische Gesellschaftskunde*, 43.3 (1937), 225–328.

Erasmus. *Acta S. Erasmi*, in AASS, 2 June I, 23.

Erhard. Conrad of Megenberg, *Vita Erhardi*, in AASS, 8 January I, 541–4.

Facio of Cremona. John of Cremona, *Vita Facii*, in André Vauchez, ed., "Sainteté laïque au XIIe siècle: La vie de bienheureux Façio de Crémone," *Mélanges de l'Ecole française de Rome: Moyen âge*, 84 (1972), 13–53.

Francis of Assisi. Thomas of Celano, *Tractatus primus super vitam Sancti Francisci*, ed. H. G. Rosedale (London, 1904).

————. idem, *Tractatus de miraculis*, in *Analecta franciscana*, X (Quaracchi, 1926–41), fasc. 3.

————. L. Oliger, ed., "Miracula S. Francisci," *Archivum franciscanum historicum*, 12 (1919), 358–401.

Francis of Siena. Christopher of Parma, *Legenda beati Francisci de Senis*, in A. Morini and P. Soulier, *Monumenta ordinis servorum*, 8 vols. (Brussels, 1902), 5: 20–46.

Galgano of Chiusdino. Fedor Schneider, ed., "Der Einsiedler Galgano von Chiusdino und die Anfänge von San Galgano," *Quellen und Forschungen aus italienischen Archiven und Bibliotheken*, 17 (1914–24), 61–77.

Gandolph of Binasco. *Miracula B. Gandolphi ante corporis inventionem*, in AASS, 7 September V, 707–12.

Garland of Caltagirone. *Miracula S. Garlandi*, in AASS, 18 June IV, 541–51.

Gauderic of Agricola. *Miracula Gauderici*, in AASS, 16 October VII.2, 1106–20.

George of Cappadocia. *Translatio reliq. S. Georgii*, in AASS, 23 April III, 132–6.

Gerard Cagnoli. Filippo Rotolo, ed., "Il trattato del miracoli del B. Gerardo Cagnoli, O.Min. (1267–1342) di Fra Bartolomeo Albizi, O.Min. († 1351)" *Miscellanea francescana*, 66 (1966), 128–92.

———. Ibid., "La leggenda del B. Gerardo Cagnoli, O.Min. (1267–1342) di Fra Bartolomeo Albizi, O.Min. († 1351)," *Miscellanea francescana*, 57 (1951), 367–446.

Gerio of Montesanto. Matteo Masio, *Vita Gerii*, in AASS, 25 May VI, 158–9.

Gertrude of Nivelles. *Vita et miracula*, in AASS, 17 March III, 592–8.

Gerulph. "Miracula recentiora S. Gerulphi," *Analecta Bollandiana*, 4 (1885), 203–5.

Gilbert of Sempringham. Raymonde Foreville, ed., *Un procès de canonisation à l'aube du XIIIe siècle (1201–1202): Le livre de Gilbert de Sempringham* (Paris, 1943).

Giles. "Liber exemplorum Sancti Aegidii auctore Petro Gulielmo," *Analecta Bollandiana*, 9 (1890), 393–422.

Giovanna of Signa. Saturnino Mencherini, "Vita et miracoli della Beata Giovanna da Signa," *Archivum franciscanum historicum*, 10 (1917), 367–86.

Godehard of Hildesheim. Philip Jaffé, ed., *Translatio Godehardi episcopi: Appendix*, in *Monumenta germaniae historica: Scriptores*, 12 (Leipzig, 1856), 650–2.

Gregory of Verucchio. *Epitome vitae . . . Gregorii . . . Veruculi*, in AASS, 4 May I, 541–2.

Gundechar of Eichstadt. Philip, bishop of Eichstadt, *Miracula Gundecharii*, in AASS, 2 August I, 185.

Hedwig of Silesia. Simon of Trebnitz, *Vita maior sanctae Hedwigis*, ed. A. Semkowicz, in *Monumenta poloniae historica*, 6 vols. (Warsaw, 1961), 4: 510–633.

———. Ibid., *Vita minor*, in idem, 634–42.

———. Joseph Gottschalk, ed., "Die Hedwigspredigt des Papstes Klemens IV von Jahre 1267," *Archiv für schlesische Kirchengeschichte*, 15 (Hildesheim, 1957), 15–35.

Helen Enselmini. Sicco Polenton, *Vita et visiones B. Helenae*, in AASS, 4 November I.2, 512–7.

Henry of Treviso. Pietro Domenico of Baone et al., *Vita et Miracula Henrici*, in AASS, 10 June II, 368–92.

Henry VI of England. John Blakman, *Memoir*, ed. and trans. M. R. James (Cambridge, 1919).

———. Ronald Knox and Shane Leshe, eds., *The Miracles of King Henry V* (Cambridge, 1923).

————. Russell Hope Robbins, ed., *Historical Poems of the Fourteenth and Fifteenth Centuries* (New York, 1959), 199–201.

Hildegard of Bingen. Petrus Bruder, ed., "Acta Inquisitionis S. Hildegardis," *Analecta Bollandiana*, 2 (1883), 116–29.

Honorina. "Translatio sanctae Honorinae virginis et martyris et ejusdem miracula," *Analecta Bollandiana*, 9 (1890), 135–46.

Hugh of Lincoln. Decima L. Douie and David Hugh Farmer, eds., *Magna vita sancti Hugonis*, 2 vols. (London, 1961–2).

Humility of Faenza. *Vita S. Humilitatis abbatissae*, in AASS, 22 May V, 207–14.

Iagnolus of Callio. *Miracula sex publicis instrumenta consignata*, in AASS, 21 April II, 949–50.

————. *Vita*, in AASS, 9 November IV, 280–8.

Januarius. *De SS. Januario episc., Sosio, Festo et al.*, in AASS, 19 September VI, 852–7.

Jerome. Johannes Andreae, *Miracula Hieronimi*, in AASS, 30 September VIII, 658–9.

Joachim Piccolomini of Siena. Auctor coevus, "Vita et miracula beati Ioachimi Senensis," in A. Morini and P. Soulier, eds., *Monumenta ordinis servorum*, 8 vols. (Brussels, 1902), 5: 5–19.

————. P. M. Soulier, ed., "Vita ac legenda beati Ioachimi Senensis ordinis servorum sanctae Mariae virginis," *Analecta Bollandiana*, 13 (1894), 383–97.

John the Baptist. *De cineribus S. Joannis Bapt. Genuae*, in AASS, 24 June V, 669–84.

————. Bonino Moriga, *Historia mediolana*, in idem, 655–6.

————. *Translatio Faciei Ambios in Galliam*, in idem, 639–42.

————. *Apparitiones et miracula in Pontiscorvi oppido Campaniae facta saec. XII*, in idem, 685–9.

John of Bridlington. Hugh, *Vita Iohannis*, in AASS, 10 October V, 135–44.

————. Paul Grosjean, ed., "De S. Iohanne Bridlingtoniensis Collectanea," *Analecta Bollandiana*, 53 (1935), 101–39.

John Buoni. *Processus canonizationis Ioannis*, in AASS, 22 October IX, 693–886.

John of Caramola. Abbot of Sagittario, *Vita Ioannis*, in AASS, 26 August V, 860–2.

John Gueruli of Verucchio. Angelo Turchini, ed., "Leggenda, culto, iconografia del beato Giovanni Gueruli (1320?)," *Studi romagnoli*, 21 (1970), 425–53.

John of Rimini. Jacques Dalaran, ed., "*Liber Beati Iohannis*: Le culte d'un saint chanoine de Rimini d'après un manuscrit original du XIVe siècle réputé disparu," *Mélanges de l'École française de Rome: Moyen âge*, 100 (1988), 617–708.

Lawrence of Dublin. Myles V. Ronan, "St. Laurentius of Dublin," *Irish Ecclesiastical Record*, 27, 5 ser.(1926), 1: 347–64; 2: 247–56, 467–80.

———. Charles Plummer, ed., "Vie et miracles de S. Laurent archevêque de Dublin," *Analecta Bollandiana*, 33 (1914), 121–86.

Leonard of Inchenhofen. Eberhard of Fürstenfeld et al., *Exordium et miracula sancti Leonhardi thaumaturgi in Inchenhofen*, in AASS, 6 November III, 182–204.

Louis IX of France. H.-François Delaborde, "Fragment de l'enquête faite à Saint-Denis en 1282 en vue de la canonisation de Saint Louis," *Mémoires de la Société de l'histoire de Paris et de l'Ile de France*, 23 (1896), 1–71.

———. M. le Comte Riant, "Déposition de Charles d'Anjou pour la canonisation de Saint Louis," *Notices et documents publiés pour la Société de l'histoire de France à l'occasion du cinquantième anniversaire de sa fondation* (Paris, 1884), 155–76.

———. Geoffrey of Beaulieu, *Vita Ludovici*, in AASS, 25 August V, 541–58.

———. Jean de Joinville, *Vita*, in ibid., 672–718.

———. Guillaume de St. Panthus, *Vita*, in ibid., 671–2.

———. Guillaume de St. Panthus, *Vita*, ed. H. François Delaborde (Paris, 1899).

Louis of Toulouse. Albert Heysse, ed., "Documenta de vita S. Ludovici episcopi Tolosani," *Archivum franciscanum historicum*, 40 (1947), 118–42.

———. Patres Collegii S. Bonaventurae, *Processus canonizationis et Legendae variae Sancti Ludovici*, in *Analecta franciscana*, VII (Quaracchi, 1951).

———. Johannes de Orta, "Vita S. Ludovici episcopi," *Analecta Bollandiana*, 9 (1890), 278–353.

Lucchesio of Poggibonsi. Martino Bertagna, ed., "Note storiche e documenti intorno a S. Lucchese," *Archivum franciscanum historicum*, 62 (1969), 1–114, 449–502.

———. Bartolomeo dei Tolomei of Siena, *Vita Lucchesii et Miracula*, in AASS, 28 April III, 597–616.

Lucian, Marcian et al. *Instrumentum translatii*, in AASS, 26 October I, 812–3.

Maio of Gualdo Tadino. André Vauchez, ed., "Frères Mineurs, érémitisme et sainteté laïque: Les vies des saints Maio († v. 1270) et Marzio († 1301) de Gualdo Tadino," *Studi medievali*, 3 ser., 27 (1986), fasc. 1, 353–81.

Margaret of Città di Castello. "Vita beatae Margaritae virginis de Civitate

Castelli sororis tertii ordinis de paenitentia sancti Dominici," *Analecta Bollandiana*, 19 (1900), 22–36.

———. M.—H. Laurent, ed., "La plus ancienne légende de la B. Marguérite de Città di Castello," *Archivum fratrum praedicatorum*, 10 (1940), 109–31.

Margaret of Hungary. William Franknoì, ed., *Inquisitio super vita, conversatione et miraculis beatae Margarethae virginis*, in *Monumenta romana episcopatus Vesprimiensis* (Budapest, 1896), I, 163–384.

———. Garin de Guy l'Évêque, *Vita Margaretae*, in AASS, 28 January III, 522–5.

Margaret of Roskilde. *Translatio*, in AASS, 25 October XI, 719.

Margaret of Scotland. *Historia translationis*, in AASS, June II, 333–4.

Martial of Limoges. François Arbellot, ed., "Miracula S. Martialis anno 1388 patrata," *Analecta Bollandiana*, 1 (1882), 411–46.

———. Jean-Loup Lemaitre, ed., "Les miracles de Saint Martial accomplis lors de l'Ostension de 1388," *Bulletin de la société archéologique et historique du Limousin*, 102 (1975), 67–139.

———. Daniel Papebroch, ed., *De Sancto Martiale*, in AASS, 30 June V, 535–73.

Martin of Genoa. *Vita Martini*, in AASS, 8 April I, 802.

Mary of Cervellone. Joannes de Laes, *Acta . . .* , in AASS, 25 September VII, 180–6.

Mary of Maillé. Martin de Boscogualteri, *Vita Ioannae*, in AASS, 28 March III, 737–47.

Marzio of Gualdo Tadino. See **Maio of Gualdo Tadino.**

Maurice of Carnoët. Beda Plaine, ed., *Duplex vita Mauritii*, in *Studien und Mitteilungen aus dem Benediktiner und aus dem Cisterzienser-Orden*, 7.1 (1886), 375–93; 7.2 (1886), 157–64.

Nevolo of Faenza. F. Lanzoni, ed., "Una vita del beato Novellone composita nel secolo XV," *Archivum franciscanum historicum*, 6 (1913), 645–53.

Nicasius, Quirinius et al. *Translatio Malmundarium et miracula*, in AASS, 11 October V, 550–9.

Nicholas of Tolentino. Nicola Occhioni, ed., *Il processo per la canonizzazione di S. Nicola da Tolentino* (Rome, 1984).

———. Peter of Monte Rubiano, *Vita*, in AASS, 10 September III, 644–64.

———. *Miracula*, in ibid., 697–9.

Odilo of Bourges. *Translatio corporis S. Odilonis*, in MPL, 142: 1047–8.

Odo of Novara. "Documenta de B. Odone Novariense," *Analecta Bollandiana*, 1 (1882), 323–54.

Osmund. A. R. Madden, ed., *The Canonisation of Saint Osmund* (Salisbury, 1901).

Paulus Novus. *Translatio Corporis S. Pauli Novi*, in AASS, 8 July II, 639–42.

Peter Armengol. Marco Salmerone, *Acta Petri*, in AASS, 2 September I, 333–4.

Peter of Foligno. John of San Gemignano, *Vita Petri Fulginensis*, in AASS, 19 July IV, 665–8.

———. Idem, "Legenda Beati Petri de Fulgineo confessoris," ed. Michele Faloci-Pulignani, *Analecta Bollandiana*, 8 (1889), 358–69.

Peter of Luxemburg. *Processus de B. Petro de Luxemburgo*, in AASS, 2 July I, 494–551.

Peter Martyr. Thomas Agni de Lentino, *Vita et miracula*, in AASS, 29 April III, 686–712.

———. *Miracula Petri Martiri post mortem*, in AASS, 29 April III, 712–27.

Peter Parenti. John of Orvieto, *Vita et miracula Petri*, in AASS, 21 May V, 86–99.

Peter Pettinaio. C. Cenci, ed., "'San' Pietro Pettinaio presentato da un predicatore senese contemporaneo," *Studi francescani*, 87 (1990), 5–23.

Peter of Siena et al. Odoric of Pordenone, *Relatio martyrii . . .* , in AASS, 1 April I, 53–6.

Peter Thomas. Philippe de Mézières, *The Life of St. Peter Thomas*, ed. Joachim Smet, in *Textus et studia historica carmelitana*, 2 (Rome, 1954), 168–84.

Philip Benizi. *Legenda beati Philippi*, in A. Morini and P. Soulier, eds., *Monumenta ordinis servorum*, 8 vols. (Brussels, 1902), II, 60–83.

Philip Berruyer of Bourges. *Vita sancti Philippi archiepiscopi Biturcensis*, in Edmond Martène and Ursinus Durand, eds., *Thesaurus novus anecdotorum*, 5 vols. (Paris, 1717–26), 3: 1927–46.

———. Socii Bollandiani, eds., *Vita et miracula Philippi ep. Biturcensis*, in *Catalogus . . . Parisiensis*, 4 vols. (Brussels, 1889–93), 2: 458–9.

Philippa Castellani. *Miracula per intercessionem virginis Philippae perpetuae*, in AASS, 15 October VII.1: 98–106.

Raymund Palmari. *Miracula S. Raymundi*, in AASS, 28 July VI, 657–63.

Raymund of Penyaforte. F. Balmé and C. Paban, eds., *Raymundiana*, in *Monumenta ordinis praedicatorum historica*, 6 (Rome, 1900).

———. A. Andrés, ed., "Gastos de la canonizacíon de San Raimundo de Peñafort," *Hispania sacra*, 3 (1950), 163–71.

———. José Rius y Serra, ed., *Sancti Raymundi de Penyaforte opera omnia*, vol. 3, *Diplomatario* (Barcelona, 1949–54), 207–63.

Rayner of Borgo San Sepolcro. Bentivenga of Perugia, *Relatio miraculorum*, in *AASS*, 1 November I, 390–402.

Remigius. "Miracula S. Remigii episcopi Remensis seculo XIV ex codice Bruxellensi 5538–39," *Analecta Bollandiana*, 4 (1884), 337–43.

Richard Rolle of Hampole. *Officium de S. Ricardo de Hampole*, in *Breviarium ad usum insignis ecclesiae Eboracensis*, 2 pts., in *Surtees Society Publications*, 72 (1879).

———. Reginald Maxwell Woolley, ed., *The Officium and Miracula of Richard Rolle of Hampole* (London, 1919).

Rose of Viterbo. Giuseppe Abate, ed., "S. Rosa da Viterbo, terziara francescana (1233–1251): Fonti storiche della vita e loro revisione critica," *Miscellanea francescana*, 52 (1952), 113–278 [= *Vita I*, pp. 227–31; *Vita II*, 232–53].

Sebastian. *Miracula SS. Gregorii et Sebastiani*, in *AASS*, March II, 939–41.

———. Baudouin de Gaiffier, "Les sources latines d'un miracle de Gautier de Coincy," *Analecta Bollandiana*, 71 (1953), 100–32.

———. Leonard R. Mills, ed., "Une vie inédite de Saint Sébastien," *Bibliothèque d'humanisme et de Renaissance*, 28 (1966), 410–18.

Seraphina of San Gemignano. John of San Gemignano, *Vita S. Finae*, in *AASS*, 12 March II, 235–42.

———. John of San Gemignano, *The Legend of the Holy Fina*, trans. M. Mansfield (London, 1908).

Simon of Collazzone. Michele Faloci-Pulignani, ed., "Il B. Simone da Collazzone e il suo processo nel 1252," *Miscellanea francescana*, 12 (1910), 97–132.

Simon of Montfort. James Orchard Halliwell, ed., *Miracula Simonis Montforti*, in *The Chronicle of William Rishanger of the Baron's War*, in *Camden Society Publications*, 15 (London, 1840), 67–110.

Simon of Todì. *Miracula B. Simonis*, in *AASS*, 20 April II, 816–21.

Sperandea of Cingoli. Matthew of Cingoli et al., *Vita et Miracula Sperandeae*, in *AASS*, 11 September III, 890–913.

Stanislas of Cracow. Wojciech Ketrzyński, ed., *Vita et Miracula S. Stanislai episcopi Cracoviensis*, in *Monumenta poloniae historica*, 4: 253–318.

———. Vincent Kadlubek, *Vita majora*, in ibid., 319–438.

Thomas Aquinas. Angelico Ferrua, ed., *S. Thomae Aquinatis vitae fontes* (Alba, 1968).

———. Dominic Prümmer, ed., *Fontes vitae S. Thomae Aquinatis* (Toulouse, 1911).

———. *Processus canonizationis . . .* , in *AASS*, 7 March I, 686–716.

————. Bernard Gui, *Vita S. Thomae Aquinatis* in Prümmer, *Fontes vitae*, 160–263.

————. William of Tocco, *Vita Thomae*, in AASS, 7 March I, 657–86, and Prümmer, *Fontes vitae*, 17–55.

Thomas Cantilupe, of Hereford. *Miracula Thomae* . . . , in Oxford, Exeter College ms. 158, fols. 3–61ʳ.

————. *Miracula ex processu* . . . , in AASS, 3 October I, 610–96.

————. W. W. Capes, ed., *Registrum Ricardi de Swinfield* (Hereford, 1909).

Thomas of Costacciaro. Razzi, ed., *Vita . . . Thomassi*, in AASS, 25 March III, 593–602.

Thomas Helye. Clement, *Vita et miracula Thomae Heliae*, in AASS, 19 October VIII, 592–622.

Trypho. *De S. Tryphone*, in AASS, 10 November IV, 323–4.

Urban V. *Processus*, in J. H. Albanès and U. Chevalier, eds., *Actes et documents concernant le bienheureux Urbain V pape* (Paris, 1897), 124–365.

Venturino of Bergamo. P. A. Grion, ed., "La *Legenda* del B. Venturino da Bergamo secondo il testo inedito del codice di Cividale," *Bergomum*, 50 (1956), 11–110.

Wenceslas. "Le dossier de S. Wenceslas dans un manuscrit du XIIIe siècle (codex Bollandianus 433)," *Analecta Bollandiana*, 82 (1984), 87–131.

————. *Miracula S. Wenceslai*, in AASS, 28 September VII, 784.

Werner of Oberwesel. *Miracula Werneri*, in AASS, 19 April II, 708–40.

William of Bourges. "Vita, miracula post mortem et canonizatio S. Gulielmi archiepiscopi Biturcensis," *Analecta Bollandiana*, 3 (1884), 271–361.

————. *Vita Gulielmi archiepiscopi Biturcensis*, in AASS, 10 January I, 627–39.

William of Norwich. Augustus Jessop and Montague Rhodes-James, eds., *The Miracles of St. William of Norwich by Thomas of Norwich* (Cambridge, 1896).

Yves of Tréguier. A. de la Borderie, ed., *Monuments originaux de l'histoire de S. Yves* (Saint-Brieuc, 1887).

————. Clement VI, *Sermones*, Paris, Bibliothèque Sainte Geneviève ms. 240, 541ʳ–549.

————. *Processus canonizationis*, in AASS, 19 May IV, 541–77.

Zita of Lucca. Fatinello de Fatinellis, *Vita B. Zitae virginis Lucensis*, in AASS, 27 April III, 504–32.

Index

10

Anthony of Padua, 162n. 55, 185n. 104, 193

Anthony of Padua (the Pilgrim), 15, 121, 193–4

Antonio de Carleto, 37

Antonio (Ser) of Florence, 48

Antonio Thomasii de Parisiniis, notary, 160n. 27

Appillaterre, Berardo. *See* Berardo Appillaterre

Apt, bishopric of, 6

Aquileia, 18, 123

Aquinas, Thomas. *See* Thomas Aquinas

Aquitaine, 124, 131

arbitration, lay and clerical, 27–35

Aristotle, 80, 190nn. 4, 5

Arles, plague at, 90

Armagnacs, 127, 144, 187n. 39

Arnold of Batsoa, priest, 41

Arnold de Prades, priest, 39

art, saints in, 2, 38, 98–9, 105, 122, 142–3, 145, 153–4, 190n. 92

Ascension, vigils of the, 98

Ascoli, 168n. 14

assurement, 30

Atto of Pistoia, 161n. 36, 194

Aubin of Angers, 29

Auch, diocese of, 40–1

Aufhofen, 137

Augustine of Hippo: on miracles, 12, 147; on sexuality 58–9; on suicide, 80, 147, 190nn. 1, 2

Aunay, 39

Aurelian (pseudo-), 130

Aurillac, abbey of, 42

Austria, miracles in, 25–6, 137–8

Auvray, battle of, 142

Avestone, 19–20

Avignon, 5, 7, 40–1, 128, 132; miracles at, 45, 124, 135, 167n. 58, 183n. 71. *See also* canonization; Peter of Luxemburg; Urban V

Azande, 2

bakery, 82, 99–100

Baltic Sea, 112–3

baptism, 89, 91

Barcelona, 111–2

Bartholomew (St.), feast of, 71–2

Bartholomew of Pisa, 166n. 47

Bartolomeo Albizi, friar, 11, 17, 19, 70–2, 87–9; on Devil, 75–6. *See also* Gerard Cagnoli

Bartolomeo Tolomei, hagiographer, 72

Baudin, 194

Bavaria, miracles in, 5, 26, 69, 137–8

Bayezid (Sultan), 138

Béarnais, 129

Beauport (Dol), monastery of, 33

Beauvais, 138

Becquerel, siege of 143

Bede, 12

Belforte-sul-Chienti (Marche), 81–3

Benedict XI (Pope), 160n. 30, 194

Benedict XII (Pope), 12

Benedicta, mother of Genteluccio, 96

benedictio thalami, 69

Berardo Appillaterre, notary, 87, 89, 162n. 54

Berardo Giacomo of Montemilione, judge, 169n. 32

Bernard Garneri, accused homicide, 57

Bernard Gui, inquisitor, 138, 160n. 30

Bernard Vernet, student, 36

Bernardino of Siena, 2, 18, 123, 157n. 8, 163n. 63, 186n. 12, 193

Bernardo Nuctii, accused murderer, 49

Bernward of Hildesheim, 66, 173n. 31, 194

Berry, 56; duke of, 132

Bertha of Cambrai, 150, 194

Bertrand de Beaumont, 143–4

Bertrand de Born, 128

Bertrand Gale, notary, 6

Beynac, 136

Biblical precedents. *See* Scripture, citation of

Black Prince, 132

Blasius 170n. 39

blasphemy, punishment for, 6, 20, 23, 36, 62, 71, 131, 133, 141–4, 150, 154–5

Blezvanna Gasqueder of Tréguier, victim of theft, 33–4

Bloch, Marc, 25

Boccaccio, Giovanni 26, 110